The Last Book

Also by Sam Pickering

books of essays

A Continuing Education
The Right Distance
May Days
Still Life
Let It Ride
Trespassing
Walkabout Year
The Blue Caterpillar
Living to Prowl
Deprived of Unhappiness
A Little Fling

literary studies

The Moral Tradition in English Fiction, 1785–1850
John Locke and Children's Books in
    Eighteenth-Century England
Moral Instruction and Fiction for Children, 1749–1820

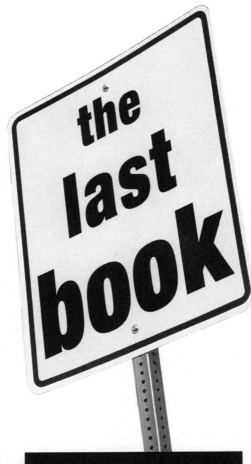

the university of tennessee press
knoxville

Copyright © 2001 by The University of Tennessee Press / Knoxville.
All Rights Reserved.
Manufactured in the United States of America.
First Edition.

The author and publisher gratefully acknowledge
the following publications in which essays in this
volume first appeared: *Creative Nonfiction, The
Purple Cow, The Southern Review, Southwest
Review, Traditions, The Texas Review,* and *The
Virginia Quarterly Review.*

The paper used in this book meets the minimum
requirements of ANSI/NISO Z39.48-1992 (R 1997)
(Permanence of Paper). The binding materials
have been chosen for strength and durability.

Library of Congress Cataloging-in-Publication Data

Pickering, Samuel F., 1941–
The last book / Sam Pickering.— 1st Edition.
    p. cm.
ISBN 1-57233-147-X (cl.: alk. paper)
I. Title.
AC8 .P663 2001
081—dc21   2001001463

Contents

Preface	vii
Auctioneering	1
Split Infinitive	12
After Christmas	18
Lies and Consequences	30
Waiting for Spring	37
Cult	50
Vetted for the Prom	63
May's End	69
Familiar Things	79
Camp Letter	90
August	98
September Rain	115
Road Warrior	120
News	145
Shadow	166
The Last Book	181

Preface

For an essayist pencil is all. One night early in January I followed the Nipmuck Trail along the Fenton River. Snow pillowed, and my boots soughed as I walked. Ledges of ice tilted across the river, and water gushed through gaps, rolling akimbo then splaying like sheaves of paper sliding from shelves. Snow frosted hard pools. The pools stretched flat as mirrors and were easily recognizable. After two hours of tramping, though, I grew careless. Suddenly I found myself lying on my side, hoping I hadn't broken my pelvis. That night brown seeped across my hip. Three days later the bruise turned literary and spread like the Ottoman Empire. "From small beginnings in Phrygia and Bithynia," I said to Vicki, tracing welts as they galloped in a jihad across hip and thigh, "through Syria, Mesopotamia, the Arabian Peninsula, and North Africa, into the Crimea and west to the Danube." Similes work better on paper than in life. "Hoist your pantaloons, Suleiman," Vicki said. "Geography lesson is over. I have to cook dinner. We are having breast of chicken, not bruised haunch of turkey."

Montaigne said essayists depict passing. A page turns. Snow melts, and bruises vanish like the palace at Bursa. At the end of January I flew to Tennessee for a poetry festival at Sewanee. My plane landed in Nashville late one afternoon, and I spent the night in the Marriott Courtyard near Vanderbilt. I didn't sleep well. At five in the morning the clock radio beside my bed burst into preaching. "From the Voice of Prophecy of the Seventh Day Adventist Church," a man exclaimed before I unplugged him. Two people were in the dining room when I ate breakfast, a doctor and his son, a medical student. "Renal cell carcinoma," the doctor said. "The first patient who died on my watch suffered from that. Things weren't pleasant at the end." "Jesus," I thought, staring at the patty sausage and grits lumpish and tumor-like in front of me. I pushed the plate aside, and walking to the buffet, fetched half a grapefruit and a packet of Kellogg's Low Fat Granola. As I sat down, the doctor and his son laughed. *Cancer* rang through their hilarity, not a word that brings guffaws to my gullet. "Buttons for self-medication," the son said. "Think of the possibilities for suicide." I did not. Instead I studied the packet containing the milk for my granola. "Ultra Skim Southern Belle Fat-Free Milk," the label declared.

My essays amble, and the passings I describe meander across days and topics. Perched atop a spur of the Cumberland Plateau, the Sewanee campus consists of ten thousand acres, much of the land forest. The day after leaving Nashville, I roamed the woods with my friend Neal Bowers. We ambled down Morgan's Steep to the dry creek below Bridal Veil Falls. Atop the plateau, fingers of ice wrapped twigs. At the knuckles of branches, ice tightened into stitches like yarn drawn through loops. Frost clung to the upper surfaces of limbs, slipping lacy over sides, in the sunlight fraying into ribbing. While ice transformed clusters of privet berries into slinky handbags, beaded and blue; it rolled cuffs around the sterile flowers of mountain hydrangea. Under the lip of the plateau, cold panes glazed greenbriar then melted and slipping down the tips of leaves froze into glassy thorns. A pileated woodpecker shrieked, and deer tracks skidded across a slope. Neal pried the nut of a shellbark hickory from the ground, and I picked up a sconce of sourwood seed capsules. The capsules were gray on the outside; inside, they were orange, almost as if winter had burned seeds to wicks.

Tattered pods hung from bladdernut. While mice gnawed holes through some lobs, others were cottony with cocoons. Reddish brown, the seeds themselves were small and round. I munched a handful, but they refused to crack and made my teeth ache. West of the falls, steam billowed from a seam in the ground. The sun was setting, and the falling light turned the steam smoky, first orange then brown. "What kind of music is snoring?" I asked Neal as we stared at the steam. On Neal's not answering, I said, "sheet music." "Did you read in the *San Francisco Chronicle*," I continued when Neal didn't react, "about the grammatical ornithologist who spent a decade correcting birdsong, urging the feathered tribe not to carol, 'tu whit tu who' but 'tu whit tu whom'?" "Did you did dig those questions out of a buried book?" Neal asked. "Yes," I said, "but I don't think I'll use them in an essay." "Going to let the author keep his lines?" Neal said. "You've always been more generous than most essayists."

Essayists are scavengers and rummage days for material. Instead of stringing theme tightly across a page, good essayists, my friend Josh wrote three years ago, "baste tale and description together in hopes of mirroring the weave of life." An essayist, Josh said, should ignore genre and definition. "Truth is heavy," he once told me. "That's why few people tote it." "Right," I answered, not certain what he meant. Josh's literary advice aside, however, I spent last week in the basement of the university library reading *Moore's Rural New-Yorker*. In the number published on January 29, 1876, appeared a stanza from a hymn written for the dedication of Vanderbilt University.

> Patrons and benefactors bless—
> To teachers, students, give success;
> We pray in faith, assured thou wilt
> Shine forth upon our Vanderbilt.

"This sort of thing," the *Rural New-Yorker* commented, "is depressing and tends to discourage all donations to colleges."

People hurt others by actions, themselves by worry. When worry makes tomorrow as heavy as today, the weight is often more than a person can bear. In part I roam the present in order to escape the future. Instead of pondering filling my "last cavity," as Loppie Groat said after pallbearers lowered Pindar Field, a dentist, into the grave, I delight in the moment, smiling, for example, when a correspondent of the *Rural New-Yorker* observed that "soar throats help singers reach high notes." For the essayist who keeps his pencil sharp, every day brings pleasure. In February I sent my friend Don a copy of my latest book. Don lives in Texas and like the dog's tail is a wag. "Sam," he wrote, "I received that book you sent me. I see that it is some more of that trash you keep churning out. As much as I enjoy reading your name in print, please send me something more spiritual next time." Don's letter cheered me, and all seemed right with the afternoon until I went to the English Department. Tacked to my door was an advertisement lifted from the Internet. For sale at eBay, the on-line auction house, was a copy of *Still Life,* a collection of my essays published a decade ago. "Item # 250650194," the copy was autographed. On May 11, 1991, I wrote, "For Sean, with best wishes and in hopes that you will write a great novel someday. It will take work. Sam Pickering." A line of blue ink curved from the inscription and running along the margin ended in an arrowhead at the bottom of the page. At the tip of the arrowhead, a student wrote, "Perhaps starving, working on Chapter 47, Sean sold his most prized possession to purchase a six-pack of Budweiser and a bag of Nachos." Neither autograph nor time increased the value of the essays, the minimum bid being seven dollars. Increments were set at fifty cents, a matter of abstract interest. No bids had been received during the four days the book had been on the block.

Because fiction is not true, happenings in novels usually occur logically. A character drives too fast and wrecks his car. In contrast essays lack plot. While driving too fast, a man unaccountably recalls a remark overheard at the dump six weeks earlier. "The more I read the less ignorant I feel. The less ignorant I feel the less I read." In an essay graphite does not coat sentences, and paragraphs rarely slip smoothly one under another. Saturday morning I had coffee at the Cup of Sun. Three teenagers were in the café, two boys and a girl eating breakfast in the smoking section. The boys were skinny and wore loose sweat pants and hooded sweatshirts, the hoods hanging like cups down their backs. A blue baseball cap sat atop the head of one boy. The bill of the cap had lost definition and pointing to the right sagged over the boy's ear. The girl wore gray jeans and a red sweatshirt with a gold star stamped on the chest. The boys were high, and profanity punctuated their conversation. Their speech was erratic, and phrases exploded, "crystal meth," "white lightning," "blue thunder," and then "truck-driving school." Tied to a post outside the café was a furry brown dog. Occasionally the dog yelped, and four times during breakfast, the boy wearing the cap left the table, opened the door to the restaurant, and spoke to the dog, twice saying, "Don't worry sweetheart. We'll be out in five minutes." Later the same boy asked his friend the name of the "bad guy" in the movie *The Nightmare Before Christmas*. When his friend said, "Scrooge," the boy replied, "that's him. That's the fuckin' guy's name." When the threesome finished eating, they cleaned the table, the boys stacking plates and the girl wiping the tabletop with a rag she fetched from the counter. I watched them leave. They untied the dog and walked west along 195. From a distance they looked slight and pitifully sweet. At Gilbert Road, they entered university grounds and disappeared. In a novel the what-happens-next matters. In an essay passing is enough. Still, in class Monday morning, I asked students to write stories in which the teenagers appeared. "I don't want to," a girl said. "Can't we let them vanish without stamping them into narrative and stripping hope away?" "Yes," I said, "in an essay, we can let them go. Who knows? Maybe one of them will be lucky?"

Writing makes liars of us all. I shade, exaggerate, and conveniently forget. I season nonfiction in fiction. The marinade is not to every reader's taste, but the result perks up the everyday fare of my life. Unlike the novelist, the essayist can beget himself and shape past and present. In April I address a conference on autobiography. Last week the director of the conference asked me to send him the title of my talk and for a brochure, a biographical sketch. "My Autobiography Consists of Lies," I entitled the talk. No foundation has ever awarded me a fellowship. In the sketch I corrected the neglect. Not only, I wrote, had I received fellowships from the National Endowment for the Arts, the Guggenheim Foundation, and the Lila Wallace Reader's Digest Fund, but I had also won the Pulitzer Prize and the National Book Award. Most recently the MacArthur Foundation bestowed "one of its coveted genius grants" upon me, awarding me $398,749 over a five-year period, so that I could devote more time to my "inestimable prose." "Did giving yourself those grants make you feel good?" Josh asked. "Damn straight," I said. "Great," Josh said. "Few people have strength enough to force what-ought-to-be into being."

Satisfaction is fleeting. A day of domesticity usually saps enthusiasm generated by any grant, even five-year lollapaloozas. After informing the English Department and the university administration about my success in garnering fellowships, I grew tired of accolades. My essays are modest and weedy. If pages can be landscapes, then Carthage, Tennessee is my county seat. When sentences spin dizzily, I head for Carthage. Many sensible fictional friends live in Carthage, and after reporters from the *Hartford Courant,* the *Boston Globe,* and the *New York Times* telephoned and asked Vicki about my genius grant, I decamped.

Not much had happened in Carthage since my last visit. To advertise the Haskins Funeral Home, Slubey Garts bought a motorcycle. To it he attached a sidecar shaped like a coffin. Both car and motorcycle were black, and on weekends, Proverbs Goforth donned dark goggles and a black helmet and motored around Smith County. People soon christened the car, some dubbing it the Bone Box, others the Glory Crib. Proverbs also rode in the Homecoming Parade. This fall the Carthage Owls played the Crossville Tigers. On the front of the sidecar, Slubey screwed a hood ornament, a brass owl with wings extended in flight. While blue and white streamers were attached to the handlebars of the motorcycle, "GO OWLS" appeared in big white letters on the door of the car. Inside the car slumped Tessie Dewberry's stuffed tiger, Horace, his tail a hangman's noose around his neck.

The sidecar proved useful. Occasionally Sarey Garts dispatched Proverbs to Barrow's Grocery, the car, she told neighbors, making a sturdy shopping cart. Professionally, the sidecar proved, as Slubey phrased it, a godsend for fetching bodies from deep country or when rain swept roads into trails. Proverbs could not cram big corpses into the car. Still, after swaddling them in slumber clothes, he was able to tie them atop the car, "even behemoths," he testified. For small cadavers the car was a fine basket, just the right size for children, men gnawed to silhouettes by disease, and most women, excluding those who died in childbirth.

When funerals are common, undertakers prosper. Since my breakfast at the Marriott, goners had rarely been out of mind. Summer is widow-making season in Carthage. According to Loppie Groat, heat sours the Milky Way producing virulent bacteria that fall to the earth as dew. A decade ago on his eighty-fifth birthday, Wesley Pitaras proposed to Allegra Sheetz. Allegra was twenty-four, and supposedly Wesley said, "Will you do me the honor to be my widow?" Wesley owned two fat farms and appeared frail. Despite her youth, Allegra had been handled, pinched, and bruised. Consequently she wasn't a fresh marriageable commodity, and she accepted Wesley's proposal, expecting him to go to grass shortly after the ceremony. She was mistaken. Appearances aside, farming toughed Wesley, and despite Allegra's exertions, Wesley thrived until this past July and the week before his ninety-sixth birthday. Proverbs laid Wesley out in lavender, and when Loppie Groat saw the corpse, he exclaimed, "I've never seen a dead man look so natural. Why I could almost swear he's alive." Because Wesley had been a deacon of the Tabernacle of Love, Slubey preached the funeral. He placed a hickory switch in the coffin beside Wesley's right arm then said, "This gray stick ain't much timber. On earth only mourning doves will nest in its branches. But as soon as Wesley soars into Beulah, the stick will bloom, one branch becoming golden chaintree, yellow and the circle unbroken; another, sweet crabapple pink; another, white sugar persimmon. Then the doves will blossom into a choir of thrushes singing 'Amazing Grace,' the notes rising in a rainbow. Squatting atop the arch and grinning will be a possum, his coat silver as morning, his teeth not jagged like that of road kill, but smooth and regular, bound by golden braces, hammered in place by the Celestial

Orthodontist. Down the possum's chops will run royal nectar, the drops turning into asphodel as soon as they touch the ground, circling the flowers, bugle bees, their notes melting like butter."

Wesley's decade of stout health embittered his widow. Convention led her to unscrew the hydrant eye at the funeral, but, according to Turlow Gutheridge, she tightened it immediately after the burial. When Loppie Groat inquired about her plans, she said, "Only our Blessed Savior knows the future. But I'll tell you what. I'm not sharing nobody's lot unless there is a building or two on it."

I enjoyed the funeral and returned to Storrs rejuvenated, ready to master celebrity. In class the next morning, students discussed occupations. "Avoiding stereotypes is difficult," a girl said. "Even today people think some jobs suitable for men, others, suitable for women." "Yes, indeed," I said. "Did you know that 73 percent of the proctologists in this country are female?" "I can't be sure, however," I continued, "that this results from social pressure." In a recent issue of *Forbes,* an anthropologist argued that women were naturally drawn to certain medical specialties. He speculated that "changing diapers imprinted an affection for the proctologic region upon the female mind." For several moments the class scribbled silently. Then a boy raised his hand and said, "Did you make that up?" "Certainly," I answered. "This is a university. What do you expect?"

I am not sure what readers should expect from these essays. However, the percentage of the made-up is considerably less than 73. Still, amid the batter of words, I have dissolved a smidgen of yeast in hopes the writing will rise entertaining and nutritious. Perhaps some of the passing will stick to a funny bone, maybe even a rib or two, and help readers enjoy their moments. If that happens, I will have done well. ❖

Auctioneering

n November I read *The Pleasures of Academe,* a book describing university life, written by Jim Axtell, an old friend. "Whatever else they are," Jim wrote, "colleges and universities are institutions designed and sustained by society primarily for *intellectual* purposes." "Would that were so," I muttered, dropping the book into my lap. I'd just returned from speaking to student affairs administrators in Kansas. While faculty growth has been limited during the past decade, student affairs has expanded faster than other parts of the American university, faster even than athletic departments. The folks to whom I spoke were good people all, but their model of a university was not intellectual but emotional. At many schools enrollment determines not simply state grants but also existence. To maintain enrollment schools accept numbers of unqualified students. In places where retention of students is important, the university becomes support group. As a result administrators emphasize comfort and preach sensibility, often to the point of deferring to weakness. Instead of snuggling warm and platitudinous around the mind like eiderdowns, ideas ought, occasionally, to make people uncomfortable.

Much as dog in a sausage can make a person fidget, so thoughts about the innards of academic doings, no matter how thoroughly scraped and scalded, often make me bilious. Happily, university matters fill only side dishes of my days. As I sat mulling myself into indigestion, Vicki called from upstairs. "The auction starts in

2 Auctioneering

an hour. If you want a shower, you better take it before Eliza comes home from soccer practice." At seven-thirty, the auction to benefit the Mansfield Council for the Arts began. The auction was staged in Tolland Cottage on the grounds of the Mansfield Training School, once home to retarded adults. I was auctioneer. I dressed the part. I wore cowboy boots, gray trousers, a double-breasted blue blazer bought at Aquascutum in London in 1965, a black-and-white checked shirt, a scarlet necktie speckled with green dots, and an Akubra hat, picked up five years ago in Australia and which, as Vicki put it, brought the outback to town: cockatoos, goannas, and red flowering gums. "Daddy," Eliza said when she saw me, "you are one cool cat."

Members of the Arts Council filled the meeting room at the cottage with card tables, decorating them with green tablecloths and vases of red roses. While items to be auctioned were displayed on shelves along one wall, tables heavy with food stretched before another: casseroles, bacon and seafood quiches, tossed salads, breads, plates of hummus, then cakes, fudge, carrot, and caramel, among others. I was not in munching mood. My throat was sore, and instead of eating I drank hot cider. Moreover, worry about Edward sapped my appetite. That afternoon in a high school football game, he got knocked out. Two linemen hit him simultaneously, one high from the left, the other low from the right. Edward spun like a wheel and landed on his head. Immediately the crowd became silent. Edward didn't move for four minutes. As he lay motionless, Vicki turned pale, and Eliza cried. For a moment I felt alone. I was not alone long. As I stood on the sideline watching a doctor bend over Edward, parents of players hurried out of the stands and stood behind me. One man was a diesel mechanic; another, a school superintendent. A woman was a secretary. A man and wife sold gutters and siding. When Edward's right foot moved, hands touched my back. One person said, "Shitfire"; another, "Thank God." Twice during the auction Vicki telephoned Francis at home and asked about Edward, signaling when she returned to the room that Edward was well.

Seventy people attended the auction. To jolly folks into expansive, buying moods, I began by telling tattered country tales, all occurring in Carthage where goings-on are swifter than in Storrs. One lunchtime Hoben Donkin asked the crowd at Ankerrow's Café a question. "If your mother and wife were drowning and you could only save one of them, who would you save?" Discussion having boiled beyond temperate and forks having been raised above mouths, Turlow Gutheridge asked the opinion of a visitor, Cerumen Hooberry who lived in Castalian Springs. "Well," said Cerumen, first rubbing his chin with his left hand then scratching the back of his neck. "I'd save my mother. A fellow might could get another wife, but he couldn't get another mother—at least not easily."

My stories were down in the long Johns, tales I hoped would unravel pretense and relax dignity. When Turlow ate breakfast at the Peacock Diner in Lebanon, the waitress served him coffee in a cup without a saucer. "Could I please have a saucer?" he asked. "No," the waitress said. "We don't dish out saucers no more. When we did, like as not, some fellow would drift off the street and drink out of his saucer. This is a first-class restaurant, and bad manners ain't good for business." Real business was the subject of my last story. In October Hopp Watrous brought his mule Red Bone to Carthage for the horse sale. "How much will you take for that mule?" a buyer from Nashville asked. "Red Bone is a fine mule, but I'll give you a special price," Hopp replied, "one hundred dollars." "I'll pay five dollars," the buyer said. "Sold," Hopp responded. "I'm not going to let a little matter of ninety-five dollars disrupt a new friendship. Red Bone is yours."

I auctioned sixty-three items. The afternoon before the auction I received a catalogue, estimating the value of each item, naming the donor, and providing a one-sentence description. While "The Homestead," donated a "wall basket with sunflower decoration" worth thirty-two dollars, Ermine Cichowski contributed a "blue pitcher with large spout" valued at thirty dollars. The highest estimate was three hundred dollars for a painting depicting a kitchen table bosomy with fruit. Bidders paid mule, not horse,

4 Auctioneering

prices, and the painting sold for one hundred dollars. After receiving the catalogue, I walked to the university bookstore and for sixty-nine cents purchased a packet of three-by-five-inch note cards. In the upper right corner of each card I wrote a number, the numbers running one through sixty-three. Next I jotted down a comment about each item. I auctioned nine gift certificates, for such things as pizza, "dance wear," massage, and cut flowers. I also auctioned six bowls, three tapestries, and four paintings.

I stood behind a lectern at the north end of the room. I worked fast, hawking all sixty-three items in an hour and fifty-eight minutes, the time including a twenty-one minute break following the sale of item thirty-four, a set of note cards decorated with watercolors and valued at fifteen dollars. Because I spent an average of 1.539 minutes an item, commentaries were short, the longest being about the first item, an autographed copy of *I Know This Much Is True*, a novel that topped the bestseller list for several weeks. Although the audience knew the author Wally Lamb wrote fiction, few people realized he was also a poet, his most famous poem, I explained, being "Mary Had A Little Lamb." I read the poem, the last four stanzas not being so familiar as the first four. "When Mary has been good," the fifth stanza began,

> Her daddy gives her lamb.
> She puts it on her little plate
> And covers it with mint jam.
>
> When Mary chews the little lamb so sweet,
> She thinks about the pasture green where lambkin
>   used to bleat.
> No more will little lambkin kick up his tiny feet.
> From fuzzy tail to woolly head he now is Mary's
>   dinner treat.
>
> But don't you worry little children,
> For lambkin is not there.
> The kindly butcher helped him climb
> The golden heavenly stair.

And there he sits with angel wings
The happy lambkin in the sky
Blissful in the shining thought
Baby Jesus don't eat mutton pie.

Oral strutting stumbles on the page. Grimaces and smiles become literary bruises. Much of my commentary was terrible. Before bidding began on a painting depicting three purple plums, I said, "As my friend Rudyard Kipling whispered to me on his deathbed, 'You'll never plumb the oriental mind.'" "Toss your Tupperware out the window," I urged, holding up a brown pitcher. "Fill this with creamy, natural buttermilk." To introduce a mahogany bowl, I paraphrased Byron, the British poet, declaiming, "The Mahogany came down like butter on a roll, / And the salad forks were gleaming in silver and gold." To dampen dry commentary, I sprinkled maxims through my conversation. Most of the sayings were as old as creosote plants: "One fool can ask more questions than ten wise men can answer," "Better wear out than rust out," "Let's not kick at each other said the rooster to the stallion," and "Nature's rule is that just enough of everything is just everything enough." Because this last statement puzzled the audience and seemed liable to break the gallop of buying, I tacked an ancient quip to *enough,* declaring, "the hand that rocked the cradle kicked the bucket."

For several items I created lists. "Imagine the dishes," I said, describing an Elizabethan dinner for six, "haunch of starling, wither of owl, braised paps of pregnant unicorns, hogs' pizzles wrapped in kudzu, white bread marinated in dragon's blood, and possums stuffed with sweet potatoes and floating in a broth of camphor and ambergris." Caprilands Herb Farm donated a twenty-five-dollar gift certificate to the auction. "Herbs," I said, "can mend cracked maidenheads and undo hasty marriages. Herbs can teach people to fry grits and read the Bible backwards and the Torah upside down. Herbs can make a person's faults better than other people's virtues." I urged bidders to choose well

6 Auctioneering

and recommended Buds from the Garden of Babylon, Pillow of Cupid Stalks, and Sprigs of John the Conqueror Root smoked in Emerald Mystery, adding that if a person was especially adventuresome, he could use the certificate to buy basil or oregano.

The successful bidder for a certificate donated by Holiday Spirits could purchase "a wine well-hung on the south side of the slope—a wine the bouquet of which smacked of walnuts and green tomatoes—a wine that slapped the tongue like Vidalia onions and tickled the palette like black-eyed peas." "In short," I said, "a wine for that migrant relative who appears at your front door every Christmas, a bushel of grapefruit in the trunk of her car, good cheer bubbling chemically from her like New Jersey Champagne." To fertilize interest in a "one-hour landscape consultation," I noted the appearance of a new magazine, *Shack and Garden,* the doctor's-office accompaniment of *Gentleman's Quarterly, The Watchtower, Vogue,* and *Tacky Cheap Caribbean Vacations.* "If you learn where to place crab grass for the best effect and when to plant burdock and Jimson weed, your home might appear in *S&G.*"

Chained to the ordinary, my patter rattled. If wit never fluttered toward the sublime, often it descended to the absurd. "My advice," I said while discussing two tickets to the Jorgensen Auditorium, the theater on the campus of the University of Connecticut, "is to attend a concert. Don't simply use these tickets to visit the auditorium. If you don't listen to a concert or see a performance, your evening at Jorgensen will be rather dull." I limited bidding on a car pass to the Mansfield Drive-In to courting couples capable of breeding, saying the drive-in was "America's contribution to Romance." Only once did my palaver undermine a sale. Until I spoke, my friend Sarah was going to bid on a "canvas tote bag and a twenty dollar gift certificate" donated by a video store. "Hide," I said, "X-rated movies from the back room in the bag. No longer will you have to creep like a shadow out of Video Visions. Swing the bag confidently, and acquaintances will assume you plan to spend the evening tapping your fingers to *The Sound of Music.*" "After Sam spoke, I couldn't bid," Sarah said. "People would have thought me a sex fiend."

The only item that didn't sell was "an overnight stay for two at the Grand Pequot Tower in Foxwoods Resort Casino and a dinner for two at the Veranda Café." The council set two hundred dollars as a minimum bid. Although I plugged the night energetically, I think gambling evil and owners of casinos parasites. Consequently I was pleased when the stay did not make the minimum. In truth I considered turning the item over to someone else to auction, telling Vicki that even a dog would wash such proceedings from his paws. "Don't be priggish," she said, "and spoil people's fun." In addition to the overnight at Foxwoods, I had trouble selling several items, the most difficult being a "weekend stay for two" at the Sleep Inn in Willington, a town four miles from Storrs. "Here is a little getaway," I said, "but one close enough to home so that you can rush back to the house if the kiddies catch the epizootic." "Spend nights in the Sleep Inn and wake up refreshed, eager to explore scenic Willington and Ashford." The value of the stay was one hundred and fifty dollars. Bidding quickly tumbled to fifteen dollars, and only started rising, ending at fifty-five dollars, when I observed that the Inn was the perfect place to dump Uncle Henry and Aunt Martha when they showed up unexpectedly, the trunk of their car an orchard ripe with oranges, pears, and waxed delicious apples, in addition to grapefruit.

That night I woke Edward every two hours to check his health. The next morning, aside from being sleepy, he seemed fine, the concussion not causing dizziness or headache. In contrast my thoughts circled back to academic doings. Recently administrators at the university gave Pfizer permission to build a "research facility" on Horsebarn Hill, the most famous drumlin in Connecticut. The university spokesman for the project had been on campus eight months. He hadn't sledded the hill in winter or watched sheep dog trials in summer. He had not flown a kite from the top of the hill or followed a gray fox as it floated along a stonewall, hunting mice. His child had not attended the local high school, and he'd never stood beside the football field, breath quickening as he watched a doctor straighten a son's legs. Unlike administrators who, more often than not, come from without academic

8 Auctioneering

life and who "jump," as a vice-provost in Kansas put it, every four or five years, faculty stay in place for decades, building and becoming community.

Last month I asked a friend why he didn't apply for a national grant. "I don't want to take Mary out of school. She's happy," he said referring to his daughter. Then after pausing, he said, addressing members of the English Department sitting around a lunch table, "To tell the truth, I really like you guys. I don't want to leave you. I'd be lonely." My friend Roger, a faculty member, wasn't at the auction because he was attending a dinner to raise funds for the library. Last year's auctioneers, Lee and Tom, both faculty members, missed the auction because they played lead roles in *Lend Me A Tenor,* a play staged by the Willimantic Players.

"Why are you so down in the chops?" Vicki said, ambling into the study. "I've been thinking about university administrators, not one of whom has been here for longer than three years. More pigs, fewer parsons, an old saying advises." "Last night's sales amounted to more than two thousand dollars," Vicki said. "Forget schooling and suck the fat out of life." "Did you hear," she continued, "about the countryman who spent a fortune on his wife's funeral, explaining to friends that 'she would have done as much or more for me, with pleasure.'"

Just then the mail arrived. I received a letter from Tom, a former student who had joined the Peace Corps and had been sent to Morocco. Tom lived in a mud hut in the Rif Mountains. "I'm working on a reforestation effort," Tom wrote. "I give farmers olive trees to plant. They keep the money from their crops, and erosion in the area is slowed—at least that's how it should work. More often than not, farmers let their goats eat the olive trees, and they use the fertilizer I give them on marijuana plants. A Peace Corps mission is often an exercise in futility."

"Yes," I thought, realizing I could do little about Horsebarn Hill. I could sketch an auction on note cards, but I couldn't script life. Only on paper can life be plotted. Actual events occur beyond margins. I dropped my pencil into the cup Eliza gave me for my birthday, "MY FAVORITE COACH" circling the mug in orange. Then I left the house and wandered the woods below the sheep barns. My observations seemed as random as donations to the auction. A red-tailed hawk kited around the Ogushwitz meadow then rode an overdraft across a ridge. In brambles lay a flap from a cardboard box that once contained five hundred Brass Eagle "Tournament Grade .68 Caliber" paintballs. Golden-crowned kinglets foraged brush by the beaver pond, the yellow atop their heads glazed and ceramic. A dogwood leaned over the Fenton River, fishing line tangling through it in plastic bundles. A juvenile red-winged blackbird dangled from a twig, the line cinched around its neck. The bird was five and a half inches long, and its beak was silvery and puckered, like bark on yellow birch. Down exploded in a topknot from the back of the bird's head, and its feet curved back and pinched inward, resembling first basemen's mitts.

Doings of a day are diverse. Knotted together by time and sequence, they resemble the items I auctioned: a purple bowl followed by an acupuncture treatment then a link bracelet, a bicycle helmet, and four tickets to a minor league baseball game. Occasionally something binds items together. In my life words form twine. On the way home from the walk, I stopped at the university bookstore. As I perused *Wild Orchids of the Northeastern United States,* a graduate student approached me. The man had spent the past two years in Italy. "Mr. Pickering," he said, "you are a role model." "What?" I said, glancing up from a photograph of rose pogonias. "You are so well-preserved," he explained. "Your appearance hasn't changed in years. I hope I look as good when I reach your age." Fall had loosened tongues, and odd remarks spilled across days like leaves blowing from trees. Tom ended his letter from Morocco, writing, "Thank you for your help and guidance. I can honestly say you're one of the coolest cats I've ever met." "Maybe I'll apply for a college presidency," I said at dinner after reading Tom's letter. "Don't," Edward warned. "You wouldn't last long." "Why not?" I asked. "You'd say something stupid," Edward said. "Not stupid," Vicki said, laying her fork across her plate. "Your father would say something intelligent, and that would get him fired." "What's for dessert?" I said. In class the next

10   Auctioneering

morning, a girl said her grandfather suffered from "Halfzheimers, not Alzheimer's, at least not yet." Later I recited the first lines of Tennyson's "Tithonus."

> The woods decay, the woods decay and fall,
> The vapours weep their burthen to the ground,
> Man comes and tills the field and lies beneath,
> And after many a summer dies the swan.

Because students could not identify the author, I supplied hints. "He was an Englishman who wrote in the nineteenth century, and his first name was Alfred." A boy's hand exploded from his side. "Alfred Hitchcock," the boy shouted. "In life," Hap said at lunch, "it's prudent to be bold. Smite the sounding interrogatory and rattle the tinsel so loudly it seems silver."

That afternoon I received a letter from Turlow Gutheridge. Slubey Garts, he recounted, had begun to modernize religious talk. Since people now used *dinner* rather than *supper* to refer to the evening meal, Slubey suggested that his congregation call Christ's final meal "The Last Dinner" instead of "The Last Supper." "Change," Slubey wrote in the church bulletin, "isn't always bad. "The pig in the serving dish," he declared, "is in his second cradle." Turlow's next bit of gossip seemed far-fetched. Still, happenings in Tennessee are more extravagant than those in Connecticut. Last month Onnie Feathers took the excursion train from Nashville to New York. While in New York, he bought a parrot and sent it to Juno, his wife, as a present. On returning to Carthage, he didn't see the parrot, and he asked Juno if she'd received it. "Parrot?" she said, "I don't know nothing about no parrot. Some fool sent me a fancy-pants green chicken. By gum it was tough. Chewing it almost ripped my bridge out."

During the auction my remarks slipped into a herringbone of quips and lists. Since that night words have clung tweedy to my days. When Juno complained about the price of sardines in Barrow's Grocery, Matthew Lanktree, the clerk, said, "Jesus Christ owns this store. He sets prices. I'm just a sinful worm crawling past the cash register to Glory." Yesterday I gave a student a special examination. The examination for the other one hundred and twenty-three people in the class takes place the day after tomorrow. Molly, however, consulted an airline timetable before she looked at the examination schedule. Eager to celebrate Christmas with her family, she booked a flight that left four hours before the regular examination began. Molly was supposed to take the special test at eight o'clock in the morning in the English Department. At eight-thirty she hadn't arrived, and I made several telephone calls. A dean roused her out of bed. Twelve minutes later she rushed panting into my office. I handed her the test and told her to relax. I wished her Merry Christmas then left the office. Three hours later I returned. Atop the examination was a note, thanking me for "preventing" her "from messing up." During a lecture I'd mentioned that my son Francis took courses at the university. "Thank you for being kind," Molly concluded. "You've been nice, nicer than anyone could have been. Nice people are hard to find, and I'm just wondering—does your son have a girl friend?" ❖

Split Infinitive

"Mr. Pickering," the reporter from the *Hartford Courant* began, "the new edition of the *Oxford American Desk Dictionary* accepts the split infinitive. What's your reaction?" When the reporter telephoned, I was pushing my foot down the left leg of a battered pair of trousers. Earlier I cleaned the air filter on the lawn mower, readying myself to mulch leaves, not verbs. As I pulled up the trousers, I almost said, "I don't give a fart about infinitives." Then for a moment I pondered a serious answer, saying the vitality of English depended upon democracy. Rules changed with seasons. Like mushrooms in fall, words suddenly appeared, some spilling spores through the language, others vanishing overnight, being cropped by the voles and squirrels of usage. English sprawled vulgar and alive, unlike French, which academicians labored to freeze into propriety, deadening it cryogenically at the top in hopes of insulating it against change. Because people skim newspapers, however, I jettisoned the thoughtful for the brisk and said, "I do not dine with those who split infinitives." And that remark, I thought, slapped a declarative end on the subject. I was wrong.

The last week in October an article on the infinitive appeared on the front page of the *Courant*. My picture also appeared. Percolating in black type under the photograph was my gastronomic assertion. The statement made people bilious. My friend

Josh reported that the quotation provoked indigestion in the business school, "that stew," as he put it, "of short-order cooks able to fry numbers but in whose skillets fine language clumped in unpalatable heaps of comma splices and dangling participles." So many people bearded me about the infinitive that I fashioned shaggy remarks. To some people I said, "Oral transgressions such as the split infinitive and the misuse of *lie* and *lay* betray out-of-grammar conceptions." "In this age of family values, patriots must not turn deaf ears to illicit couplings." "Youth and the aristocracy," I told others, "forever fornicate across linguistic strata," adding that for an aristocrat dining with the illiterate was another matter. "Can you imagine," I asked, "sharing a meal and conversation with someone who placed gerunds where participles belonged and who forked through agreement oblivious to the nominative and the objective?"

My tone stopped acquaintances from ruminating endlessly about usage. Alas, the statement in the *Courant* turned transitive. The Associated Press reprinted my quip. *Newsday* made it "Quote of the Day," and a score of radio programs interviewed me, including the Voice of America. Rarely do remarks on radio constitute a sound byte. Almost before I opened my mouth, I was off the air. Form determines content, so I cooked up several crisp statements. I began interviews with "To be or to not be, that is the question." "Republicans," I asserted, "had mulled making me an independent linguistic prosecutor." On some shows I declared my patriotism, asking why an *Oxford* dictionary. "Why not a Nashville, a Wichita, or a Peckerwood Point dictionary containing apple-pie American Speech?" Unfortunately my literary petits fours rarely sweetened interviewers. Nobody recognized the paraphrase of *Hamlet.* "Is that a quote?" a man asked. "Yes," I answered. "What's it from?" he continued. "It sounds good. But what does it mean?" "I've heard of Nashville and Wichita," a woman said, "but not Peckerwood Point. In what state is it located?" Even worse talk-show hosts took my statements literally. "Wow," a woman said, "I didn't think people in Congress cared enough about speech to appoint a prosecutor."

14 Split Infinitive

The day after the Associated Press printed my remark, I received a transformer of electronic mail. I shouldn't have been surprised. Discussions of language short-circuit common sense. Near the end of September, Turlow Gutheridge wrote me from Carthage. Piety Goforth's son Reuben, Turlow reported, eloped with Hymettus Clopton. The Cloptons being Pentecostal, Piety disapproved of the marriage. Later when he saw Reuben outside Barrow's grocery, Piety said, "I heard tell that you is married. Is you?" Not expecting to meet his father at the grocery, Reuben paused for a moment then said, "I ain't saying, 'I ain't.'" "I ain't asking you, 'is you ain't?'" Piety responded, "I'm asking you, 'ain't you is?'"

Unlike Turlow's story electronic mail did not celebrate language. Many correspondents were angry. Several urged me to get a "real life." "In some place," Josh said, "smoky with erasures where sentences are fragments and people double negatives." I crafted an answer to one message rough with inappropriate demonstratives. "Dear Anonymous," I wrote, "you didn't sign your name. What a pitiful chickenshit you are." Eliza saw my reply. "Don't send that, Daddy," she said, "the person is such a pitiful cackler that he is liable to flutter into Storrs and lay addled eggs on the front stoop."

Several correspondents hugged the remark to their bosoms. "I'm glad someone maintains high standards in the classroom," a man wrote. "Standards are so low today that a one-legged grasshopper could bound over them." Under the heading DISAPPOINTMENT, a woman wrote, "it has come to my attention a horrible quote attributed to you in a recent AP news update regarding the latest edition of the OED. The article quoted you as saying that you do not dine with those who split infinitives. I would hope this is not true and if it is, it was in jest. How crude it would be to say such a thing in real life, removing oneself from opportunities to dine with those who would benefit perhaps from your life experiences. Have you ever taken it upon yourself to dine with children or young adults who would benefit from educated mentors and perhaps imbed a spark in a young mind to succeed in life? Would that be possible if you were only to dine with those who avoid splitting infinitives? How unaccomplished your life must be to be so haughty and removed."

In contrast to notes written by people suffering from fused intelligences, several messages flickered good-naturedly. "I saw your remark about the infinitive in *Newsweek*," a woman wrote. "In June I heard you give a commencement address. In the speech you mentioned a son but not a wife. Might you be single?" "Seven years ago," another woman wrote, " I bought one of your books. On the title page you wrote, 'May your garden be green with children.' I just wanted you to know that I think of that comment often. I am married now, and Bill and I are looking forward to starting our garden." A sophomore in high school wondered if there were sentences in which an infinitive might sound better split. That question out of the way, the sophomore asked sixteen more questions, among which were: what are some of your main interests, do you enjoy your current job, how would you describe yourself, could you list some important events of your life along with the dates, and lastly, what is your opinion on war.

Every morning I have coffee with friends in the Cup of Sun, a café near the university. As I was reading the student's questions to Ellen, a stranger approached the table. "I saw your statement in the *Courant*," she said, handing me a sheet of paper. "I'm not sure what an infinitive is, but I know you'll like this story." Yellow with age, the paper had been folded into tenths, a crease running smudged down the middle. Written in blue ink in a firm upright hand was a tale of low usage. A preacher who wanted to earn money for his church learned that a fortune could be made racing horses. Consequently he decided to purchase a horse and race him at the local track. Because prices were steep, "the preacher ended up buying a donkey." "He figured that since he owned the donkey, he might as well enter him in a race." To his surprise the donkey finished third. The next morning the headline on the sports page declared, "Preacher's Ass Shows."

The preacher was so pleased by the donkey's performance that he entered the animal in a second race. This time the donkey won. The next day the headline proclaimed, "Preacher's Ass

Out In Front." Publicity about the races so upset the local bishop that he ordered the preacher not to run the donkey again. Having already registered the donkey for a third race, the preacher immediately withdrew the animal. Accordingly, the next day the headline stated, "Bishop Scratches Preacher's Ass." The headline gave the bishop high blood, and he demanded that the preacher get rid of the animal. The preacher wanted the donkey to go to a good home, so he gave it to a nun living in a nearby convent. The next day the paper announced, "Nun Has Best Ass In Town." On reading the paper, the bishop fainted. As soon as he recovered, he told the nun to rid herself and the parish of the donkey. The nun sold the donkey to a farmer for ten dollars. The next day the paper reported, "Nun Peddles Ass For Ten Dollars." "Twenty-four hours later," the story concluded, "the bishop was buried."

"And all of this," Ellen said after reading the story, "because of your asininity. What a period the story puts on the split infinitive!" Ellen is a novelist, not a grammarian. For her, the end of a story is "The End." In contrast linguistic matters stretch through endless run-on sentences. Instead of a period, the story was a colon. That afternoon I received a packet of letters.

In nineteen lines a woman used twenty-two split infinitives, ending her letter with a postscript explaining, "to quickly come up with so many infinitives to wantonly split was not easy, but it was fun to hardily try." From Toronto came an advertisement for a "Diksionari uv Kanadan" written in something akin to phonetics. "Prof Pikrin," my correspondent explained, "Yu ar a linggwistik aktivist. Dherfor, I hoop dhat yu will organaiz ful, staffd diskussiones uv Kanadan, dhe fiinal tranzformasions uv ingglis." "I well remember," a man wrote from Vermont, "that nothing caught a teacher's eye like a split infinitive. My cousin would deliberately include one deep in any lengthy report he wrote as a test to see if the teacher actually read it with attention." At the end of the letter appeared a list of questions. Why, for example, "when English was being codified, did the academics involved decide to make the infinitive two words?" Suddenly, I tired of the parenthesis life had become. Condemning the infinitive to the pen, the page, and the dictionary, I split. I dropped the letters into the recycle bag, and slamming the door behind me, headed for wood and field.

Below the sheep barn the afternoon sun planed through sugar maples, painting the scrub orange. Along the cut for the power line, ferns curled bony and bronze, and green drained out of barberry, turning leaves orange then red. Early the next day silver halos leached from the leaves of northern red oak, buffing the sky. Along an old road a breeze streamed cool as water. At the edge of a marsh a female osprey perched atop a shattered tree, clutching a fish. I had never seen an osprey in Storrs. The bird's white breast and epaulettes gleamed in the light. Later that day in the English Department, Tom asked, "has there been any reaction to what you said about the infinitive?" "Yes," I said, "but this morning I saw an osprey." ❖

After Christmas

One Friday night early in December, Vicki and I drove Edward to St. Philip's Church in Ashford for the high school football banquet. Vicki and I grazed across a landscape thick with ham, turkey, and roast beef. We chatted with parents and marveled at size of our boys, small without helmets and shoulder pads. Edward won a letter and received a black sweatshirt, a white panther toothy and scowling stamped on the chest, E. O. SMITH FOOTBALL printed below in capital letters. Although Edward sat with friends, he seemed preoccupied. "The banquet was great fun," Vicki said later as we drove home. "Not for me," Edward said. "December is a basketball month. Football ends in November. The banquet was out of season." Order and definition appeal to Edward. He dresses carefully and organizes shelf and drawer. He finishes books he starts. He believes directions and handwriting should be clear. At fifteen Edward resists the truth that life is disorderly. He does not understand that categories are artificial, imposed by men in vain attempts to neaten days. "Doings cannot be confined to season. Life sprawls," I preached. "Rules deaden. Once life tumbles over man-made barriers, days quicken into promising chaos." "Why do you make me speak correct English if rules destroy?" Edward asked, folding his sweatshirt neatly and placing it on the seat. "Language enables a person to hide thought," I said. "Rules are nails which enable people to conceal feelings behind structure. While readers study sentence and idea, a writer scales verb and noun and, slipping through the sill of meaning, escapes into the disorderly world." "What did all that you said to Edward mean?" Vicki asked in bed that night. "I don't know," I said, turning the light out.

The next morning Vicki and I returned to St. Philip's for the annual "Christmas Ethnic Bake Sale." Tables sagged, heavy with Slovak and Polish pastries—nut, poppy seed, and lekvar rolls. I bought thirteen dollars worth of rolls, and Vicki, two Teddy bears for four dollars, one dressed in pink shorts, the other in blue. I chatted with a secretary who managed a dean then with a woman whose granddaughter I'd taught. Afterward Vicki and I ate mango tarts, the crust rich with almonds. Before leaving St. Philip's I went to the lavatory. Taped on the wall were signs reading, "PLEASE flUSH AFTER USE—FR. JOE." "Maybe Father Joe thinks carelessness a venial sin," Vicki said as we drove home. "Maybe," I said, adding, "we haven't been to St. Philip's in fifteen years. Now we have been twice in two days. Isn't that odd?" "No," Vicki said, "it's Christmas." When we arrived home, Vicki prepared breakfast for the children, and I looked out the kitchen window. Perched on opposite sides of a bird feeder, two juncos tried to intimidate each other, extending necks, pointing bills, then flattening their tails on the wood, fanning them so that the white outer feathers almost snapped. A Carolina wren landed on a bar of suet, the first Carolina wren I'd seen since last winter. "The wren is back," I said.

The wren was not a harbinger of wintry order. Christmas is a disturbing season. Schools close, and routines crumble. Out of kindness, people disrupt the comfortable, pedestrian lives of relatives and acquaintances, in cards and letters reminding them of loss. People exhume memories and, in trying to breathe life into dry bones, cause others to cough and weep. Friends so long vanished that they seem strangers clamber up from the dead year, filling minds with ghostly what-might-have-beens. Thoughts about beginnings in other places and other times soon become worries about endings. As people age, their ponderings resemble those of Rog Wilkenfeld and Jack Manning, two reprobates in Carthage. In December a preacher at the Baptist Church on Main Street declared eternal punishment a myth. "Did you hear what the reverend said about there being no Hell?" Jack asked Rog after the sermon. "Yes," Rog answered, "but so what?" "Well," Jack said, "if the preacher is right, then what's going to become of us?"

In hope of thinking less about the ends of things, people entertain more during Christmas than during any other season. Late on December 23, Sam and Ellen came to the house for shrimp and new Beaujolais. The wine bubbled, and Ellen recited her favorite holiday poem, "Grapefruit." "Fresh from Florida when they arrive, / We know Grandmother's still alive." After the shrimp vanished like krill, Vicki tossed a salad and put candlesticks on the dining room table. I ordered a pizza from Paul's, a large one loaded with olives, mushrooms, and pepperoni. I uncorked more wine, and we ate an early Christmas feast. Later that night Fennel the cat met Ellen at her front door. "I served Fennel a big dinner," Ellen said the next day. "Unfortunately I missed his bowl and poured cat food all over the kitchen floor."

Christmas Day made me melancholy. Wrappings scattered across the living room seemed husks, remnants of happiness thinned by time. I tried to remember Mother and Father. I shut my eyes and attempted to force memory into sound. I didn't succeed. I studied the tree in hopes that old ornaments would light association and boyhood Christmases in Nashville would flash into mind. Alas, recollection remained dark. So that my mood would not cloud the children's day, I went for a walk before lunch.

Chickadees gleaned hemlocks above the Fenton River, turning twigs into trapezes. Bluebirds foraged swamp dogwood. A red-bellied woodpecker clacked, and four crows swept over the Ogushwitz meadow, their shadows lingering like moats at the edge of vision. A vole raced through grass and spun sideways into a tunnel. Nearby, an owl had brushed the ground, feathers spread like fingers, pulling snow into angel wings. Water in the beaver pond was low, and from willows mats of roots hung down in scouring pads. Like a hand-me-down ornament, a hornets' nest hung from an oak, the sides of the nest knocked into shreds, the three tiers of cells akimbo. Ribs of snow curved down the ridge above the meadow. At the top of the ridge, sunlight whisked yellow through trees. Walks are opiates, sights alkaloids numbing the past. I returned home in good spirits. For lunch Vicki cooked leg of lamb, Edward's favorite meat. When Vicki set the lamb on the table, I said, "Ah, yes, a wing of the old wool bird." "What bird?" Eliza asked. "Never mind," I said, "Merry Christmas."

The following Monday I drove Francis to the eye doctor. To pass time while the doctor examined Francis, I thumbed magazines. Season influenced content. A full-page advertisement in the December 21–28 issue of *New York Magazine* startled me. "One in three suffer from *Gynecomastia,* an embarrassing condition that causes masculine breasts to become enlarged," a paragraph asserted. A plastic surgeon with an office on Park Avenue placed the ad in the magazine. Fatty and glandular tissue, separate or in cohoots, caused *Gynecomastia.* To remove fatty tissue "only liposuction" was "needed." "When extra glandular tissue" caused "the problem," it was "removed in sections through a small incision around the nipple-areola complex." I showed the advertisement to the woman sitting next to me. "I don't think my HMO will pay for that," she said. "A third of all males in a population of 280 million," Josh calculated, "would be 46,666,666 people. Of course most would be dry. Not more than 20 percent would be milking." "Still," Josh continued, "men capable of breeding should be freshened." Josh noted that the advertisement appeared just before the New Year when all the oafs in the nation resolved to tidy their hopeless lives. For his part Josh said he was pleased to have a little suet on his bosom. Every night before bed, he pranced back and forth before a full-length mirror, sticking on pasties, twirlers attached to the ends. "I can make one breast rotate clockwise while the other spins counterclockwise," he said. "Unfortunately my titties are too small for me to balance a glass of champagne on them, and the most I reckon I'll ever balance is a liqueur glass. But I'm training hard, and some night I will invite you over for a nip and a show."

That night Vicki and the children watched *Washington Square,* a movie adapted from Henry James's novel. After Christmas I avoid meaningful experiences, especially those on film, and I didn't see the movie. "What does it teach the children if you will only be part of the family for explosion movies?" Vicki asked. "Plenty," I said then went upstairs and read P. G. Wodehouse's novel *Full Moon*, a book populated by Christmas ninnies, among others, Tipton Plimsol, Galahad Threepwood, Lady Hermione Wedge, and the Empress of Blandings, this last a sow owned by Clarence, the Ninth Earl of Emsworth, and the perennial winner of the Fat Pigs Class at the Shropshire Agricultural Fair.

At the end of December I received a bundle of tardy Christmas mail. "You are on a list in my address book," a friend wrote from Georgia, "because you have touched my life in such an important way that you have become the fabric of my life. Thank you for being there and holding our hands when we needed you the most. What a wonderful time to remember the meaning of life, and how lost we would be without our Savior, who came 1999 years ago." Smacking more of April than December, several messages promised spring. Emma sent Edward a card from Durham, North Carolina. On the front a little girl in a snowsuit stood on her toes and slipped an envelope into a mailbox decorated with ribbons and holly. Printed on the side of the box was the name "S. Claus." At the girl's feet a baby seal lay in snow, a flipper against the post supporting the box, the animal's eyes round marbles and its mouth curving upward whiskered and smiling. "Dear Ed," Emma wrote inside the card, "I hope you have a wonderful holiday season and hope to see you at camp next summer." Emma ended writing, "Love ya," the love being drawn, a heart instead of four letters. On New Year's Eve, I received a letter from Britain, the kind of letter that warms winter with envy. "We have bought," Brian wrote, "a small farm in Provence. The farmhouse has a fabulous view looking south over its own vineyard and out over rolling ridges toward Cézanne's Mt. Saint Victoire and north to Grande Luberon Ridge."

By year's end pattern stamped days. On New Year's Eve, Vicki, the children, and I visited the Wadsworth Athenaeum in Hartford, a trip we make every December. I spent the morning at an exhibit of "19th Century American and Australian Landscapes" entitled "New Worlds From Old." Soon ritual would transform the new into an old year, indistinct from the haze of previous years. According to Greek tale, Noah glimpsed the tops of mountains on January 1. Not until February 17, however, did he send the dove from the ark. Perhaps he suspected that once the ark ran aground, routine would harrow his life, burying excitement beneath sandy clods. For eight minutes I studied Eugene von Guérard's "Ferntree Gully." Bushes of tree ferns swept the earth like green feather dusters. In the distance the sky curved porcelain, and slipping downward like a teacup sat atop a saucer-shaped ridge. I'd first seen the painting six years ago when we spent twelve months in Australia. The painting made me sentimental, and that night I chose the entertainment, *Harvey,* my father's favorite movie, starring Jimmy Stewart and his companion, an invisible white rabbit.

On New Year's Day, Vicki, the children, and I drove to Princeton to visit Vicki's mother, a trip we make every year after Christmas. In the basement of the house, Edward found a silver centerpiece manufactured by Gorham in Providence, Rhode Island. Eighteen and a half inches long, the centerpiece was a female dachshund lying on her side, feeding eight puppies. The puppies screwed onto their mother's nipples, four atop four. Order mattered, and each puppy was numbered, the number stamped on the puppy's navel. In the mother's navel appeared a boar's head, indicating that Gorham made the centerpiece in 1885. Next to the centerpiece was a copy of *The Rubaiyat of Omar Khayyam,* "the Astronomer Poet of Persia," printed by Houghton Mifflin in 1894 and illustrated by Elihu Vedder. Illustrations were ornate, hybrids of William Blake and the Pre-Raphaelites, wings and robes fluttering across pages.

In June, 1900, Elizabeth Teresa Dale, Elizabeth Congdon, Alice Dillingham, Marjory Cheney, H. Jean Crawford, and Anne Maynard Kidder, the board of the *Fortnightly Philistine,* Bryn Mawr's undergraduate magazine, presented the book to Grace Latimer Jones, the journal's editor-in-chief and Vicki's great-aunt. I flipped through pages. Stuck to the top of the page on which appeared the

Rubaiyat's ninety-sixth verse was a snapshot of two professors striding along a path, gowns rippling around them. I read the verse under the photograph.

> Yet Ah, that Spring should vanish with the Rose!
> That Youth's sweet-scented manuscript should close!
> The Nightingale that in the branches sang,
> Ah whence and whither flown again, who knows!

Beneath the book in a cardboard box lay a parchment, a heavy orange seal four and a half inches in diameter and five-eighths of an inch thick attached to it by a sturdy ribbon. Signed October 3, 1767, the parchment deeded 28,971 acres "more or less" and "all Manner of Mines unopened excepting Mines of Gold Silver Lead Copper & Coals in and upon the said Tract of Land" to a list of settlers of the "Township of Yarmouth." "To all whom these presents shall come Greeting," the scribe began, "Know Ye That I Lord William Campbell Captain General and Governor in George The Third under The Great Seal of Great Britain have given granted and Confirmed and do by these presents by and with the Advice and Consent of His Majestys Council for the said Provence. . . ." "Daddy," Eliza asked, "why are these things in the basement? What do they have in common?" "The hand that put them here," I said, adding, "let's go to the Princeton bookstore."

I explored the bookstore much as I had the basement. The arbitrary nature of title and subject intrigued the children. "Write a book entitled *Searching for the Fairy Godmother*," Eliza said after perusing self-help manuals. "Call yourself Tulip McGee. Every nincompoop in therapy will buy it." For his part Francis studied literary criticism. "Daddy," he said, "I know the title to get you a named chair, *Transgendered Racial Stereotypes in the Bible Belt.*" At the store I bought only one book, *Caesar's Gallic Wars*, the Loeb Classical Library edition for Edward. Later the children and I met Vicki in Kitchen Kapers in Palmer Square, and Vicki purchased wooden tongs for three dollars, useful, she explained, "for pulling muffins from the toaster." While Vicki explored the store, Edward sat beside the front door on a pile of copra doormats and read. The mats were colorful. Pansies bloomed on a lattice of green leaves, yellow thumbs in the middles of blossoms, clovers of black, blue and green petals surrounding them. A man looked at the mats then Edward. "What are you reading?" he asked. "Julius Caesar," Edward answered. "Stella," the man said to a woman eyeing a large frying pan, "I told you stores in Princeton would be different. This boy is reading Latin. You won't see that in Home Depot."

"What was odd about my reading?" Edward asked later. "Nothing," I said. "The man didn't expect to find Latin in a hardware store. Someone else might think a football banquet in December unseasonable." Vicki, the children, and I returned to Storrs on January 4. "After Christmas" had ended. The next morning school opened. In the mail appeared harbingers of spring, flower catalogues, their pages, yards; their sentences, Iris and dahlias, lilies, hollyhocks, and butterfly bushes. White Flower Farm advertised yellow ladies' slippers. I imagined yellow waltzing through the wood behind the house. Winter dreams rarely fit the rest of the year. The arch of my pocket was too flat to support flowers costing sixty dollars apiece or three for $167.95. For a moment I considered buying a dozen astilboides for $112.95. With leaves two feet wide, the plants would soften light, turning it smoky and pliant. In November the dogwood I planted in the dell twelve years ago died, and I decided to order a tree. Bark appeals to me, and I considered planting a clump of river birch, the Heritage cultivar, the bark of which peeled into buckskin. Because shade slips over the dell like a glove, however, I bought a hybrid witchhazel from Wayside Gardens, the Diane cultivar that blooms coppery each fall.

As cold weather drives dogs mad, so winter makes people behave oddly. The first week in the New Year, a man who dubbed himself Zammariel wrote from Missouri. He addressed his letter to "Appropriating Pikeryng." At the top of the page he wrote, "as cats hunt rats, so would you rifle / The dustiest books to steal a trifle." The letter contained two quotations, "The Finding of Moses" and "Belshazzar's Feast," verses Zammariel said he discovered nailed to Resurrection Gate. "On Egypt's banks contagious to the Nile," the first quotation began,

Great Pharaoh's daughter came to wash in style.
And after having a tip-top swim,
Ran about the sands to dry her skin
And kicked the basket the babe lay in.
"Gals," says she in accents mild,
"Which of you is it as owns this child?"

The second quotation was snipped from the same biblical papyrus.

When all the nobles stood appalled,
Someone suggested Daniel should be called.
Daniel appears, and just remarks in passing:
"The words are Mene, Mene, Tekel, and Upharsin."

After Christmas my thoughts run to religion. Every January a theological tiff startles the "outstrapolous flocks," as Turlow Gutheridge dubs congregations in Carthage. Late in December Cumpton Hardress died. Immediately after the funeral, Roavea his wife became ill. Two days later she died. Cumpton was ninety-four at his death, Roavea, a year younger. They married when they were fifteen and fourteen respectively. "Seventy-nine years," Slubey Garts said at Roavea's funeral. "Death cannot untie a marriage knotted by God. In the next life Cumpton and Roavea will be one angel." Five years ago Malachi Ramus seceded from Slubey's Tabernacle of Love and founded the Church of the Chastening Rod. After learning that Slubey said the Hardresses would become a single angel, Malachi preached a sermon in which he said such doctrine could only be found in *The Devil's Bible,* "bound in ass's hide, sewed together with spider webs, printed on snake skin, and with a wishbone for a bookmark." Slubey, Malachi asserted, deceived people into thinking he could read in the dark and teach ants to mine gold. During the years that Slubey preached in Carthage, Malachi said, he had not grown upward like a swan's neck. "No, brothers and sisters," Malachi declared, "He's sunk down like a cow's tail." Malachi labeled Slubey a malignant bookworm, "not *genus homo,*" he declared, "but *anobium pertinax* gnawing the Holy out of Holy Writ."

"A person needs a sense of humor to be a Christian," Turlow told the lunchtime crowd at Ankerrow's Café. For his part Slubey treated insults as compliments. Instead of criticizing him, Slubey called Malachi "a trumpeter in the Hallelujah Band, always blowing glory notes, no matter that the tunes were sometimes distempered." Undeserved praise is satire, and Slubey's remark infuriated Malachi. Slubey, he declared, was a Luciferist, a snake with glue for skin. The Luciferist sticks to whoever touches it, Malachi elaborated, "and coiling slowly through his days like a vine, loosens faith, the mortar binding soul to God."

Unlike Slubey, Proverbs Goforth, deacon at the Tabernacle, did not remain above the fray. Although Malachi thought himself Commissioner of the Christian Highway Patrol, Proverbs said, he was only "a Pentecostal Caliph wearing a store-bought badge." When Malachi first appeared in Carthage, he was specter-thin. Later after feeding on parishioners' purses, he put on flesh, becoming "a talking sausage, thick as an elephant's trunk."

Money is often the taproot sustaining weedy religious doings. Slubey was a successful Christian entrepreneur. In September Malachi opened a shop, The Gospel Cabinet. The Cabinet sold Scented Glue. "Adhesive frankincense," the label on the jar stated, "for repairing Bibles, Prayer Books, Hymnals, and Precious Family Documents." From Juno Feathers, Malachi purchased suet, and members of the congregation coined fatty pennies, quarters, and half-dollars sized for kitchen and "sacramental needs." Stamped on one side of the penny was the phrase "NOBODY BUT JESUS." On the reverse side a pot of snaps cooked on a stove. "SHINE ON ME" and turnip greens appeared on the quarter. "GOD WALKING" and a bottle tree with a chicken roosting on the lowest limb were stamped on the half-dollar. The shop also sold Bibles, Malachi writing on title pages, "With the Author's Compliments." Sales at the Cabinet so disappointed Malachi that Proverbs accused him of suffering from "The Golden Dropsy."

In part desire for publicity contributed to Malachi's attack on Slubey. In November, Malachi published a collection of sermons. Aside from purchases made by his parishioners, sales languished. Dedicated to "The Redeemer," the collection consisted of seven sermons: "A Pleasant and Profitable Tour of Hell"; "Sores of Sickness, God's Germs for His Beloved"; "High-Heeled Shoes for Dwarfs in Holiness"; "Spiritual Mustard to Make the Soul Sneeze with Devotion"; "A Blast Aimed at the Devil's Backside"; "Crumbs of Comfort for the Hens and Roosters of the Church"; and "Reaping the Stubborn Ears for Heavenly Succotash." Proverbs labeled the sermons "elbow writing," saying that instead of transforming clay into life the sermons changed life into clay. Proverbs aside, however, the sermons contained elevated moments. In the preface Malachi praised his mother. "The Womb of Grace that bore me and the Nipples of Righteousness that gave me suck made my Soul hunger for Christian Bread." In "Crumbs of Comfort," inspiration rose yeasty as he urged readers "to nibble biscuits baked in the Oven of Charity, buttered by Sparrows of the Spirit, over them the Swallows of Salvation spreading preserves sweet with eternal life."

Commerce aside, what really set Malachi against Slubey was losing two members of his congregation to the Tabernacle. Shortly after Through-Much-Tribulation-We-Enter-The-Kingdom Crabb changed his Christian name to Henry, he left the Chastening Rod, taking with him his wife Gospody, who, for her part, changed her first name to Primrose, thus becoming Primrose Crabb. A skilled seamstress, Primrose sewed a quilt on which she depicted Adam digging peanuts and Eve spinning a rug, between them David playing his harp. Around the edges of the quilt Primrose sewed a verse:

> Goliath Armed Led An Host From Gath
> Defied The Lord And Provoked His Wrath.
> Young David Came, In His Hands A Sling
> And With A Stone The Giant Down Did Ding.

Malachi didn't think much of the quilt. Primrose sewed a beard on Adam, "unbaptizing him" and transforming him from a Gentile into an ancient Hebrew. "Adam was the first man, and we are his descendants," Malachi said, "and if he hadn't been a Gentile, none of us Christians would be here in Carthage today."

After the holidays religious controversy wilted as congregations prepared for planting. In Maggart, Hamlet Toothaker, a hermit, died. Hamlet retired to the hills after Freelove his wife started stepping out. To keep a cat from wandering, an owner butters the animal's paws. Hamlet, Turlow recounted, spread lard on Freelove's feet, but she "just hunkered down on all fours, wagged her tail, and scampered away." After his wife vanished, Hamlet appeared in Carthage only twice a year. Each spring and fall he stuck a stick through the nose cartilage of Thumb his cow, or she-bull as he called her. Attaching strings to the ends of the stick, he rode Thumb into Carthage, stopping whenever he got thirsty to milk her. Failure of his marriage curdled Hamlet's nature, however, and no one mourned his death. Above his grave someone hammered a slab of wood, chalking on it,

> Whether He Lived, or Whether He Died,
> Nobody Laughed, and Nobody Cried.
> Where He's Gone, and How He Fares,
> Nobody Knows, and Nobody Cares.

Early in January Hollis Hunnewell's carnival visited Carthage and staged a series of pantomimes, the most popular being: "Oh! My Poor Husband," "The Country Wedding," "No Kissing at All," "Tell Me Why," "Mrs. Graves," and "Preserved Fish." I don't know much about the performances, hearing about them only on Twelfth Night, just before Vicki and I stripped ornaments from the Christmas tree. "After Christmas" had ended. Three days later a fund-raiser at the university forwarded a card to me, writing, "Thought you would like this." Inside the card a former student wrote, "This gift is in honor of Professor Sam Pickering, a man who believed in me before I believed in myself." "How sweet," Vicki said. "That should make you feel good." "I'd feel a hell of a lot better," I said, "if the man had sent the gift to me and not to the damn university." "Christmas has come and gone," Vicki said, taking pork chops out of the icebox. ❖

Lies and Consequences

The more cultured a man the more he lies. "Rarely," my friend Josh said recently, "can the truthful be trusted to do the right thing." Capable of delicacy and civility, the liar is concerned more for the particular than the abstract. Weaving fancy across the gulf separating what is from what ought to be, liars are imaginative and nurture hope and dream. "Lies," Josh continued, "are the sauce of conversation and appetite. Nothing spoils a meal quicker that bacterial truth." Liars are tolerant, realizing that ultimate truths rest upon stretchers. "Unfortunately," Josh said, shaking his head, "once kind lies become established they evolve into inhumane fact." Liars are at ease outside Zion. Because they are not enthusiasts, liars don't bully wayward human nature into hypocrisy. For the liar life is not a pilgrimage but a meandering, freeing people from narrow, straight ways. Only after children learn to lie can they have lives of their own. Towering over the child, the ogreish adult says, "I can forgive anything but a lie"—a statement that is itself a lie.

Lies curve through my essays like Frisbees. Pony Boguski was the most notorious miser in Carthage. Some years ago Pony had his tonsils removed at Baptist Hospital in Nashville. After the operation Pony telegraphed his wife Amanda. Western Union did not charge customers for their names. "I want to wire Carthage," Pony said to the operator. "What's your name?" the operator asked. "Well," Pony said, "I know I look a little pale, but I'm a Cherokee

Indian, and I've just had an operation. My Christian name is 'I-Will-Be-Home-Friday.' My middle name is 'On-The-Evening-Train,' and my last name is 'Hold-Dinner-And-Meet-Me-On-The-Platform-At-Eight-O'clock.'"

Many lies are visual not verbal. Juliet hangs lace from her bones, so that when Romeo looks at her, ribbons flow in sweet distraction. In November Enos Mayfield opened a bar in Crossville. He named the bar "The King's Arms." Above the front door Enos nailed a sign painted by Labelle Watrous. On the sign appeared two legs wrapped in thick black socks, the calves round as whiskey barrels, staves bulging fermented, the hoops a pair of garters decorated with yellow violets framing the motto "IT AM I."

Writers know lies provide mortar for both fiction and nonfiction. Occasionally, a seeker after truth chisels at paragraphs and reduces fancy to ruinous common sense. When St. Jerome translated the Bible into Latin in the fourth century, he discarded clumps of prose from other versions, particularly those used in North Africa. How nice to know that in an earlier, "Old Latin" Bible, Matthew explained that the dog's nose was cold because Noah used it to plug a hole in the ark and that caterpillars couldn't eat leaves growing on trees touched by rainbows. Today no schoolboy reads about the siege of Metiosedum, described in the *B* version of Caesar's *Gallic Wars*. Inhabitants of Metiosedum refused to surrender to the Roman commander Labienus. Facing starvation, they chopped off their left arms and ate them, so that they would have strength enough to fight with their right arms. The bravery of the "barbarians" so impressed Labienus that on the fall of Metiosedum he spared the survivors. Unlike truth, bed-bound by spade and hoe, lies create landscapes weedy with possibility. Metiosedum was located on an island in the Seine. Today a majority of the islanders are right-handed, a condition the inhabitants explain, not by the fact that most Frenchmen are right-handed, but by a story describing behavior centuries ago.

Taking pride in truth or accuracy leads to inflexibility. In contrast to liars who alter fact and change perspective, truthful people eschew intellectual play. Incapable of holding multiple and

32   Lies and Consequences

contradictory interpretations of events in mind, the truthful delude themselves into certainty. Sure his explanation is correct, the truthful person rarely hesitates to speak. Consequently he spreads misinterpretations which smack, if not of lies, at least of fiction. In Carthage Nazarenus Honeybone was a potter. An outspoken devotee of truth, Nazarenus was a shallow thinker and as such was responsible for some of the lankiest tales circulating around town. Nazarenus toured Tennessee and Kentucky in summers, searching for neglected graveyards. Clay for jugs, he told the lunchtime crowd at Ankerrow's Café, "rises from tombs like Lazarus." He dug his best clay, he said, from the graves of slaves, "field hands whose strength leached into the ground making the soil lumpy and muscular." Almost as good and suitable for prime kitchen pots was clay spaded from the graves of yeomen, "folks so yoked to plowing that their bodies became tongue and axle." In contrast, the graves of bankers and lawyers yielded sorry clay. Because the color was rich, such soil, Nazarenus recounted, fooled him at first. "Pots made from pinstripes," he declared, "don't wear well in honest farmhouses." The worst grade clay, however, came from the graves of professors. "Thin as skim milk," he said, "lacking gumption and grit."

Like a diffuse root system the fictional impulse runs fibrous through people. In the Café last Thursday, Hoben Donkin said the Book of Jonah had a curious history. "I read an article," Hoben reported, "in which an historian stated that the first version of the Bible didn't include the account of Jonah and the whale. For three hundred years the story was lost. Then one afternoon a fisherman caught an angelfish in the Sea of Galilee. That night when the man gutted the fish, he discovered the Book of Jonah." "Surrounded by roe?" Turlow Gutheridge asked. "Yes," Hoben said, "a bushel of golden eggs, all larger than pearls." The eggs made the fisherman fabulously wealthy. "Holy mackerel," Loppie Groat exclaimed. "That reminds me of an article I read." "Like the Book of Jonah, early Bibles did not contain the Gospels," Loppie began. To provide meat for his daughter's wedding a wealthy Egyptian living near Luxor slaughtered one of the Pharaoh's lean kine. Because his daughter was fond of tripe, the man boiled the stomachs himself. "Imagine his surprise," Loppie said, "when he sliced open the first stomach and the Book of Matthew oozed out." As might be expected Mark popped out of the second stomach, while the third contained Luke and the fourth, John.

Humans are classifiers, delighting more in ordering than in creating. Separating truth from lie then labeling results accurately is almost impossible, however. Many stories, which on first sight smack of exaggeration, later prove startling truth. Eighteen years ago the *American Archaeologist* described the opening of a burial mound in Reynolds County, Missouri. At the center of the mound was a small tomb containing a square coffin fashioned out of flat granite pink with feldspar, "the long home," the account stated, "of the world's smallest mother." Inside the coffin was the skeleton of a woman. Measuring fifteen and five-eighths inches from the top of the skull to the underside of the toes, the skeleton lay on its back, ankles crossed and head to the east. The woman's left arm curved outward like the waning moon. Cradled in the semi-circle was the skeleton of a child, a boy four and a half inches tall. Clothes worn by the woman and child had turned to dust. However, scattered amid the woman's ribs were ninety-four small beads. With holes drilled through their centers, the beads had slipped from a necklace, the string of which had rotted. For the society of which the woman was a member, the article surmised, "beads probably signified wealth, and more than likely elders believed beads would serve mother and child well in the afterlife." Lending credence to the theory was the variety of minerals composing the beads, "some obtained," the article speculated, "through trading rather than mining." Among the minerals were smoky quartz, amethyst, green kyanite, galena, white calomel, leucite, yellow sphalerite, and leadhillite tinted blue and green.

Early in February I flew to Atlanta and spoke at Emory University. Interest determines hearing. In describing an acquaintance, the man sitting next to me on the airplane said, "the only way you can tell whether he is lying or not is to look and see if his mouth is open." At Emory I spent a morning roaming the campus.

34 Lies and Consequences

A woolly bear caterpillar lay in a tight curl on a walk outside Callaway Center. I put the caterpillar under a bush atop a nest of pine needles. Afterward I sat on a bench overlooking a small gully running east and west from Ashbury Circle toward the chapel. The gully was a hundred yards long, and its sides pitched into a drainage ditch, creating the impression that the earth had collapsed like cake. A bridge crossed the gully at Ashbury Circle. Three thin lampposts stood on the bridge, the glass around their bulbs tapered, making the lights waver like flame. Attached to the side of the bridge were black bundles of electric cables. Under the bridge on a concrete platform was a grid of white and silver pipes, six wheels attached to them. A wooden ladder leaned against a wall, and a blue cloth hung on a railing. Nearby stood two white plastic buckets, probably containing sealant.

A shawl of English ivy rumpled down the sides of the gully, catching on rocks then the entrances to storm sewers, rusty and big as tree trunks. A lone patch of daffodils grew amid the ivy, twenty-eight blossoms and a score of yellow buds. Although mockingbirds called rollicking from other parts of the campus, I didn't see a bird in the gully. Occasionally the storm sewers belched. Overhead planes rumbled incessantly, pushing air down and confining imagination under an iron lid. Gardeners planted dogwood and magnolia along the lips of the gully. While pink loosened buds on dogwood, transforming the minute turbans into caps, dieback browned the tops of magnolias. In the gully, orange leaves clung to a beech. Twenty feet above ground the trunk of the beech broke into three limbs. While two limbs thrived, pressed together in a fleshly embrace, the third limb rolled to the side, cankered and alone.

I didn't learn the name of the gully. "I've been here twelve years, and I don't know the gully's name. Actually, I have never thought about it," said a man wearing a red sweater, gray trousers, and a blue beret. Students staggered by in clutches, full of words but not one knowing the name of the gully. A man with a long nose and teeth orange as pumpkin seeds lit a cigarette. "Hurry up, Gall Bladder," another man said pulling an old bulldog on a leash. The name of the dog brought Carthage to mind, and I forgot the gully and pondered the yearly poetry contest sponsored by the *Courier*, the weekly newspaper. This year Googoo Hooberry took first place, albeit rivals accused Googoo of lifting the prize quatrain from a forgotten periodical. Entitled "Ovenbird," the verse began,

> If 'tis joy to wound a pigeon,
> How much more to eat him broiled.
> Sweetest bird in all the kitchen,
> Sweetest, if he is not spoiled.

Piety Goforth took second place with "Evolution." "Man comes from a mammal what lived up in a tree, / And a great coat of hair on his outside had he."

Much in life smacks of the lie. Gardens are visual lies, hot houses without grass in which plants that would never grow beside each other in the honest wild rub together stem and inflorescence. On returning to Storrs, I spent two days roaming field and wood. In three Old Latin versions of the Bible, St. Paul told the Corinthians that on the Second Coming "the World will shed its winter skin." Comfortable with fiction and dieback, winter is beauty enough for me.

I walked across a cornfield. Stubble tottered sideways. Cold had baked rocks and deer tracks into puddingstone, and winter rains had swept silage into frozen swirls. Three bluebirds sunned themselves in scrub. Behind them, trunks of big-toothed poplars glowed white and yellow, buds turning up from branches in wicks. Later I watched the sun sink behind Horsebarn Hill. Swabs of clouds seem to brush the top of the hill then tatter, tired and gray. In the distance, workaday denim clouds lumbered across the horizon. At frayed edges sunlight broke through holes. To my left, orange stained the sky. On my right, horses clustered eating hay, their dark winter coats thick on bony hangers. In the damp below the horse shed, a plastic balloon shaped like a heart sank into the ground. Printed in gold in the middle of the balloon was "Happy 50th Anniversary."

The next morning I wandered below the sheep barns. A mouse dozed in a grass blanket beneath an abandoned grill. A red squirrel

36   Lies and Consequences

hunched against the trunk of a hemlock, looking like a loop of fur. The head and front feet of a dead raccoon draped from a hole in a broken red maple. Although dried, the coon's body was whole, its skin leathery, its nose black and shiny. Insects tied cocoons to the animal's fur, dappling it. From the path above the gravel pit, the Ogushwitz meadow looked like a sweater worn out of blocking. Cattails had become mothy, and tussock grass sagged into knots. Fronds of sensitive fern fell ragged to the ground. Atop willow herb empty seed capsules peeled into loose eddies. Lint clung to milkweed pods, and wool-grass rolled like socks that had lost elastic.

What I noticed was so partial that I distorted season into illusion, something writers do in pressing life between pages. Of course seeing life whole is not possible. Bits, though, are wondrously satisfying, particularly to people not bound to truth. Fragments are trellises on which tales can bloom. On my return from the second walk, a letter was waiting for me. "Thought you would like to know," Turlow wrote from Tennessee, "that Baldy Skarth died last Wednesday in Carthage. He was eighty-six, and his obituary appeared in the *Courier* on Saturday. That afternoon I overheard a conversation between the Tweddle girls, Dede and Sadie. 'Look,' Sadie said pointing to the obituary, 'Mr. Skarth the octogenarian is dead. I knew him, but I don't know what an octogenarian is. Do you have any idea, Dede?' 'Not really,' Dede answered, 'all I know is that octogenarians are awful sickly. You never hear about one unless he is dead or dying.'" "Is there any truth to that tale?" Vicki said after I read her the letter. "You bet," I said. "It's all true, right down to the last adjective and adverb." ❖

Waiting for Spring

The last snow slipped from February like a dishcloth tumbling from a clothesline. The snow rolled along the yard then collapsed, bunched against oak and maple. Over the back stoop, wind dropped a handkerchief of white dust. Early in the morning juncos stitched the stoop into pattern. The tracks seemed needlepoint of season. In fall when chickadees groom the house, plucking egg and cocoon from the siding, I know that soon skies will darken and clouds hang like iron over Connecticut. Similarly when season wears snow threadbare, I realize spring is greening. The next day sun brushed snow from the yard, and I roamed the woods. Turkey tail glazed logs, the browns, grays, blues, and whites gleaming in the sunlight. Below the sheep barns a raccoon sprawled dead in grass, seeming to melt into the earth. In December I found a starling frozen to the ground, its bill pointing straight down like a pencil sharp over a page.

As I looked at the raccoon, a cloud rolled shadow through the woods, darkening the trunks of white oaks. For a moment winter grasped the day. But then the shadow loosened, and a small flock of bluebirds flew into scrub and preened in the light, their orange breasts polished like fingernails. A week later a pair of finches hovered side by side atop the carriage light over the front door. While a male cardinal offered sunflower seeds to a female perched in a lilac, a titmouse plucked buds from dogwood and fed his mate. A yellow-bellied sapsucker punched holes into black birch. Sap ran from the holes and pooled down the tree trunk. For three days the bird lingered about the yard. Buckling itself to the tree, it drank sap and then from the air pinched insects drawn to the liquid.

In hopes of discovering signs of spring, I studied the nearby. Throughout winter I imagined planting dove trees in the yard. In spring white bracts would flutter like feathers. In March, however, I potted fancy. Storing thoughts of dove trees in the cold room of the mind until next winter, I meandered the immediate. At the beginning of March a friend wrote from Atlanta. "While waiting for spring," he recounted, "I made my death arrangements." "Not that I contemplate forcing the final flowering like paperwhites," he added. "Still, I directed Matthews's Spring Hill to lay me out in a solid cherry casket with a cover of long-stemmed carnations, eucalyptus, and magnolia leaves." Many letters I received in February and March smacked of paperwhites in gravel, the stones, however, not external and pastel but internal and gallish. "Yale accepted John," a friend wrote from Pennsylvania. "He made 1260 on his college boards, but he is a 1600 linebacker." "High scores for an athlete," Josh said. Harvard, he told me, admitted a kicker from Lineville, Alabama. The boy's college boards warped and sprung well below twelve hundred. But he had "twin toes" on his kicking foot, a condition in which the big and second toe are joined by a ridge of flesh. Not once during his last two years of high school, did the boy miss a field goal, the longest traveling forty-eight yards and winning the Alabama State Championship in overtime. Moreover, the boy was religious. Before the boy's senior year a Church of Christ minister, and booster, baptized the twins in the Tallapoosa River, christening them Tryphena and Tryphosa, the names taken from the Epistle to the Romans, describing, in St. Paul's words, those "who labor in the Lord."

Francis spent fall applying to universities. By the end of February, he hadn't heard from any colleges, and Josh's anecdote stoked my blood pressure. "One hundred and sixty-one over one hundred and four," Dr. Dardick said. "You have to monitor this." That afternoon I bought a "Lumiscope." Until the weekend my blood pressure remained high. But then I spent Saturday and

Sunday reading student essays. By Sunday night the numbers had slipped to one hundred and fourteen over sixty-five. The cure for one ailment often causes another problem. Too much reading is dangerous. That night white bolts slashed down the side of my right eye. The ponderous weight of prose had torn my retina. On Tuesday a doctor in Hartford machine-gunned the tear with a laser after which he froze a corner of my retina. Freezing made me wiggle my feet, but for someone waiting for spring, laser surgery was not unpleasant. Each blast burst through my eye like a flower budding and blooming yellow. As the blossoms wilted, crystals of blue and green sparkled then turned brown blighting the flowers.

A tear in the retina of any beholder produces hybrids, most pollinated by strange floaters. Two weeks after the surgery I returned to the doctor for an examination. A nurse dilated my eyes and led me to a waiting room. In the room was a woman whose eyes were also dilated. The woman was a Pentecostal, and while we huddled together in the benighted dark, she tried to save my soul, or as she put it, labored "like the Celestial Locksmith to pick the Doors of your Heart." While listening to the woman, biblical phrases, not bits of retina, drifted through my head: "the blind leading the blind" and "let there be light," this last a condition devoutly not to be wished for.

What was once inclination has hardened into philosophy, buttressed by slogan. As my days unspool into tangles, so my essays wander. Happily the person who dabbles, waiting for season, eventually stumbles upon justification. "Your style," a man wrote from France, "is unique with each page unfolding like the hand of a gypsy to reveal some new and unexpected delight." "Yes," I exclaimed, transforming the gypsy's light felonious fingers into a hearty palm patting me on the back. Unfortunately my correspondent's next sentences slapped like horny reality. "I have been trying to locate other collections of your essays. But I cannot find any. Why is that?"

I didn't ponder the question. "Daddy," Eliza suddenly shouted, "Hurry up. I can't be late." That afternoon the Middle School Jazz

40   Waiting for Spring

Band performed for residents of Juniper Hill, a senior citizens' center. The band played in the dining room. Translucent white vases stood on tables, *alstroemeria* jutting out in orange tufts. I sat in a folding chair. Hanging on the wall above my head were reproductions of two paintings by Winslow Homer. I recognized both paintings and knew the name of one, "Boys in a Pasture." In the other a line of barefoot children snapped across a field playing Crack the Whip. Behind the children stood a one-room schoolhouse. The building was red, and its walls curved warm and friendly, smacking more of recess than rulers and slates. Above the gable of the school a mountain hung like a shadow. "If the soft pasture represents childhood," I thought, watching Eliza unpack her French horn, "the mountain must be life itself—a landscape broken into steep ridges, its dells not pillows in which travelers can rest, but hurdles, cords of brambles and underbrush, grasping and tearing children into old age."

When the tangles of a day knot feelings, I fiddle with numbers, the resulting tune cacophonous enough to banish grim refrains from mind. The Jazz Band, I noted, consisted of twenty-seven children. Twenty-four parents, seven siblings, and the band director and her husband accompanied the players. In the audience were two cafeteria workers, and thirty-one residents, twenty-five of these last being women and six men, figures that elevated my blood pressure. High blood did not turn the concert wintry, however, for suddenly I noticed two women wearing straw hats bigger than platters, one of the hats pink, the other yellow, a giant rose twisting purple and thornless through the hatband.

Winter makes Edward morose. "He's the life of the funeral," Vicki said. "I'm not going to play sports any more," Edward announced when I returned from the concert. "But you were the starting quarterback," I said. "Coaches want too much," Edward said, ending the conversation by going into his room and shutting the door. When knots get too tight for numbers to pick, I leave Storrs and travel to Carthage. Well-bred, my Carthaginians exhibit *nonsense oblige.* Turlow Gutheridge, the mayor, is my age, and "in his anecdotage," as Josh puts it, has a keen sense of rumor. This past fall Crossville measles swept through Carthage. "Mathuzalum Guppy brought them home from an experience meeting," Turlow recounted. "Thank goodness they weren't so bad as the Knoxville measles Cetus Blodgett picked up in East Tennessee two years ago. Happily folks around here aren't great travelers. Because no one has been to Europe, much less to Russia, we've been spared the ravages of German and Red measles. Of course, homegrown varieties can spot a fellow badly. For a fever nothing can beat the August measles in Red Boiling Springs."

Juno Feathers's hogs have a genius for obesity. For the third year in a row Juno's sow Phryne won "Best Pig" at the state fair, retiring the trophy, a silver-plated trough, twelve inches long, four wide, and five high. Juno drilled holes in the bottom of the trophy and converting it to a planter, placed it on the mantle in the living room, stuffing it with wildflowers—pigweed, sow thistle, and hog peanut. Above the mantle hung a portrait of Phryne painted by LaBelle Watrous. Phryne lay on her side, an odalisque, blue ribbons draped over her spigots so the painting would not offend viewers. Many Carthaginians have artistic hankerings. The last week in January Willie Busler staggered into Ankerrow's Café. Circles under Willie's eyes were thick as wool grass. "Willie," Loppie Groat exclaimed, "you look exhausted. You best get some Sick Man's Salve. What have you been up to? I haven't seen you since last spring." "I spent the past year writing a novel, and it liked to have killed me," Willie said. A couple of boys from the School for the Afflicted in Buffalo Valley sat across from Loppie at the table, eating ham and fried grits. "Fancy going to all that trouble and spending twelve months to write a novel," one of the boys said after Willie sat at the counter. "That fellow must be simple. Why he could have gone right around the corner to Read's drugstore and bought a novel for a quarter or maybe thirty-five cents."

Religion being more profitable that art, Carthage contained a strip of Christian warehouses, "Temples Housing the Commercial Ghost," as Turlow put it. At the bargain end of the Sacramental Mall, the Pilgrim Rest Here Pentecostal Church discounted ritual and hawked salvation at Robert E. Lee Day prices. In January

42 Waiting for Spring

Obed Ells preached at the church, declaring, "Christianity is almost as old as the Creation." To drum up a congregation, Obed's wife Samsonetta performed before the service. In earlier, less theological days Samsonetta worked in a circus, appearing as "The Female Hercules." Samsonetta's hair hung down to her knees, and before the sermon, she braided it into two ropes. Afterward Obed tied the ropes around the ends of an anvil. Then Samsonetta stood and lifting the anvil off the floor strode between pews shouting, "Come, butter, come" and "Kill the snake." Once the tongues of parishioners were resurrected, Samsonetta lay on her back, and Obed covered her with an asbestos blanket, leaving only her face visible. Three men then placed the anvil on her stomach after which Elkannah Wookey, the blacksmith in Red Boiling Springs, removed a lump of iron from the wood stove beside the back door. Next he placed the iron on the anvil and beat it into a horseshoe. While he hammered, Samsonetta sang hymns, old favorites, including "Dwelling in Beulah Land," "I'm Kneeling at the Door," "There'll Be Light at the River," "The Solemn Somewhere," and lastly "Like a Mighty Sea," the refrain of which she repeated three times.

> Like a mighty sea, like a mighty sea,
> Comes the love of Jesus sweeping over me;
> The waves of glory roll, the shouts I can't control,
> Comes the love of Jesus, sweeping o'er my soul.

Obed crowed raucously, but it was his hen who produced a clutch of silver. Samsonetta's performance wrung so much enthusiasm out of the congregation that Obed took collection in a bucket. Despite the bright gleanings Obed was an itinerant practitioner, hustling the sawdust trail, peddling words chapel to chapel. In contrast, Slubey Garts possessed the shining entrepreneurial hand, able to transform "poor befeathered pigeon's milk," Proverbs Goforth said, "into the honeyed colostrum of Abraham's bosom."

Recently several people in Smith County decided to be cremated rather than buried. To serve his brothers and sisters in Christ better, Slubey sold funeral urns. Ceramic, the urns were heart-shaped. For spinsters and bachelors, the urns consisted of single chambers. For couples who wished to enjoy eternity in one another's dust, the urns were divided into ventricles, the right ventricle containing the husband's or Adam's ashes, the left those of Eve. Drilled through the membrane separating the halves were two arteries, one at the top for spiritual, vegetative embraces, the other near the bottom for vital, appetitive communion. For a time Slubey pondered selling an array of urns. To this end, he commissioned Isom Legg to design two additional "vessels," the first a two-foot-tall version of Michaelangelo's David, the second modeled on Bottecelli's Venus, the thorny, laboring parts of both statures buried under pelts of plaster of Paris roses, old garden roses, the sort, Slubey instructed Isom, popular in Carthage, the Damask "Mme. Hardy," or the Bourbon "Boule de Neige." Slubey said he thought the urns would buck up the spirits of the homely, putting them at ease in Zion by enabling them "to trip less fantastic grimaces across the clouds." This explanation aside, Slubey jettisoned both urns after Quintus Tyler criticized the enterprise. The statues, he said, appealed to pride and made the dying vainglorious. "On the Register in God's Hotel, no one signs in as a prince or a counselor, a Venus or a David. Only immortality is immortal," Quintus said, noting that flesh was crabgrass. "Not even old families," he concluded, "last longer than three oaks."

In the fall an article in the *National Geographic* describing "Treasures of the Vatican" furnished Slubey with an idea for another biblical enterprise. Depicted in the article was a page from an illuminated manuscript. For people hereabouts, he told Proverbs, "the Book of Life is a barn," adding that its pages should be consecrated to Glory instead of to sheep dip and chewing tobacco. In church the following Sunday Slubey distributed paint, generally the heavenly colors—blue, gold, and white—albeit some farmers requested hellish red and yellow. Slubey gave away the paint free, asking only that somewhere on their barns parishioners paint the name of the church, The Tabernacle of Love, and the address, Carthage, Tennessee. On learning that a book in the Vatican inspired the project, Mathuzalum Guppy accused Slubey

44   Waiting for Spring

of "setting up housekeeping with the Devil's father-in-law." The Agrarian Renaissance, as the Head of the Yale Center for British Art later referred to the painting, rolled across Smith County stall and loft. As a result Mathuzalum's jeremiads had no more effect upon public opinion, Proverbs said, than the Flood did upon fish.

Initially painting consisted of simple warnings and exhortations such as, "The Lord Knows Who's Drinking," "Baptize that Juke Box," and "Sinner Man, You So Hard to Lead." Traditional questions and statements appeared almost overnight: "For the Wages of Sin Is Death" and "Who Taketh Away the Sins of the World?" Occasionally a statement seemed almost Elizabethan. "To Be Nameless in Worthy Deeds Exceeds an Infamous History" decorated a tobacco barn in Buffalo Valley. After the first burst of conventional epigram and warning, painters embraced poetry, exhibiting, as the Head of the Yale Center put it, "growing self-awareness and assurance, revealing themselves as enlightened individualists and humanists, not so much rejecting the Gothic barnyard as rediscovering the innate greatness of tin and wood." In their verses, "these poets of the soil elevated theological rhyme into magnificence." Among the first poems to appear were "Holy Bible, Book Divine / Precious Treasure, Thou Art Mine" and

> Young Ladies All, Attention Give,
> You That in Wicked Pleasures Live;
> One of Your Sex, the Other Day,
> Was Called by Death from Friends Away.

Man is imitative, raising new verses upon old. Consequently, later barn poetry was more sophisticated.

> Oh, Mother dear, Jerusalem!
> When shall I come to thee?
> When shall my sorrows have an end?
> The Joys when shall I see?

Eventually the Renaissance turned reflective, and in place of inspiration, humor flourished. "Old Mrs. Potiphar was a very great flirt. / She caught hold of Joseph and tore his shirt. / There's a happy day a-coming." Satire marked the end of the Renaissance. Five weeks after Slubey distributed his last gallon of paint, satire appeared on the roof of a barn in Maggart.

> Tears so overflow my sight,
> With waves of daily weeping
> That in the careful night
> I take no rest for sleeping.

From its inception, pictorial and literary aspects of the flowering were entwined. In fact illustrations on many out buildings were iconographic. Doubters who worried that sacred images could mislead quizzed Slubey about the pictures. Christ, he reminded critics, permitted St. Luke to paint His portrait. "The Lord is not a mystigogue," he said. "Barns aren't Rosetta stones. To read the Lord's hieroglyphics, a Christian doesn't need a key." On his barn Ben Meadows painted a slice of Humble Pie. The slice was flat and brown and lacking meringue had a thin, scaly crust. Atop the pie a knife and fork lay at right angles to each other, forming a stainless steel cross. For his creative part Hink Ruunt painted the head of a snake on the door of his barn. While the snake's mouth was spread like an outfielder's mitt and its fangs dripped green venom, its eye was orange and flickered like a dying candle. The door of the barn not providing a large canvas, Hink shrank the snake's coils into a cloven hoof. As a result from a distance the snake resembled a monkey wrench, the handle of which had melted sideways.

Isom Legg painted the most impressive icon in the county along the side of his cattle barn. From the ground flames flared up in a volcanic rush. Near the middle of the barn, two arms clawed upward through the fire, the forearms charred black, but the hands white, the fingers writhing in agony. Hanging under the eaves of the barn was a white cloud shaped like the underside of a ewe. From the sheep's belly dangled eighteen pink teats looking like a chain of uncooked link sausages. Clinging to the nipples of the sausages were small sticklike humans, two grandmas, an old grandpa, an uncle and an aunt, a man and his wife and their

46   Waiting for Spring

eleven children, "a good farm family," Isom told Sunday tourists who drove up from Nashville to study the barn.

I don't believe in making work out of pleasure, as the man said when he buried his wife. Essayists are impatient. When painting became tiresome, I shoveled the barnyard off my page. In hopes of jumping into spring, I flew to Hanover College in Indiana. Instead of landing in a budded world, I arrived in heavy snow. I spent a week at Hanover as visiting professor. Schedule did not afford me the leisure to wait for season. I ate breakfast with students at eight o'clock. At twelve then again at six, I ate lunch and dinner with faculty. Every morning I taught two or three classes. One evening I discussed writing at a coffeehouse. Another evening I gave a public lecture in Fitzgibbon Recital Hall. Yellow posters announcing the lecture blanketed bulletin boards across the campus. Essayists are willful, and beside my name on posters I scribbled comments. My literary abilities being inferior to those of worshippers at the Tabernacle of Love, my comments were drab, consisting of phrases such as "Hey, like Wow!" and "He's the Cat's Ass." I considered unflattering, naughty remarks, but then I worried that a student might catch me and lug me off for discipline to my host, the head of the English Department.

When not teaching or eating, I roamed. Duggan Library divested itself of seconds. For twenty-five cents I bought *Plant Galls and Gall Makers* written by Ephraim Felt and published by Comstock in 1940. On the steps of the Campus Center, a girl asked, "Are you the visiting Egyptian journalist." "Yes," I said, "Allah is merciful and compassionate. I cannot talk now. I must pray." In the lobby of the Horner Health and Recreation Center, a square gray board rested on an easel. Printed in white on the board was "Hanover College Football Welcomes Bart Darmody, Decatur Central High School."

The college sat on a bluff overlooking the Ohio River, and I spent most of my free time away from buildings, roaming trails that creased the bluff and sliced into a ravine called Happy Valley. Deep snow hid trails the first time I hiked, and I followed a path four deer beat through woods. Walking was difficult. Run-off from the ridge top furrowed the slope, and boulders and fallen trees clumped in hurdles. I grabbed saplings and yanked myself through brush. I stumbled often. Many saplings snapped, almost as if they'd been potted then forgotten, the soil around roots drying, turning trunks papery. The next morning the temperature climbed into the eighties. By afternoon most snow had melted from the ridge. At the beginning of Bluff Trail, periwinkle swung over rocks in ropy ladders. A tuft of daffodils splashed lemony from a dish of snow. Rain had dug pits in dolostone ledges, and amalgams of gray and green moss filled cavities, softening overbite. Weedy clumps of paulownia hung over the path. Buds bunched on branches and looked like orange mittens clipped onto racks. Clay oozed red from the ground greasing the trail, forcing me to walk slowly. I stopped often and looked east toward the Ohio River. Early in the morning the river appeared quiet, the surface frosted. By afternoon currents looped in half moons as the river flexed and turned red. In the morning barges pushed through the water. Sometimes they seemed low trains, other times, primitive mechanical gars, coal on the flatbeds lumps of hide. Painted on wheelhouses were names: *Roy Mechling* and *Bill Berry,* this last appearing beneath *Ingram Barge Co.*

Robins foraged through brambles near the top of the trail. Along the bluff woodpeckers thumped: red-bellied, hairy, and pileated. Near the mouth of Happy Valley, cardinals chased through trees, and calls of titmice unwound like springs. A pair of buzzards slid into the wind and coasted along the ridge. A hawk beat across a silver pane of sky. The bird had a white breast and looked like peregrine falcon, but it must have been a northern harrier.

Beside the trail leaves from red oaks clumped in adhesive pads. On box elder fruits dangled in damp gray clutches. While grapevines wove swings through trees, winter creeper wrapped a green muff around a maple. At the beginning of Happy Valley, trunks of river birch unspooled into cinnamon. Sycamores towered above the valley, their upper limbs thrusting into the sky like white veins. Along the trail toadshade opened, the mottled leaves looking like small tablemats. On hummocks alongside Happy

48   Waiting for Spring

Valley Creek, salt-and-pepper, rue anemone, and mertesia blossomed, the blue flowers of this last nodding above a setting of spoon-shaped leaves stained purple and medicinal. Jefferson salamanders lay under rotten logs. In the cold their blue bodies curved in small scythes. Gold splotches turned the tail of a dusky salamander into a necklace of irregular nuggets.

I walked until I reached valley's end at Dead Man's Falls. Slabs of limestone had tumbled from the falls and lay broken in the creek bed, filigreed with fossils. I picked up the end of a stalactite five and a quarter inches long, growth rings circling it like armor. Water peeled over the fall in a thin skin and slide down, at the bottom papering a green outcrop translucent. On ledges east of the falls, students carved names: Noel, Travis, Helen, Doreen, and Rose. I climbed the bluff west of the falls, something a father should not have done, especially alone. To get purchase I flattened myself against rock and soil. Suddenly I saw things I hadn't noticed: owl pellets sharp with the vertebrae of voles; the bleached shells of snails, white cocoons stuffing some; and at the trunk of a tree possum droppings beady with seeds. Walking fern hitched across boulders, and atop the bluff, squawroot burst through oak leaves, the cones bristling with yellow scales edged brown.

When I returned to Connecticut, I entered a chiller time and lost track of season. Travel influences observation, however. Having studied Felt's book, I noticed galls: oak bullet galls then on silky willows, pineapple, beaked, and potato galls. Almost imperceptibly, spring drew near. One afternoon a song sparrow sang in brush above the Fenton River. A cowbird landed on the birdfeeder outside the kitchen. Red maples bloomed, flower buds opening like mouths, the edges of the buds tawny red lips, the throats tonsilly and scarlet. On Easter morning I hid thirty-three eggs in the yard. A brown snake curled under plywood in the Ogushwitz meadow. Because I'm colorblind, the snake looked green, and I brought it home for Eliza to identify. "Brown, not green," she said. "Black marks behind the eyes are the key." That night I returned the snake to the meadow. At the beaver pond elementary school students hunted spring peepers. The children wore headlamps and carried pond nets. The next day Eliza found red-backed salamanders in the wood behind the house. That night she dreamed a cult created an elixir capable of changing salamanders into dinosaurs.

This past Thursday the university library held a spring sale, piling books on tables on the patio. In hopes of finding a book comparable to *Plant Galls,* I went to the sale. Amid a stack of books I noticed *Bedford Forrest and His Critter Company,* a biography written by my old teacher Andrew Lytle. I opened the book. Written inside the front cover was "S. F. Pickering, November 2, 1965." Under the date appeared the name of an emeritus English professor: "Max Putzel. Storrs, 1979. Gift of Sam Pickering—God Bless Him!" I copied the inscription on the back of a card I pulled from my wallet. Afterward I turned the card over. On it appeared the date of my next eye appointment, June 18, 1999. If the Pentecostal woman showed up at the same time, I decided I would describe barn paintings to her. That afternoon a letter arrived from Turlow Gutheridge. "Spring is about over," he wrote, "and I'm waiting for summer." Obed Ells, Turlow recounted, was in Monteagle. Samsonetta accompanied him, "reluctantly, however." Late one night a small earthquake struck Carthage, disturbing Obed and Samsonetta's sleep. Afraid that the chimney might collapse, Obed leapt from the bed and bounded toward the door, abandoning Samsonetta, her legs tangled in the sheets. "Wait for me, Obed," she shouted. "When the Lord calls," Obed answered, dashing out of the house, "his redeemed captives can't wait for nobody." ❖

Cult

Early in April, Vicki, the children, and I spent a weekend in Princeton. Saturday morning Eliza and I watched the Princeton heavyweight crew row Harvard. We stood at the finish line at the north end of Carnegie Lake. Spectators near us wore baseball caps, crossed oars stitched across fronts like military insignia. Resembling toothy camp counselors, a school of middle-aged men swirled the shoreline, binoculars spinning about them like krill. The men were officials of the United States Rowing Association and wore brown shorts and shirts. Veins seamed their legs, and their calves looked like beer mugs. Several spectators wore khaki trousers, creases sharp as knives; tasseled loafers; blue blazers, and regimental neckties, campaign ribbons of orange and black striping them. A kennel of registered mutts accompanied owners to the races. An old Corgi waddled across the grass, an orange handkerchief around its neck. A golden retriever wound an orange and black leash about the legs of a man in a blazer. While a Lakeland terrier stood immobile by water's edge almost as if he expected a fox to lope across the current, a team of black Labradors pulled a woman along the beach. "Casey, Nicky," the woman commanded, "whoa!" "How do you think the names of those dogs are spelled?" Eliza asked. "The usual way," I said. "Wrong," Eliza said, "KC and Nikki. No animal on this beach is normal, Daddy. We are surrounded by a cult."

The next Saturday, Vicki, Eliza, and I attended the spring horse auction held in the Ratcliffe Hicks Arena at the university. Thirty-four "lots" sold. A froth of sawdust covered the floor, and a woody broth of chips, ammonia, and manure seasoned the air. Around the border of the ring, flats of pansies sat atop bales of hay. In the center of the arena stood ten round tables, all covered with blue cloth. Families brought lunches in baskets and picnicked while members of the university drill team showed horses. Beside the tables stretched four rows of gray folding chairs. From a strut at the top of the building hung a rectangular wooden sign. Printed in white on the sign was the question, "Got Milk?" Above the sign house sparrows chattered nervously. We sat on steps that circled the arena, transforming the building into an amphitheater. To the right and on the floor of the ring, two auctioneers sat behind a raised platform.

Buyers got bargains, many horses selling for less, Vicki said, "than I paid for our new washer and dryer." Although two orthodontists from Fairfield County bought pets for children, most purchasers were big-bosomed and bellied people who dressed rough. "Owners of stables who pay more attention to equine overbites than they do to human molars and bicuspids," Eliza said. Rudy an "aged brown Thoroughbred gelding 15.2 hands" sold for $750. "He's honest," the auctioneer said. "He's played polo for ten years and needs a nice home for retirement." Woodsong Leader, a seventeen-year-old Morgan stallion 14.3 hands high went for $2,050. Two mares at the university were in foal to him. "His semen is good, a 300 x 106 concentration," the auctioneer declared. "He's got a lot of breeding years left." Selling for $4,000, U. C. Windsong, a three-year-old bay mare, brought the highest price. "This mare has show horse written all over her," the auctioneer said. "She's destined to be a star." Jackies Chances Are, a seven-year-old registered Quarter horse, sold for $900. "You've just bought yourself a nice horse," the auctioneer told the purchaser. "That horse really was nice," Vicki said, looking at me. "I wish we could buy a horse." "Could we, Daddy?" Eliza added quickly. "No," I said.

"People are going to look at you when you ride this horse," the auctioneer said on the appearance of U. C. Three Times a Lady, a six-year-old registered Morgan mare. Jessica, one of my students in a poetry class, rode Three Times a Lady. "We hope she is in foal to Windsong Leader, but it has only been twelve days, so we don't know yet," the auctioneer said. "Did he say something about your student?" Eliza asked. After the mare sold for $2,900, the auctioneer remarked, "I like a Morgan breed." As horses went for $1,100, $1,250, and $1,500, I studied the crowd. A girl in a green blouse cradled a minute yellow and white kitten. Three beagle hounds stood by the door to the arena, tails flicking. A boy dropped a chocolate-covered doughnut on the sawdust. He reached down, brushed it against his overalls, and after pinching off chips that clung to the icing, bit into the doughnut, swallowing it in five bites. Members of the audience knew each other. "Another cult," Eliza said. "The people dress the same: sweat shirts; khakis, the legs worn into stovepipes, and baseball caps with the names of tractors printed on the fronts, John Deere and International Harvester." "It is hard to be a nay-sayer here," Eliza punned, adding, "if I hadn't decided to row for Princeton, I'd own a stable."

The following Sunday, Vicki, the children, and I went to the Windham County Kennel Club show at the fairgrounds in Woodstock. Pods of trailers rumbled across the small hills, curving around the fairgrounds, their tops silver in the sun, awnings stretching over make-shift pens bristling with dogs: jovial Irish wolfhounds; Dobermans, ears sharp as thorns; dachshunds galore; English spaniels with the faces of waiting maids; candied poodles, their hair brushed into white chocolate meringue; and Chinese cresteds, professors, skins coffeed with spots, hair along their muzzles and over their heads electric, wacky with idea.

The Bulldog Club of New England raised a tent and sold silver lapel pins depicting bulldogs in full, heavy stride, and then neckties, jowlish with packs of blue and yellow bulldogs. I watched owners lead bulldogs around the show ring. Dogs' hips rolled like footballs, and their thick skins hung loose like melted Tootsie Rolls. When not on show, the dogs sat quietly by owners' feet, occasionally looking up to have jaws wiped or receive flat, wafer-like treats. I liked the dogs. "Shells and horses are not for me," I said to Vicki. "I'd really like a bulldog. Watching them makes me feel good." "You've gone round the bend," she said. "Bulldogs are the ugliest animals in the world." "No," I said, "they are beautiful."

"Members of rowing and horsy sets," Josh lectured me later, "are enthusiasts." "Most enthusiasms," he continued, "wear thin after a day. Only when an enthusiasm endures for years and narrows life does it smack of cult." "I judge people by their redeeming vices," Josh declared. "Only zealots lack an exaltation of vices. Incapable of sympathizing with suffering, tempted humanity, they are damned." As a person ages, life constricts. Thoughts of where they should or might be dissatisfy some people. As a result, not only do people celebrate the present and the known, but they also shape the past so that vanished dream does not make them uncomfortable. In the process such people blind themselves into certainty. Others create idealized youths and become boosters, enthusiasts, and loyal alumni.

No man can so insulate himself that he is oblivious to seasons of thought. Once the new delighted me, seeming to offer promise. Now instead of change, I embrace pattern. Hope and satisfaction have proved delusions, and simple continuance reassures me. On May 10, examinations started, and my students behaved as they have done for thirty years. Early Thursday morning after distributing an examination, I strolled into a hall in Arjona. Suddenly a girl rushed through the front door to the building. She looked around frantically then raced toward me. "Are you my English teacher?" she asked breathlessly. "Maybe," I said, "what class are you looking for?" "Oh, gee, I forgot," she exclaimed. "Are you looking for the Short Story?" I said. "Yes, that's it!" she shouted. "Then I'm your teacher. The test is in room 104," I said, pointing to my right.

As usual students appended notes to examinations. "Thank you for a great class," Matt wrote. "I have thoroughly enjoyed the lectures, and I have learned a great deal about poetry." Matt signed the note *love*. An arrow pointed toward *love*. Instead of feathers, a comment was attached to the end of the shaft. "We theater students," Matt explained, "can write to men and sign the letters 'love' because we are so in touch with our feelings." "Professor," Adam declared, "I'd like to thank you for teaching me so much about writing. Normally when I write this kind of letter at the end of a blue book I'm just kissing ass. But I want you to know I'm not kissing your ass. I am trying to be sincere here. I really did learn a lot about writing."

Each semester oddities occur. Phillip and Michael were good students. After the examination I bumped into Phillip in the library. "Michael and I enjoyed your course," Phillip said. "We had great fun. Michael never took any notes of his own. Each day in class he looked over the shoulder of that Jennifer sitting in front of him and copied her notes verbatim. She wrote down everything you said. 'Go to the piggery behind Horsebarn Hill. Look at the boars. They have big testicles.' She underlined *look* and *testicles*. After class Michael and I had coffee together in Bookworms Café, and he read Jennifer's notes aloud. What a gas!"

Albeit not an enthusiast, Josh is an accumulator like me. Instead of the ordinary, he collects the strange. In June he leaves Storrs for the summer. Before going he visits my office. This year Josh collected unanswerable questions: "What song did the sirens sing?" and "If novelty impresses man so strongly, why does virtue affect him so little?" "Suppose," he speculated, "St. Peter lived next door to Lot in Sodom, and when Lot and his wife fled destruction, Peter had been part of their caravan. If Peter had joined Lot's wife in giving the old homestead a final goodbye glimpse, would he have been transformed into a Pillar of Salt or Salt Peter? Of course the latter would have caused a theological explosion." Curious knowledge appeals to Josh. Vermont, he informed me, was originally named Verdmont, or Green Mountain. At the end of the eighteenth century, a careless scribe omitted the *d* in the name, transforming the state to Vermont or Mountain of Maggots.

Midway through examination week I usually explore a graveyard or two, unconsciously hoping, I suppose, to exhume prose more lively than that written by students. In 1872 Ophy Tumpkins died in Chaplin. She lived only eight months and sixteen days. Carved on her tombstone was a quatrain,

> Silent and cold in her cradle-bed,
> Our little baby lies,
> With never a flush on her marble cheek,
> Or light in her winsome eyes.

Occasionally continuance doesn't reassure. When I returned from Chaplin, two letters lay on the kitchen table. The first contained an obituary of my grandfather clipped from the *Carthage Courier* in 1953. "Rites Set Friday For Sam Pickering," the headline declared. The second letter came from The 1209 Society, Cambridge University's development office in the United States. The "OFFICE OF PLANNED GIVING" invited me to a "discussion of estate planning over English afternoon tea" held on June 3 at the Colony Club located at 564 Park Avenue. "Perhaps," Vicki said, "the convergence is significant." "No," I said, "I'm too fat to die. Only a skeleton key can open Death's Door." "Teeth dig graves faster than shovels," Vicki said.

The next morning I tacked the obituary to the bulletin board outside the office of the English Department. As I admired my work, a student started reading clippings on the board. "Oh, no," she said, seeing the obituary. "I planned to take Pickering's course in the fall. Now I will have to redo my schedule." "Is he really dead?" she said turning to me. "Plucked and fried," I said. "He's roosting in the holy sanctum now. Never again will he teach writing." "Damn it," the girl said, "what an inconvenience! My friend told me getting an *A* from him was easy. Now I'll have to find some other gut." That night I described the girl's reaction to Eliza, explaining that I was going to squeeze the conversation into an essay. "Then when the Angel of Death scoops me up and totes me away so the undertaker can afford to buy his babies candy, you'll have my books and their stories." "Yes, and one day thirty years from now," Eliza said, "I'll read them and actually believe what they say."

After examinations ended, I spent much of the rest of May in the basement of the library, hunting stories, "botched plagiarisms,"

Josh labels them. While browsing, I always discover inconse-
quential matters that entertain me. Pressed between pages fifty-
eight and fifty-nine of the July 1869 issue of *Ballou's Monthly
Magazine* was a yellow card measuring three by one and three-
quarters inches. Printed along the top of the card was "ALLYN
HALL." While "Tickets, 25 Cts." appeared at the bottom, stamped
in the middle was "Benefit Of HARRY BRYANT, Tuesday Evening,
Mar. 28." Two-thirds the way down page fifty-nine, the story "The
Yankee Officer and the Partisans" ended. Written by James
Franklin Fitts, the tale described the escape of Ned Sly from a
band of Confederate guerrillas in Western Louisiana in April 1863.
Sly swam a bayou to safety. The leader of the partisans was not so
fortunate. As he pursued Sly into the bayou, a roar suddenly
erupted, followed by cries of "the alligator, the alligator." "The
increasing darkness," Fitts wrote, "hid the scene from view, and
its worst terrors could only be imagined. For a few yards, unseen
in the darkness, the life-blood of the unfortunate man crimsoned
the muddy stream, while his mutilated body floated down."

Printed on the lower third of page fifty-nine was the beginning
of "My Trip In the Sally Ann," an autobiographical account of a
journey to Nova Scotia written by Miss Camilla Willian. Willian
did not enjoy the excursion. "Dear reader," the first paragraph
began, "did you ever go to Nova Scotia in a schooner? If you ever
did, then you need no advice of mine; but if you have not had that
experience, read mine and be warned. I went to Nova Scotia once,
and I went in a schooner; and ever since then I have hated that
corner of the Atlantic through which my route led, and make a
point of scratching out that odious little peninsula on all the maps
I get hold of."

After having jibed through the library and taken on a cargo of
musty tales, each May my winding route leads to Carthage. I
always run aground atop a church. Four years ago Slubey Garts
purchased a radio license and started WGOD. Time has brought
sophistication to the station, and, as might be expected, criticism.
A rival divine, Malachi Ramus damned Slubey's Saturday night
show, The Evening Gospel and Holiness Hour, as "a matinée

religieuse." Malachi aside, however, in Smith County the Hour was more popular even than WSM's Grand Ole Opry. Slubey polled his audience after collection at the Tabernacle of Love, distributing questionnaires to the congregation. He studied responses and shaped programs accordingly. "Anybody can reap knowledge from reading," he told Turlow Gutheridge, "but only thinking separates wheat from chaff." As a result when Proverbs Goforth opened the hour exclaiming, "WGOD—broadcast from Carthage, 10AC, the shining cross on your dial," practically all radios in Smith County were turned to the station. Proverbs began the show with "Hospital Admissions" followed by "Obituaries of the Air." While Coralee Ollerenshot had been admitted to the infirmary in Cookeville suffering from glanders after having been sneezed on by Pimma, Pappy Farrell's purple mule, Vester McBee entered Vanderbilt Hospital in Nashville, "suffering, poor soul, from a stricture of the gall duct, near the outsquirts of the lights." During the third week in May, only one Carthaginian died, Beswick Rooney. "A lawyer by profession," Proverbs said, "but a honest man by practice." For forty years, Beswick urged the legislature in Nashville to appoint educated people to the judiciary. "The judge who doesn't know grammar," he said, "is liable to pronounce an incorrect sentence."

Bits of advice ran through the show like seams of fat through ham. One or two cautionary nuggets also served as advertisements, Burma-Shave, for example, sponsoring

> Fat and well-fed today.
> Skinny and dead tomorrow.
> Today a comfort to all.
> Tomorrow under the pall.
> Buy Burma-Shave.

Most advice was aphoristic, consisting of a single sentence, "There ain't much good in evil," "The only way to double your money without hard work is to fold your bills," "Folks are always happier for having been happy," and "Natural beauty is God's handwriting." Malachi Ramus objected to this last statement, calling Slubey a "haughty culturist" and the next morning at the Church of the Chastening Rod warming people against WGOD. "The Hand of Providence," he said, "does not wink at transgressions. The sensuousness does not come in clear at first hearing, but hidden in luxuriant verbiage, it coils through the static like a snake. Unplug your ear. Turn off that radio. Instead of the warbling of the distant toucan, Garts harkens to the whispering asp." Coveting the station's audience, Malachi called Slubey a "Christian Mammonite." At the Chastening Rod, Proverbs said in Ankerrow's Café, "the Lord's Prayer begins with 'Hollered be thy name.'"

During the Hour Slubey himself referred to the Lord's Prayer, advocating humility and simplicity, noting that of the sixty-six words in the prayer, forty-eight consisted of one syllable, for "good and saving measure," adding that fifteen of the seventeen words in the Golden Rule also consisted of a single syllable. Several times during the Hour, Slubey ran commercial banners up the Gospel Flagpole. Each week he interviewed a successful Carthaginian then "scattered the sunshine of Love" over new businesses in hopes they would grow fertile "by the light of the Cumberland River." Late in May, Slubey interviewed Pappy Farrell, owner of a prize herd of Holsteins. When asked how he came to be a dairyman, Pappy said, "I come to it naturally. I've been milking since I was two days old. Mammy told Grandma I was the beatenest boy for pulling Smith County's ever seen." On the same program Slubey announced that Hink Ruunt had started farming possum. "Possum fritters and Injun batter / Makes you fat and a little fatter," Hink sang, noting that when served with greens, sweet potatoes, and pecan pie, possum made a stout meal, "just the dish to put lard on consumptives summering in Red Boiling Springs." "Those folks are so thin," Hink said, "that if you brush against their shadows you'll bleed." After six weeks of possum cake, he continued, the sickly will grow so fat that if their shadows fall on you, you'll be "smothercated."

The highlight of each broadcast was the testimonial of a repentant sinner. Before he became a Child of the Kingdom, working without pay in the Lord's Department of Life's Great Store, Jubal

Arnold ran a mail order business. Although named The Mirror of Mercy in the Midst of Misery Mail-Order, the business was really Arnold's Dead Letter. Among other items, Jubal hawked water-logged coffins. "If the coffin doesn't fit the corpse," Jubal wrote prospective purchasers, "he doesn't have to pay." Jubal sold a cabinet of patent medicines. A rub-down with Queen Elizabeth's White Owl Liniment, Jubal advertised, stripped away age, "transforming an old man into a young buck, leaving enough gristle behind to make a poodle dog puppy." For a dollar and twenty cents, the gullible could purchase plans for an infallible mousetrap. "Open mouth," instructions read. "Place a teaspoon of sweetmeats far back on the tongue. When whiskers of mouse tickle teeth, bite down swiftly." "To keep eggs from spoiling," he advised customers, "eat them while they are fresh." Even worse, Jubal moaned, "twice I sold the bodies of mad dogs to butchers for sausage meat, and once I made butter from the milk of a cow suffering from bovine venereal disease."

Throughout the broadcast the choir from the Tabernacle sang hymns. Near the end of the Hour a visiting preacher delivered a pithy sermon. Usually the hymns and the sermon were connected. In late May the choir sang, "Little One Come to Me," "Called Home," "If I Come to Jesus," "He Lifted Me," "The Sweet Olden Story," and "The Great Physician." After this last hymn, Pharaoh Parkus, who was leading a revival in Buffalo Valley, preached a sermon on the death of children entitled "Taking Up His Own." "Everyone knows the sad old rhyme," he began:

> We cannot see through the clouds, sweet wife.
> They tell of a golden track.
> But if we followed it out, t'would be
> To bring our darling back.

"God lops off soft underbranches," Pharaoh explained, "to strengthen trunks so they can grow higher toward heaven."

Each May during the week before graduation I follow spring's green track. In a sermon, Slubey called field and wood "sacramental waysides." For my part communion with the outdoors doesn't nurture thoughts transcendent. Still wandering invigor-ates, if not restoring lost youth like Queen Elizabeth's Liniment, at least rejuvenating enthusiasm for life. Love of God often con-stricts sympathy, transforming men into dreadfully good people. Only rarely does affection for nature harden into doctrine. To the music of birds I always dance soft-shoe. Before graduation a killdeer nested in the disturbed land below the sheep barns. When I approached the nest, the mother bird cried, tilted to the side, dragged her left wing across gravel, and fanned her tail, orange flaring from a white sun, cooling at the edge of feathers into a black and white border. Atop Ski-Tow Hill redstarts foraged ashes, and catbirds scraped through brambles. Yellow warblers twittered, and a pair of blue-winged warblers tumbled in a gold braid from a scarlet oak. Thrushes called from the deep shade down the ridge, their songs damp with blue.

On the hill I met a man wearing hearing aids. "I'm not deaf," he said. "I only wear hearing aids on weekends so I don't miss birdsong." For my part I hear only a few spring birds. "But you see most," Eliza said. "Study Ezra. Verse twenty-one, chapter seven, is the alphabet verse. In it Ezra uses all the letters of the alpha-bet, except the modern *j*. If *i* and *j* are considered a single letter, then he used the whole alphabet. Collapse warblers under the heading *yellow* then you'll have practically every spring bird."

Often I imagined pruning spring. May was so lush that occa-sionally I became melancholy. As a busy child, I hurried through days, oblivious to rich season. Now that my flowering was over, profusion overwhelmed. Like a dry twig I lacked the capacity to bud and capture light. Still, despite no longer being able to absorb season like the high leafy mantle, I leaned toward the sun plant-ing two shrubs in the yard: Oregon grapeholly, dug yellow and blooming from the pharmacy garden; and a Japanese maple pinched from the backyard of Vicki's home in Princeton. The grapeholly may not live, "another patient for the plant hospital," Vicki said. Nevertheless, many of my adoptions survive, giving the yard a ragamuffin, lived-on look. In November I planted a pani-cled goldenrain tree beside the drive. In May leaves bristled pink and serrated through branches, resembling heads of spears.

Bugle wove itself across the backyard, some of its spindles white, others lavender or dark blue. A chipmunk perched on the root of a shagbark hickory, jowls swollen. At dusk a reddish groundhog fed on violets. The groundhog lived in the brush pile in the woods. Across the street a female groundhog lived under Miss Sochor's porch. One afternoon a car ran over the groundhog. Before Vicki saw the body, I shoveled it out of the road and buried it in the woods. I covered the grave with a pall of bugle, six armfuls, and then a swatch of bleeding heart. The animal's teats were swollen, and she was heavy with milk. Several times I explored her burrow, but I didn't hear mewing. "Groundhogs are nuisances," Francis said. "Why would you want to raise the babies?" "To each creature there are seasons," I answered. "I'm at the time of life when every death diminishes."

The day after I buried the groundhog, warblers blossomed in the backyard: myrtle, Wilson's, and black and white. "Suppose," Eliza said, "the earth is a huge animal which breathes every six hours causing tides." "Then trees and shrubs would be fur," I said. "And people?" Eliza asked. "Perhaps we are vermin. But what are birds?" "Birds," I thought later, as I drifted down Ski-Tow Hill, "are fragments of dreams, rainbow shards fluttering through the unconscious." I didn't think long. At the bottom of the hill a woodcock broke cover. Gaywings bloomed in sunny eyelets looking like purple pins pushed through lapels. Toothwort, wood anemone, and dwarf ginseng mottled a rag of gray leaves, ginseng's minute white globes almost revolving.

A dead white pine towered above the beaver pond, its limbs barren pews, a congregation below, lively in the wet lowlands, grackles, red-winged blackbirds, and yellow warblers. A northern water snake slid across the pond. An oriole whistled from an oak. A bullfrog crouched in mud, its head a broken stick covered with algae, the eyes buds. An eastern dusky wing basked in the grass beside the dirt road. A kingbird sallied from a willow hawking the air, and an eighteen-spotted ladybug clung to a blossom on shadbush. I followed a pair of ovenbirds through the woods. From a maple a barred owl stared at me, not flying away until I was fifteen feet from the tree.

"Professional basketball is boring," Eliza said that night, "because it lacks plot." Would that I could impose structure, if not plot, upon my meanderings. Only entertainment, basketball needs plot in order to remain popular. Ambles are formless, however, and I am free to marvel at cinquefoil and wild strawberry, yellow and white across dry, stony land, or notice scrub white oak calf-high along a bare ridge, new leaves hanging down in pink wads. One morning I got up early. Mist steamed over Valentine meadow. Horses stomped behind wooden fences, and pigeons bubbled gruffly atop silos. As the sun rose, light toasted the new leaves of cherries. Looking like drops of sugar, dew clung to the tips of grasses, bending the blades into spoons. Frost streaked false hellebore and turned the bright yellow of winter cress doughy.

"Why don't you quit teaching and become an undertaker?" Vicki said later that morning when I returned from the woods. "You'd charm people and have more fun." "A narrow house, a home of clay, a palace for another day," she continued. "Not only that," she added, "You could weave palls out of wildflowers and call yourself a Christian florist. You might become a cult figure." "Maybe," I said, "but I'm not in a theological mood just now." Turlow Gutheridge, I suddenly began, was so known for charity that two or three times a week a tramp appeared at his back door and begged a handout. Turlow sympathized with everybody except alcoholics. Last Tuesday a tramp fermenting like a distillery banged on his door at six-thirty in the morning. "I'm here on the Lord's business," the man stated, "and I want alms." "The fellow who attends to the Lord's affairs," Turlow said, shutting the door firmly, "has gone to Memphis and won't return until Saturday night." ❖

Vetted for the Prom

"I have to eat at Emma's house tomorrow night," Francis said at dinner. "Her parents want to meet me." The star of *Anything Goes*, the school play, Emma was in eleventh grade, and Francis had invited her to the senior prom. During Francis's four years in high school, I had not met many of his friends. Most remained faceless names attached to high grades or sometimes to a discreditable anecdote. Emma was an exception. Vicki saw the play and said Emma was "great." One noon this past spring while I was writing, she walked home from school with Francis and ate lunch in the kitchen. I did not want to embarrass Francis, so I didn't talk long to Emma. I told her I was writing about snakes. She didn't say, "Yuk," a silence I interpreted as a good sign. Knowing nothing about Francis, Emma's parents wanted to inspect him before allowing him to cart their daughter away for half a night. "Good sense," I said to Vicki later.

At dinner, however, sense did not season conversation. "You're being vetted. Your inoculations had better be up to date," Vicki said before dishing out a nine-course meal of advice, serving platters heaped with sartorial and culinary suggestions. "Remember you are away from home, so don't lick your dessert plate," she said. "And don't part you hair down the middle," Edward added. "Bathe before going, and do not wear one of those polyester Hawaiian shirts that your nerd friends like," Eliza said. "When you sit down at table," I added, "don't swish your bottom back and

64 Vetted for the Prom

forth and say, 'ooh, this seat is so comfy.'" "And don't break wind," Edward said. "But if you do let fly a rouser," I interrupted, "pretend to be offended. Scowl and say 'ugh' loudly." Thinking Emma's parents might ask Francis to say grace before the meal, not something done at our house, Vicki recited a blessing for him, urging him to memorize it. "Oh, Lord, we thank thee that while we are enjoying health and prosperity, so many others are tossed upon beds of pain and denied the comforts of life. Amen."

After being dutiful parents and providing Francis with an etiquette book of advice, the family urged Francis to vet Emma's parents. "After all," Vicki said. "We know nothing about them, and, heaven forbid, they may be people about whom we should know nothing." We instructed Francis to ask if they enjoyed the benefits of means, and if so, to discover if their assets were new or old. "Ask where the family came from," Vicki said. "Ascertain if they sprang spontaneously into being or if the family has fermented in the muck for generations in some gothic dungeon like Rhode Island or Louisiana." We emphasized that Francis's inquisition should be thorough. Twice we told him to ask Mr. Hippophagy about the origin of his name. "Now what exactly was your name before you came to this country and changed it to Hippophagy?" Edward suggested.

If Mr. H inquired about college plans, Francis was to say *Princeton* in a haughty, stuffy tone. "Practice the haughtiness for twenty or thirty minutes," Edward said. "Stand in front of the mirror upstairs and scowl." "And say," Vicki chimed in, "but, of course, Princeton is de rigueur. Old WASP, you know." "And you, what is your Alma Tomato?" I urged Francis to counter. After Mr. H replied, Francis should say, "Oh, yes, quite a goodish place. I do think I've heard of it. But my memory is a sieve, and there are just so, so many colleges in this country, especially west of New York. Where exactly is that institution located?"

If conversation dragged, I told Francis he should ask if Emma was a virgin, "an interrogatory guaranteed to stir a nubbin or two of fruit cocktail into most Jell-Oish chatter." If Mrs. H should turn the question back to Francis and ask if he had indulged in fleshy delights, Francis should respond, "Of course, every chance I get, and for your information such chances occur with great frequency. But for heaven's sakes, what a question to ask a gentleman!"

Suddenly Edward interrupted. "Good Lord," he exclaimed, "do you suppose they could be Catholic?" "Impossible," Eliza answered, then paused, her face turning white. "Suppose, they are," she began then stopped. "Suppose they are—well, you know." "Damnation!" Vicki exclaimed. "I'd never considered that." "I doubt they are," Francis said. "Emma plays on the school tennis team. A person does not learn tennis down on the farm or at the you-know-what." "Don't be too sure," I said. "Perhaps she learned the game by whacking balls against the side of the barn." "No, the expense of replacing balls which bounced into manure would be too great," Vicki answered. "Perhaps the balls were not replaced," Eliza said. "Heaven forbid!" Vicki exclaimed. "Exactly," I said and turning to Francis asked him to report on the shoes worn by the family. "Pay particular attention to fragrances loitering about the soles like tassels." "If they wear shoes," Edward said.

Without a hash of story, meals sink like soufflé, and I provided Francis with a seasoned smorgasbord of old standbys. The Reverend Slubey Garts, minister and owner of the Tabernacle of Love in Carthage, Tennessee, I began, spent Stonewall Jackson's birthday visiting a cousin who owned a rice farm outside Whistle, Arkansas. At night, mosquitoes rose from the fields in black mists. "Mosquitoes in Arkansas are huge," Slubey said on returning to Tennessee, adding, "A great many of them weigh a pound." "Not only that," he told the lunchtime crowd at Ankerrow's Café, "they climb trees and bark." Two days later Proverbs Goforth stopped Slubey outside Read's Drugstore. "Those lies you told about the size and climbing ability of Arkansas mosquitoes have upset the congregation something fierce. Folks hereabouts will excuse anything but a lie: drinking, running around, murder, even Sabbath-breaking." "Lies?" Slubey said, looking puzzled. "I haven't told any lies. It would take many mosquitoes to weigh a pound, maybe as many as million or two. As for climbing trees and bark, any fool knows that if an insect climbs a tree, he climbs the bark, too."

The good storyteller, I instructed Francis, heaps paragraph upon paragraph, just like a waitress serving mashed potatoes in a family-style restaurant. If the H's chuckled at Slubey's doings, "then you, Francis," I said, "should inform them that the reason people laugh is because they don't have tails to wag when they are pleased." If this last remark caused biliousness, I advised Francis to tell a riddle. Not only do riddles effervesce, but reaction to a riddle is a better indicator of family intelligence that a battery of Scholastic Aptitude Tests. As could be expected, I supplied my son with an appropriate conundrum. What word is pronounced quicker when a syllable is tacked on to it? Obviously, the answer is the word *quick*.

The good vetter always probes family, even if he does not ask riddles and dig into the quick and the slow. On the chance that Mr. H inquired about me or my doings, I told Francis to muster a tear, clap his hands above his eyes like the bill of a baseball cap, shudder, then say, "Father? I'd rather not talk about him. Mommy doesn't let us mention him in the house. All families have such people. But if you must know about the bastard, you can look the trial up in the *Tolland County Court Reporter*." Immediately, thereafter, before the H's responded, I urged Francis to mention his mother in diverting detail. "Throughout the whole son-of-a-bitching affair, Mommy was the image of long-suffering virtue. When a reporter tried to interview my little brother Edward, Mommy chased the man down the street with a butcher knife. She had the knife because she was chopping the head off a chicken when the reporter appeared. She's a gourmet cook. You should taste her onions and tripe, and she makes divine bread. She has tiny toes and is very fastidious, and she likes to bake because dough cleans her hands. She can't stand dirt, and water gives her the all-over shivers, especially when it is stirred with soap. So she makes bread because she values personal hygiene." "That's dandy," Edward said, "but add, 'damn it to hell, I should have brought a loaf tonight. I'll give Emma one for you tomorrow at school. Will sourdough be all right?'"

Our family's roots run deep and when soaked in water, stories bud. "Don't forget to tell the Hippophagys about Uncle Elroy,"

Eliza said. "He wanted badly to be a published author. After being released from the institute, he started writing *A Dictionary of Anonymous Heads of State*. Unfortunately he couldn't get pass the first letter of the alphabet and suffered a conniption collapse." "For years afterward he experienced difficulty with his medication, getting slightly addicted to that prescription," Vicki added. "And then the manner of his death," Edward said, "though after all those things he did, it was a blessed relief." One Sunday afternoon when he was fishing on Dunphy's Pond, Slubey Garts noticed a bottle bobbing on the surface of the water. "A Jim Beam bottle, if memory serves," Eliza said. Slubey hooked the bottle. Wrapped around the mouth of the bottle and trailing down into the depths of the pond was a clothesline. Rolled inside the bottle was a scrap of paper. Written on the paper was, "I'm down here at the end of the string. I just couldn't take them statesmen no more." Sure enough Elroy was at the bottom of the pond, hunkered over like a mud turtle, his feet strapped to cinder blocks, "elevated sandals," Slubey said, "to help him climb to Glory." "Poor Elroy," Vicki said, "just thinking about him gives me a sore tit."

"The most surprising thing," I said, "was that Elroy got up enough courage to drown himself." Like Francis's mother baking in the kitchen, Elroy didn't fancy water. He was a good Christian, and twice he signed up at the Church of Christ to be baptized. He went the whole hog, buying the white robes and for three days abstaining from all spirits except the holy one. But when the chosen day arrived, and he got to the riverbank, he couldn't go through with the submersion. Staring at the water, he stood in a stand of willows weeping and muttering, "this river is just too damn snaky."

"Daddy," Francis said, "suppose the H's don't believe our family stories. What should I do then?" "Just say, 'it's awfully hard to determine exactly where the truth lies with regards to the facts.'" "Before Mr. H responds tell him about the time Elroy suffered a constriction of the bowels and went to see Dr. Sollows." "I'm going to have to give you an emetic," Dr. Sollows told Elroy. "That won't do no good, doctor," Elroy answered. "I've done tried them twice before. They wouldn't stay in my stomach, and I throwed up something awful."

The next night Francis ate dinner with the H's. "How did things go," I asked when he came home. "Fine," he said. "Did our advice come in handy?" Vicki said. "You bet," Francis answered. "What were the Hippophagys like?" she continued. "Nice," Francis said. "Did you like them?" Edward asked. "Yes," Francis said. At this point the conversation stopped. Vicki and I had moved on to other things. In three weeks Eliza graduates from the Middle School. In September she starts high school. At dinner that night, she said she'd finished William Thackeray's novel *Vanity Fair*. No one else in the grade had read the book. "Eighth-grade boys," she said, "are Philistines," adding, "I'm afraid high-school boys won't be any better intellectually. I'm just going to have to date graduate students." ❖

May's End

Near the end of May sentences become seasonal. Days leaf so fast that definition blurs, and topic vanishes. In hopes of noticing green before life slips through memory, I wander field and hill. Instead of scrolling pages, I drift beyond margins, resisting the temptation to force phrase into idea. Along Golf Hill, Japanese honeysuckle yellowed into old newsprint. Petals sifted through branches of autumn olive and rumpled along the ground. Racks of minute flowers opened on Amur maple, their soft fragrance wavering distilled in the quiet air. On black cherry, buds jutted out in sudsy brushes while on bigtooth aspen catkins shredded and blowing low through roots caught and twisted into loose twine. The tips of pistillate flower candles on white pines glowed like embers. I measured eight candles. The longest was seven and a quarter inches; the shortest, four inches.

Spongy oak galls fruited on scarlet oaks. I peeled a gall the size of a lemon and ate the flesh. Wet and grainy, the gall tasted like apple. In the middle of the gall, the grub of a wasp curled in a larval chamber. I ate the grub, the worm being of no gastronomic consequence and my sight too poor to locate it anyway. During May's End galls filled sidebars of hours: blister galls swollen on the leaves of quaking aspen; erineum galls splotching maples; wild cherry pouch galls, spindles whirling red at the tips; and on willows pineapple galls, not weathered into shakes but whitewashed and silvery.

70   May's End

From the dorsal awns of sweet vernal grass, white threads waved light as silk. Atop Ski-Tow Hill flowers hung in ladders from black locust. Along the edge of the Ogushwitz meadow willow down slid linty across the beaver pond. In a clearing near the Fenton River, iris unraveled into yellow stars. A black racer shed skin under plywood, its blind eyes blue. Beneath a refrigerator door a pair of milk snakes tied themselves together. At May's End gardens of snakes bloomed in cool hothouses under hunks of wood and metal, black racers, garter, brown, and ring-necked, the abdomens of these last bright runners. Beneath a thick slab of cardboard, a white-footed mouse wove sweet fern into a nest, lining it with willow. On my lifting the cardboard, the mouse scurried into a field birch and perched on a limb, tail curled and ears cupped.

Most of June belongs to May's End. Only after schools close and Eliza and Edward leave for camp does season change. Before then hours flow impressionistic, colors rarely hardening into the articulate. During the first week in June the perfume of maple leaf viburnum eddied musty through woods. From land bruised by an abandoned development, verries called, their notes a lotion, at first tingling then soothing. Only occasionally did worldly doings scratch days into irritation. In September Francis was slated to enter Princeton. Because applications blistered my leisure for two years, sometimes I mentioned college. "When we drop Francis at school," I told Vicki one day after the mail brought Edward a college advertisement, "I suspect the parents we meet will be happier to be at Princeton than their children." That night I found a green fruit worm on the kitchen floor, and schooling slipped from mind. The next morning a walnut sphinx moth clung to the screen outside the study window. I stopped writing and leaving the house roamed the battered land west of the university landfill.

Near a mound of stumps, blue flags blossomed, twelve of the flowers white. Close by lamb's ears bloomed, the flowers slivers of blue paper pinned to pale wands. Leaves grew along the stem in pairs, one leaf directly opposite its companion. Below each twosome grew another two leaves, this second pair at right angles to the first, forming a series of struts, making the plant appear boxy from above. Snout weevils foraged on mullein. The weevils clamped themselves to plants at points where leaves joined stems. When I touched leaves, weevils unhooked and falling tumbled to the ground or snagged leaves lower down the stem. On nettles, ants with amber abdomens and red thoraxes herded aphids. Under the remnant of a yellow raincoat, a wolf spider clutched a speckled egg sack. In damp shadowed by phragmites, scores of rose pogonias bloomed, petals and sepals feathering startled, centers of flowers buttery, the fringes purple.

I ambled into woods. Gullies were bushy with sumac, staghorns itching with bees. A little wood satyr bobbed ahead of me. I dragged my left hand across the corky bark of sassafras. Afterward I munched a leaf, pulling my tongue slowly along the hairy underside before tamping the leaf against my lower teeth. Later I chewed a wad of mugwort. Beside a cornfield, fragrant bedstraw grew in loose bales, the rich perfume not the stuff of small, white, country flowers, counterpanes, and oilcloth, but of salons smoky with Gauloises and garish with women red and enpurpled. Meadow fescue hung over a dirt road, stippling shoulders, its jointed green stems, brush strokes and its ribbony leaves, slashes.

During May's End death blooms, providing yeast for life. In the Ogushwitz meadow, a barn swallow lay splayed in high grass, looking as if it died cutting the air. Beside a woody path stretched a fledgling ruffled grouse, its body unmarked and warm. Feathers at the tips of the bird's wings looked like small oars, shafts blue, blades brown, the ends creamy white. Above a marsh a fox sank into the ground, red fur pooling around the bones. The skull was intact, and I brought it home and cleaned it, soaking it in Clorox. Under brambles ruffling the edge of Unnamed Pond lay the left hind leg of a fawn. Aside from ropy tendons, the flesh had been torn from the bones, leaving the hide loose, looking like a red muff, white splashed across it in mustaches. By a stone wall I found the leg of a rabbit. May had been so dry that, as Vicki put it, the university had to sprinkle the Fenton River to keep dust down. As a result the leg was cured, and snapping off the foot, I took it home, for good luck placing it atop the television.

72 May's End

Neither spring nor summer, May's End is in-between, a time that lends itself to sauntering both afoot and in mind, writing letters to people forgotten for a decade. Because obligation does not determine content, letters written during May's End are often quirky, paragraphs leaping fences into the personal. Chris graduated from the University of Connecticut in 1986. The first week in June she wrote me. "Thank you for your gentle attempts to discourage my writing very lame poetry," she began. "I have since found that non-fiction is my genre—non-fiction of a morbid nature. I picked up a copy of Jessica Mitford's *The American Way of Death* shortly before graduation and became interested in what goes on behind funeral home doors (the physical stuff, not economic matters). I began reading everything I could about funerals, embalming, cemeteries, then branched out into execution, cannibalism, dissection, etc. Before long, I read 1,200 books on these subjects and compiled the words I came across into a *Death Dictionary,* which was published in 1994. Still interested in the 'juicier' subject matter, I wrote a history of the corpse, mostly a compilation of facts from other sources. I found the stories of carnival mummies and other preserved bodies of this century intriguing and then wrote *Modern Mummies*, researching it by visiting many mummies and interviewing several embalmers and a taxidermist. I then thought I wanted to write about the living and began researching a book about traumatic amputees, but it wasn't to be. Instead I have returned to the dead for my material and am writing about collections of human bones."

The rabbit's foot brought good fortune, and that afternoon I ordered *Modern Mummies,* expecting the book would enliven summer reading, most of which was committed to studying *The Letters of Matthew Arnold*, four massive volumes. In late April I suffered through a bout of spring fever. The virus having larded my system with optimism and made me feel deceptively energetic, I agreed to review Arnold's correspondence. The deadline for the review was September, and during May's End, I crammed Arnold onto a back shelf and spent hours roaming the university library, arbitrarily sampling sentence and paragraph. In the January 21,

1864, issue of *Country Gentleman,* L. Wells criticized gum chewing. "It is," Wells wrote, "almost a sure step to chewing tobacco, and that, to drinking whiskey." "The boy," Wells explained, "who is continually drawing saliva from its proper deposit from the age of seven to seventeen will by that time almost physically require an extra stimulant in the form of tobacco, and thence in that of alcohol."

"Habit," Wells declared, "is what chiefly regulates our lives." During May's End a person escapes habit, or at least, those habits which chain one to task and self-improvement. From a shelf one afternoon I plucked *Fern Leaves From Fanny's Port-Folio,* a collection of sketches and essays published in 1853 and written by Sarah Parton, a popular sentimentalist who wrote under the name Fanny Fern. Rarely do books fail to surprise. Pressed between pages 98 and 99 was a small Johnny Jump Up. On the two pages themselves appeared a sketch entitled "A Night-Watch With a Dead Infant." "Moorest thou thy bark so soon little voyager?" Fern asked. "Through those infant eyes, with a prophet's vision, sawest thou life's great battle-field, swarming with fierce combatants? Fell upon thy timid ear the far-off din of its angry strife? Drooped thy head wearily on the bosom of the Sinless, fearful of earth taint? Fluttered thy wings impatiently against the bars of thy prison-house, sweet bird of Paradise?" Fruit dots of dialogue peppered Fern's leaves. In "The Partial Mother," a mother asked, "Is that you, my darling?" "No, mamma," a small girl answered, "'tis only me!" "Fancy," Fern wavered, "that little, pale neglected, sensitive child, meekly returning that touching answer to the mother of her petted, beautiful sister!"

In June the Friends of the Mansfield Library sponsored a second-hand book sale. Townsfolk donated books to the sale, and proceeds went to the library. I donated twenty-eight books. Since the sale occurred during May's End, I inscribed the books to myself, enlisting Francis to furnish a second handwriting. Inscriptions were fulsome. A naturalist declared love first of my prose then of me, writing, "The man whose sentences flutter so beautifully must himself be a butterfly. If we had met before I molted into middle age, you would have been the monarch of my bosom. Instead of wasting my sweetness on proboscises dulled by insurance and stock certificates, my nectar would have flowed like milk between your honeyed lips." A dignified member of President Bush's cabinet dubbed me, "The Dickens of New England." Despite being renown for public dourness, the man scribbled his favorite riddle across the title page of his memoirs, asking the difference between a cat and a sentence. "One," he wrote, "has pauses at the end of its clauses; the other clawses at the end of its pawses."

Alas, May's End does not turn everyone into a dabbler. Not susceptible to the in-between, some people cannot recognize dabbling. The morning of the library sale, an advertisement appeared in the *Hartford Courant.* "Many inscribed first editions," the ad stated. "Holy cow," Francis exclaimed on reading the paper. "What's going to happen?" "Nothing important," I said, adding that "on Judgement Day all straight paths will be made crooked." "That's sound doctrine," Josh said after I repeated the remark. Josh himself is susceptible to May's End. The second week in June he wrote the dean of the College of Arts and Sciences, requesting an exercise assistant. The dean had assigned research assistants to many of Josh's colleagues. The assistants slog through chores, fetching, for example, books from the library, in the process freeing faculty to devote time to "serious scholarship." "If a graduate student swam my mile each morning," Josh wrote the dean, "my scholarly productivity would rise. Walking to the pool, undressing, showering, swimming, then showering, dressing again, and returning to the library not only sucks two hours from the academic day but also so drains my energy that afterward I am too weary for research." The entire scholarly community would benefit from the dean's allocating Josh an exercise assistant. "Moreover," Josh continued, "because the assistant would be youthful, he, or she, would finish the mile quicker than I, probably saving half an hour, thus making available an additional thirty minutes, the total savings amounting to two and a half hours each day for research. On days when I didn't use the entire one hundred and fifty minutes, I would gladly assign a portion of the time to faculty members needing greater windows of opportunity for research." "Finally," Josh concluded, "the assistant would certainly be more comely than I, thus providing other swimmers with an inspiring aesthetic experience—one bound to energize weary crawls and thus so speeding exercise that other swimmers, too, would have more time for research. Indeed, assigning me a research assistant would ripple through the university community, each year leading to, I have calculated, an additional twenty-three books, one hundred and eighty-eight articles, and three grants from the National Science Foundation."

During May's End I visited Carthage. For his part Josh went to Maine, staying on Deer Island with a retired tree surgeon. Josh has never been to Tennessee and for eight books has warned me against Carthage. "Not only do the visits undermine the scholarship buttressing your essays," he said recently, "but Tennesseans are dangerous. Still, if you must visit the Volunteer State, heed the saw, 'Believe the women. Distrust the men, and fear the children.'" Although doings in Carthage shred the fabric of my essays, townsfolk are kind rather than frightening, on Christmas, Easter, and just before butchering, feeding hogs buttermilk. Language in Smith County is clear, smacking of May's End, only the occasional preacher suffering from platitudinaria of the vocal cords. Almost no one is the creation of larynx or pen, and people pay more attention to action than to talk. On hearing that a Presbyterian sultan in Nashville had ranked prayer superior to deeds, Dr. Sollows opined that he'd never read a medical study that proved God's hearing was better than His eyesight. "God's old, even older than Methuselah," Dr. Sollows said. "Since hearing deteriorates before long-range vision, I suspect that for all practical purposes He is deaf. Certainly He can't hear the whining that passes for prayer beneath Presbyterian tents in West Nashville."

In May Slubey Garts cautioned parishioners about the evanescence of earthly things, especially bank accounts and health. "If spring floods wash the farm into the Cumberland," he said, "plough resentment under ground and sow a spiritual crop. Fertilize shoots with kindness. Become the Lord's Poor, not the

Devil's Poor." "One night can change a fat man," Slubey warned, "into nothing but skeleton and bile." "To keep digestion rumbling heavenward, twine your heart about the cross like a beanstalk around a pole." Last month in Crossville after a Baptist gourmandizer chopped the head off a hen so he could fry Sunday dinner, Slubey recounted, an angry rooster spurred him in the wrist. Ten days later pain cut through the man's chest like a hatchet. Immediately he "fell to the ground on all fours, scratched, clucked, crowed, and died, rolling over on his back, dusting himself with dirt looking just like a chicken covered with flour in a skillet, his drumsticks sticking up in the air." "Gone to Glory," Proverbs Goforth said after the sermon, "before he broke out in feathers or, worse, laid an egg."

Sunday evening Slubey called on Noddy Hall. Noddy recently declared himself a transmigrationist, explaining that he'd be reincarnated after death, returning to Smith County as a mule. "A notion that came to him," Proverbs said, "while he was in his silage at Enos Mayfield's Inn in South Carthage." Slubey urged Noddy to abstain from fermented grain. "If you do," he explained, "when you return, you'll be treated like Ray Anselment's mule Otis. Every evening you'll be fed a bushel of oats and be rubbed down with soft pea-straw." "Otherwise," Slubey said, "you'll live like a railway mule, suffering from the itch, kidney worms, and the blind staggers. When you die the second time, your shinbones will be so mealy they can't be used to make ivory caneheads and knife handles."

The *Carthage Courier* did not announce any book sales during May's End. Still, news was interesting. A Pentecostal in Lebanon advertised for lodging. "In a pious family," he wrote, "in which my Christian example will be considered compensation enough for room and board." In Maggart, Judge Bell bushwhacked a path through a brambly case. While cleaning house, a servant girl neglected to shut the cage of her master's pet squirrel, Clabber. When the girl left the room, Clabber scurried out an open window, so souring his owner's heart that not only did he dismiss the servant but also he refused to pay the girl's weekly wage. "Clearly the servant is partly to blame. She should have latched the cage," Judge Bell ruled. "But her wages should not have been docked, for her master is also guilty of neglect. If he had clipped the animal's wings, Clabber could not have escaped through the window and vanished into the forest."

In May, resorts in Red Boiling Springs opened for the summer. Convalescents traveling from Nashville to drink waters usually broke trips by spending a night at the Walton Hotel in Carthage. The final Friday in May was stormy. Saturday morning a convalescent filled a prescription at Read's Drugstore. Sitting at the soda counter was a man from the School for the Afflicted in Buffalo Valley. "You certainly have loud thunder in Carthage," the convalescent said, making conversation. "Yes, we do," the man from the school agreed, his head nodding like a pump handle, "yes, we do, considering the small number of people hereabouts." The same fellow ate lunch in Ankerrow's Café and overheard Hink Ruunt complain about the racket made by Buster his hound, saying that if Buster didn't stop howling he'd have to punish him. "Don't do that," the man interrupted. "America the beautiful is a free country, and Buster is just speaking his mind. You should be proud of him. Only last week I heard a man say that none of the lowdown belly-crawling curs in the legislature dared to yip without heeling and begging permission from the governor."

The most memorable happening in Carthage during May's End was the Grand National Baby Show, staged by Hollis Hunnewell in the high school gymnasium. Hollis limited the show to a hundred children. In the *Courier,* he promised parents prizes, noting that thirty-one babies "were already engaged, including twins, triplets, and one quatern." Not monetary, the prizes were eclectic, including cider mills, lop-eared rabbits, ground bone, and a pharmacy of cure-alls: Buckworth's Lozenges, Hufstader's Vermifuge, and Zahl's Catalpa Liver Pills. From the Sin No More Press, the publishing font of the Church of Christ Deuteronimus in Chattanooga, Hollis purchased a cart of remaindered books, the most memorable being a trilogy of "Boxed and Blessed" novels, the first, *The Nun's Escape,* "An Inspirational Tale of Shedding Bad Habits" written by Sister Bernadette Verona Brangle; the second, *Mated Not Married,* "A Thrilling Account of Heathen Intrigue in the Desert," by Mrs. Bernie Massoula; and the last "A Sanctified Historical Romance" by B. V. Brangle entitled *The Maiden Unchained,* "A Fiery Dart Stabbed into the Heart of the Wall Street Dragon."

Awarded to parents of the most comely baby, the grand prize consisted of five hundred pounds of Ta-Feu, "night soil, screened, dried, disinfected, and leavened with salts of ammonia." Ta-Feu, Hollis claimed, thickened hedges of Osage Orange, made watermelons lap up moisture, and for grapes was better than Peruvian guano. All grapes, Hollis declared, waxing poetic, "Delaware, Concord, Union Village, and Hyde's Eliza; Isabella, Arkansas, Elsinburg, and York Madeira; Hebemont, Lyman Mountain, and Canby's August." "Spreading outhouse doubloons atop watermelons?" Vicki said after I described the grand prize. "Wool-witted parvenoodles might not fancy such high agronomy," I said, "but mind and word wander during May's End. Even Slubey strays from patented sermons. Last Sunday he said that Jonah swallowed the whale, not the whale Jonah." "That's fuddle-pated," Vicki said. "No," I said, "it's nothing compared to Hink Ruunt's latest invention, a toy called the Cleopatra, a tin bosom with a mechanical asp attached. After being wound, the asp snakes around the bosom, slowly twisting until it reaches the top whereupon it hisses, opens its jaws, and strikes, its mouth clamping down on the nipple just like, as Hink put it, "a big old thumb pressed against a doorbell." Before Vicki responded, Edward walked into the room. "Daddy," he said, "UPS brought you a book." "The title," he continued, opening the box, "is *Modern Mummies.*" "Hot dog," I said. ❖

Familiar Things

For six months the chancellor of the university lived next door. In May he and his family went to Disneyworld. Each morning Vicki fed his dogs, two Labradors named Mousse and Huckleberry. "Don't you think that's better?" Vicki said one afternoon, pointing to the kitchen ceiling. Last fall in Norwich Vicki bought a light fixture for the kitchen. Once home, she discovered the lip of the fixture was warped. For months the lip swayed dizzying across Vicki's vision. Then in May, while preparing food for Mousse and Huckleberry, Vicki noticed three of the same fixtures in the chancellor's house, none warped. "The darn things only cost $21.95 a piece," she said. "The university should have bought something better." In June the chancellor accepted the presidency of Louisiana State University. "Before he and Clara leave for Louisiana," Vicki said, "I'm going to switch fixtures." "Don't," I said. "I'm doing it," she said. "He's leaving, and the change won't bother him. I'd switch fixtures even if he stayed."

A week later when the chancellor and his family were visiting Baton Rouge, Vicki rid herself of the warped fixture. "I switched ours with the one in the study. I thought about removing the fixture from the master bedroom, but then Clara might have noticed. Women's minds wander to cooking, cleaning, lights, almost anything during. . . ." "Enough," I said, clapping my hands over my ears and staring down at the kitchen table. "I don't want to hear any more."

Despite refusing to glance at the ceiling, I knew not only what hung above but also what lay ahead. School had ended. Francis was riding a mountain bike in Italy, and Edward and Eliza were at camp in Maine. Summer had arrived, and the time had almost come to depart for Nova Scotia. Every June, Vicki and I debate going to her family's home in Beaver River, Nova Scotia. Invariably we decide to spend summer in Storrs. Just after the decision, however, something happens, and we leave. Two years in a row thieves stole my bicycle, and rather than remaining in town fuming, we decamped. For a moment I thought the ceiling fixture might push us toward the northern lights. But the chancellor didn't notice the switch. Four days later he and Clara invited us to a farewell party. At the party the kitchen light flickered in my mind. In hopes of dimming fluorescent consciousness, I drained a skin of red wine. For a while I succeeded in darkening awareness, becoming an incandescent bore. An acquaintance's nose was so large, I informed a vice-president of the university, that he couldn't blow it without packing his nostrils with gunpowder. After the naiads finished bathing, I asked a dean, what service did the dryads provide? On the man's looking puzzled, I explained that the dryads distributed towels.

A sociologist, not a classicist, the man didn't appreciate my *bon mot*. Consequently, I asked him a riddle. Why is the letter *B* like a hot fire? The answer—because it makes *oil boil*—not elevating him to laughter, I then described recent doings in Carthage. One chilly night in February, Horace Armitage staggered into Enos Mayfield's Inn and sat by the stove. Horace had prepared for the cold by swallowing a pint of homemade antifreeze before leaving his house. Nevertheless, the walk chilled him, and he hunkered over the stove, rubbing his hands together and spreading his fingers. "Mr. Armitage," Mayfield's son Tyrell said after five minutes. "There ain't no fire in that stove." "Damn you, you rascal," Horace exclaimed, standing up, shivering. "Why did you tell me that? I was just beginning to get warm. Now you've given me the shakes."

Like pigweed amid corn, my wit proved too weedy for the chancellor's cultivated guests. The dean having left me, I ambled over to a clump of people, including, among others, the town's representative in the state legislature. Age having uprooted several incumbents, local Democrats, she said, were having trouble finding people to plant on the town council. At this furrow of the conversation, wine blighted my intelligence. Eight minutes later the representative led me into town hall to be interviewed by the Democratic Committee. The committee sat soberly around a table. I thumped down, slapping a plastic glass brimming with wine in front of myself. I began discussion by apologizing for being "tight as a tick." I announced that I wouldn't hesitate to raise taxes, saying I'd promise the citizenry a chicken in every garage and a Lexus in every pot, wit that brought puzzled, not smiling, looks. Afterward remarks vanished in a Cabernet Sauvignon haze. Eventually my stomach turned feathery, and I walked home through the woods, suffering from dyspepsia, "the remorse," my friend Josh said later, "of a guilty palette."

The next morning I informed Vicki the time had come to leave for Nova Scotia. By summer's end my lubricated appearance at town hall would have dried and blown from mind. "Maybe," Vicki said, "but suppose the Democrats nominate you. Drunk or sober, you'd lead the ticket." "Surely," I said, "the committee wouldn't nominate a tippler." "Bad behavior provides the best possible education for office," Vicki continued. "The pure and the good cannot cope with public matters. Besides you behaved like a jackass, something that always indicates good character. No man who has been laughed at is irredeemably damned."

Four days later Vicki and I, and George and Penny, the dogs, left Connecticut, driving to Bar Harbor and the new ferry to Yarmouth. By the time I reached New Hampshire, I'd shed the cloven hoof kicked up at Town Hall. In truth banging the boards of my stall frees me to spend summers willfully. Misbehavior protects a person from distending ambition. Instead of foundering amid the poor provender of position and responsibility, I wander pastures that have nourished me since childhood. Any wise man, as Josh puts it, can run a college but only a fool can lead the good life. "Shakespeare was wrong," I said to Vicki as we passed Portsmouth. "Pharmacists are not 'pillers' of society. Essayists are." "What?" Vicki said. "Never mind," I said, dropping the speed to fifty miles an hour.

Vicki and I are experienced dog travelers. At Mackey's in Willimantic, Vicki bought a pillow cover, stuffing it afterward with two pillows purchased at J. C. Penny's, making a dog bed for twenty-eight dollars, thirty-one dollars less than the cost of a comparable bed at Puppy Love, the pet store in East Brook Mall. We walked and watered the dogs throughout the drive: at the "Welcome to Maine" rest stop near York; outside the Birchwood Motel north of Castine; across a field behind the Dexter Shoe Outlet in Ellsworth, Maine, where boat shoes sold for thirty-nine dollars, none unfortunately 10 1/2, Vicki's size; then finally along the hill above the Bay Ferries terminal at Bar Harbor. Dog days are tiring. The owner of Birchwood kept two cats. During nights the cats pounce from the railing running the length of the motel, landing on the hoods of cars. To prevent the cats leaping onto the Toyota and conducting the dogs in a chorus of howls, I parked ten feet from the railing. Still, at 5:12 the next morning, a cat ambled across the parking lot, and Penny yelped. At least she yelped until I joined her in the car, barefoot and wearing pajamas.

Later that morning Vicki and I planned to explore Castine. Because the day was hot, we didn't leave the dogs in the car long, this despite cracking all four windows and placing a plastic bowl of water on the floor in front of the driver's seat. Still, we wandered a bit. ABCD Books sold used books. A customer in the store asked the clerk the location of books describing nature. The clerk didn't know. "Next to gardening," I said, having roamed the store searching for one of my books. "Any collection of essays would have done," I told Vicki later. "You write about New England. Did you really expect to find one of your books?" she said, handing me a postcard, adding, "here's a present. I bought it at a souvenir stand." Six belted Galloways grazed across the front of the card, the white bands circling the stomachs of the steers resembling corsets. I pondered buying a muffin and a cup of coffee at Cappy's Bakery. I wanted to stroll down Commercial to the Megunticook River. I planned to sit on a bench and sip and munch. I imagined furling into the quiet and watching schooners slide through the harbor. "Sweets and doldrums kill dogs," Vicki said, steering me clear of reverie and piloting me back to the car. The ferry at Bar Harbor was a catamaran, from the side looking like a pasteboard iron, from the front, a giant ray, wings sweeping black toward the water. On board I sat in the theater. Tired from having muzzled Penny before breakfast, I slept through a showing of *Anastasia,* waking only for the death of Rasputin.

"If your heart is in the highlands," Josh informed a musical acquaintance, "it ain't here." In Nova Scotia, my heart and body can almost always be found in Beaver River. Once or twice during the summer, envy causes a chamber to skip, when, for example, a friend writes from France, his letter winy with murmuring about Tuscany or the Loire Valley. A walk, however, soon restores rhythm, ambles along the drumlin overlooking the Bay of Fundy being natural pacemakers.

Electrical problems always await us in Beaver River. The hot water heater in the house is forty-four years old. This summer it needed, as the repairman phrased it, an electrical by-pass. After the operation, I bathed, sinking under a white mound of "Wild Rose" bubbles. Before the bath, while the heater was convalescent, I'd spent days doing chores in and out of the house—inside, removing shutters, freeing stuck sashes, and jacking up the backhouse in order to open the pantry door. Vicki admires spiders, and before I vacuumed, she urged me to be gentle. "Catch the spiders and take them outside," she instructed. "They are fragile. Be careful not to suck them up when they scurry into cracks. Cleaning near spiders requires a delicate touch." Many spiders built webs under windows, bays being favorites. The spiders fed on flies and wood lice, spotting boards under webs yellow with droppings, the exoskeletons of lice drifting dry and broken across the floor like minute shields. The vacuum cleaner wheezed when I turned it on. During winter a mouse built a nest in the tank, crawling up a seven-foot hose at the end of which was a metal extension shaped like a boomerang.

The second morning in Beaver River I cut rhubarb growing along the stonewall beside Ma's Property, the field south of the house. Later Vicki bought a flat of strawberries grown in Annapolis

Valley. The next day she made eight jars of strawberry-rhubarb preserves. I spent much of the first week in Nova Scotia outside. From under the bays I trimmed bridal wreath. I oiled the scythe and mowed grass behind the barn. I cut dead branches from hawthorns and dragged away spruce weakened by porcupines then snapped by wind. I chopped Japanese knotweed with a machete, carting canes into the woods. Forty years ago Vicki's father planted the knotweed as an ornamental, a mistake because the plant spreads by rhizomes, forming dark, close bacterial thickets that smother other vegetation. Two red maples shade the front of the house. In fall they drop leaves into trenches formed where gables pitch up from the roof. Moss and twigs cling together in heaps, and the trenches become planters. This past year asters rooted, and soon after arriving in Nova Scotia I climbed atop the bays and weeded the roof, hoeing some of the soil, then using a long bamboo pole to pry up the rest, playing clumps of dirt like fish on lines.

In summer saws jump to hand. After a morning's cutting, be the slicing useful or whimsical and indulgent, I drink coffee and eat a sugar doughnut. Rocking in the kitchen, a wood fire thumping in the stove, I feel more attuned to the world than in Connecticut. Instead of hanging heavy, leaded with the metallic fumes of automobiles, air sweeps blue off the Bay of Fundy and stirring through the side meadow whisks up currents of rose and pine. In Nova Scotia summers slip together seamlessly, the appointments of days comfortable and familiar. On our arrival black alder and sheep laurel bloomed along the lane leading to the bluff. As I do each summer, I confused black alder with inkberry. Once more sheep laurel startled me, the small blossoms, cups overflowing with pink sweetened by purple. A long-horned beetle lit on my right leg as I sat on the side porch. A white-spotted sawyer, the beetle feeds on dead and dying conifers. During the summer several sawyers land on me. "Because," Vicki explained, "you are so woodenly conventional." The first moth I noticed this summer was an underwing with three glossy black spots dotting the margin of its forewing. The moth is common. In past years I tried unsuccessfully to identify it. This summer I failed again. For creatures about the farm, place is constant, something that reassures the two-leggeds who camp in the house.

Every summer a song sparrow or one of her progeny nests in the rugosa roses bordering the side meadow. Caterpillars of mourning cloak butterflies chew the willow at the edge of the meadow ratty. Batches of their castoff skins stick to the ends of branches, turning twigs black and spiky. This summer in the blueberry field a stick mimic clung to a stem of fireweed. A fleshy shelf jutted from behind caterpillar's head like a leaf scar. While the caterpillar's back legs grasped a twig, a silk thread tied the insect's head to a leaf. The head stuck out resembling a bud, and the caterpillar's legs twisted like crooked twigs from its body. I wouldn't have seen the caterpillar if I hadn't known where to look. Every July a similar caterpillar appears in the same patch of fireweed.

Trifles compose place and character. In early afternoon a cock pheasant wandered the lane, usually resting near alders shadowed by apple trees. At dusk a porcupine swam up from beneath the backhouse, or did so until I crammed buoys into holes dug under the building. Place and person are patchworks of the small. The more patches a person recognizes the more he will appreciate life. During my first amble along the lane, I heard the song of a white-throated sparrow then those of myrtle and black-throated green warblers. Tails bobbing, a small flock of palm warblers foraged low through scrub. A black-backed gull rode the wind over the headland, muttering impatiently, the sounds out of feather with the bird's unperturbed, elegant flight. Two eiders and a loon bobbed in the water, the breast of this last ballooning white like a buoy. Two years ago I lay two sheets of plywood on the open ground behind the headland. While four brown snakes curled like laces under one sheet, a vole nested under the other.

A white admiral patrolled the lane. Soon Atlantic fritillaries would sip meadowsweet in George's Field, and monarchs would perch lazily on knapweed growing above the foundation hole on Ma's Property. Deerflies had hatched, and looking at the ground, I watched their shadows swing around my head. Suddenly the sour aroma of witherod oozed through the air. Bill Grace, our neighbor, had sawed branches off saplings that leaned into the lane. As the leaves of witherod blackened, fragrance clotted and fermented, repulsing Vicki, but appealing to me, smacking of bourbony bread pudding. For twelve years Bill's cat has crossed the highway and hunted our property. Amid grass along the lane lay pieces of two meadow jumping mice, the tufts of their tails small black brooms. A northern harrier lifted herself over white spruce then slid down the headland. Near a setting of swamp candles lay the head of a hare, hunks of meat red and still attached, fur spreading in a brown puddle, scraps left by a great horned owl. I pocketed the head and later stuck it in a jar, covering it with a blend of water and Javex 2, an "All Fabric Bleach."

Even the new seemed familiar. Cardinals nested at the edge of the blueberry field, the first Vicki and I ever saw in Beaver River. In the lane a large green and yellow dragonfly hawked a skimmer out of the air. Perched on a twig, the big dragonfly ate his smaller cousin. The dragonfly swallowed the skimmer head first, eating everything except the wings. Torpid after the meal, the dragonfly didn't flutter when I pushed him off his perch onto my index finger. Later I surprised a woodcock and two fledglings in the damp near the cow pond. That afternoon the body of a hump-backed whale washed ashore at Beaver River. Rot had shrunk the whale's head, and the carcass was smallish, twelve paces from front to fluke. Time had flayed the body, slicing black skin into strips that waved in the tide like kelp. Beneath the skin gleamed hunks of yellow and brown flesh. Blubber glistened, and cables of bone bound the animal's sides. From the sides, fins swept out like loose, knobby wings. When I turned away, Penny bathed in the carcass. "No different from last summer when she rolled in dead seal," Vicki said later. The next day Vicki's brother Geoff arrived for a visit, and we pried two vertebrae from the body. After inserting a long pole through holes left by the spinal column, we brought the vertebrae back to the house, each of us carrying an end of the pole. "By next summer the stench should be gone," Vicki said.

Keeping life familiar takes effort. Grass grows amid stones above the outlet at Beaver River. Vicki's father thought the grass foxtail, and for years Vicki and her father cut clumps, arranging them in vases in his study. After her father's death, Vicki continued to cut the grass. Every July foxtails evoke memories of family summers past. For years I've known that the grass Vicki and her father cut was squirrel tail, not foxtail, a lovely, but, as botanists put it, "noxious weed." Never have I corrected Vicki when she called the grass foxtail. Better that familiar association endures, tying daughter to father, warming days with recollection.

Things that occur in Nova Scotia seem to have happened before. One morning Vicki picked 1,304 blueberries. That night she started reading *Moby Dick*. She began at page 147, the chapter entitled "The Mast-Head," having read the first one hundred and forty-six pages two years ago. Printed in Boston for The St. Botolph Society, the edition had been given to Vicki's father in 1922 by "Aunt Leila." The following night at dusk I walked to the headland. Venus gleamed near the lower horn of the crescent moon. From horn and star yellow ladders rolled across the water in rungs. Lights from fishing boats pricked the horizon. To the north waves slipped landward smooth and silver until they broke into shadows and oozed oily over the sand.

Two days later I hiked the cliffs above Bear Cove. Several years ago portions of the movie *The Scarlet Letter* were filmed at Bear Cove. Atop an outcrop builders constructed a house and barn. During the past year teenagers tattooed walls with sketches of bats, flying snakes, and headless horses. Scattered throughout the house, perhaps as a form of evangelical exorcism, were copies of a religious tract "How To Live Forever." The front cover of the tract was blue. Pasted against the blue was the skyline of Atlanta, a cross towering above buildings. The tract was distributed by Rock Spring Baptist Church located at 5900 Reynolds Road in Morrow, Georgia, "Tommy Aman, Pastor." Printed inside the back cover was an "Eternal Life Birth Certificate." "I," the certificate began, followed by a space for a name, "received Christ at." After a space for the place appeared the word "on," this followed by a final space for the date. Also printed on the certificate was an excerpt from John: "And this is the record, that God hath given to us eternal life, and this is in his Son. These things have I written unto you that believe on the name of the Son of God; that ye may know that ye have eternal life."

The slow roll of days in Beaver River quickens memory. Early in July while walking the spruce woods behind the headland, I stepped on a young hare. The hare screamed and flipped over, legs kicking spasmodically. I picked the animal up, and wrapping her in folds of my sweatshirt, carried her back to the house. I intended to drive to Yarmouth to buy an eyedropper and soybean milk, the kind of milk fed to unweaned kittens. "I can save this hare," I said. "No, you can't," Vicki said. "Break her neck and end her suffering." "Don't thwart good intentions," I said, suddenly remembering when a cat belonging to Vicki's mother ripped a mouse open. The mouse's entrails protruded. I pushed the entrails back through the tear then asked Vicki to sew the wound, saying I would hold the mouse while she sewed after which I'd cover the stitches with antibiotic cream. Vicki refused to stitch the wound, and as a result I snapped the mouse's neck, a memory that bothers me every summer. The hare fared better than the mouse. More shocked than hurt, the animal recovered in the warmth of my shirt. After examining the hare's legs, making sure no bones were broken, I returned her to the woods. I rubbed her back then placed her on the ground. Quickly she jumped away, vanishing under blackberry canes.

The next morning Vicki and I received a letter from Eliza. "Thursday was an exciting day," she began. "For breakfast I decided to be adventurous and have oatmeal instead of raisin bran. I will not be repeating the experiment. The first few bites were good, but the rest tasted like paste. After breakfast I packed for the Lake Magaunacuk canoe trip. I was in the stern of our boat with Sarah in the bow. The rest of my tent went as well as a couple of other girls. When we reached the lake, I saw an extremely large green frog sitting in reeds. The day was sunny, and although I wore sunscreen, I still got burned on my arms. The lake looked deceptively short, but it twisted and lengthened. We paddled for about five hours and covered three or four miles. Because I provided most of the real pushing power for my canoe, my arms felt like jelly at the end. I was so happy when lunch came. We had cheese Triscuits and Fig Newtons then went swimming. It was really windy on the way back and hard to paddle, but Sarah, Abby, and I belted out show tunes. Consequently we kept drifting off course and were the last to finish." "That sounds familiar," Vicki said. "Eliza must have lifted the letter from one of your books." "Yes," I said, "green frogs, Fig Newtons, sentimental old songs, and drifting—that's the good life." ❖

Camp Letter

Every night this past summer at nine, George the dachshund climbed the stairs to Vicki's and my bedroom. He burrowed under a blanket atop a pillow beside my bed. At eleven-thirty I rousted him out of the doggy motel, as Vicki labeled pillow and blanket, and carried him downstairs for his nightly visit outside. George was nine years old. At six-thirty the next morning, he woke me, and I took him outside again. Instead of the bedroom, Penny slept under a side table in the kitchen. In the morning she accompanied George into the meadow. On returning to the house, the dogs went back to sleep. I stayed up. I made tea, filling the kettle with water and putting it on the hot plate in the pantry. Next I fetched kindling from the backhouse and started a fire in the stove. The fire warmed the kitchen, making it toasty when Vicki got up at nine. After the fire blazed, I ate breakfast, over granola and a banana, dumping milk and mounds of berries—all of which I picked, blueberries, raspberries, blackberries, and shadbush berries. While eating I read, this summer the two-volume, revised edition of *Roland's Flora of Nova Scotia*. After scraping my bowl bare, I washed it in the kitchen sink. Resting on the table near the sink was the slop bucket, heaped with vegetable parings from the previous night's dinner. I grabbed the bucket and taking it outside, emptied it at the edge of the blueberry field. Afterward I set the bucket beside a larch I planted four years ago and named for Vicki's father. Then I ambled across the meadow and through alders to a mossy clearing near the stonewall bordering Ma's Property. "A real outhouse," I said, "one with a view." Not once during the past three summers have I used the lavatory inside the house, an insignificant, immodest eccentricity that deludes me into thinking my Nova Scotia self more natural than my Storrs self, the teacher cramped at a desk, scribbling paragraphs around rolls of paper.

Weather never affected my routine. I enjoyed storms, alders switching and rain pattering like keys on a piano. On the way back to the house, I picked up the slop bucket. Once in the kitchen I awakened the dogs. After pulling on boots and stuffing the pockets of my orange jacket with a notebook, a hand lens, two ball-point pens, a six-inch ruler, a knife, and three plastic pill containers in which to put insects, I slung binoculars around my neck and sauntered forth to explore the world. On warm mornings George and Penny raced ahead of me. On cold, they malingered. Eventually, though, aromas so heated their imaginations that they forgot the chill coiling around them. I meandered woods, chattering at red squirrels and rolling over logs, disrupting the quiet of salamanders and white-footed mice. Often I sat on the headland and watched waves break into doilies. Usually I wandered for ninety minutes. When I returned to the house, Vicki was puttering about the kitchen and listening to the radio. I greeted her then went into the study and thumbed guidebooks, trying to identify the morning's sights: ferns, caterpillars, and flowers. Identification dragged because I didn't harm the creeping and crawling generations. Once I recognized a creature, I freed it, taking it back to the place where I caught it. By now ten o'clock had passed, and I joined Vicki in the kitchen to await the mail. Monday through Friday, the postman drove up Route One from Yarmouth filling boxes hanging over the road. He reached our box between ten-thirty and eleven. Starting at ten-thirty, I listened to cars traveling along the highway in hopes of hearing brakes. Several times before the mail arrived, I stepped on to the side porch and peered through the hawthorns toward the road to see if the flag atop our box was flying.

Yesterday a student interviewed me for a class assignment. What aspects of my life, she asked, had changed during the past

92 Camp Letter

five years? I explained that little had changed. Unlike earlier hunks of time during which children were born and parents died, when dreams of the future made the present bubble, recent years had stretched flat and calm. "Paradoxically," I said, "the only change the past five years have brought to my life is the absence of change." In great part continuance bound Vicki and me to Nova Scotia. Days were silent, my companions not people, but petals, fruit dots, and feathers. In Nova Scotia only mail stirred mornings.

This summer Eliza spent seven weeks at Alford Lake Camp near Hope, Maine. During July and August she sent Vicki and me fifteen letters. She wrote in her tent at night, lying in bed on her stomach, a stack of books to her left propping up a flashlight. "I was always the last person in the tent to fall asleep," she said later. "After I wrote you and Mom, I read a couple of chapters of *Tristram Shandy*." Francis and Edward also wrote, but they're boys, and their correspondence was boy-like. From Italy Francis mailed two postcards, one of which arrived after he himself appeared in Beaver River. For his part Edward wrote six dutiful letters, all conveying the impression that he was alive and happy, but not much else. "Being a counselor is different from being a camper," he explained later, "and Mom wouldn't understand. Eliza is a girl, and girls write more." "Baloney," I thought.

When a letter from Eliza arrived, I fetched it from the mailbox. Sitting at the kitchen table, Vicki sliced the envelope open with a paring knife. I turned the radio off and sat in the rocking chair. Vicki read the letter aloud, often re-reading paragraphs. After she finished, we talked for thirty or so minutes. The letters were joyful, and we tossed the contents back and forth as if we were playing ball on a beach. We mulled Eliza's doings and speculated about years that lay ahead. Eventually, though, talk slowed. Vicki began a chore, defrosting the refrigerator, mending curtains, or if the mail was late and we had chatted a long time, preparing soup for lunch. For my part, I took a second morning stroll.

Eliza wrote on stationery eight and a half inches wide and eleven tall. A blue border circled the paper, reducing the length of the writing surface by two and half inches and the width by an inch. During the summer Eliza's handwriting shrank. In her first three letters, she fit thirty-seven, forty-five, then forty-six lines on a page. In the last three letters she crammed seventy-five, seventy-six, and eighty-two lines on to a page, forcing Vicki to read with a magnifying glass. Gardens of decoration illuminated the letters. Pictures adorned envelops, constellations of blue stars; a bear who punned, "I Love You Bear-y Much"; and a purple and green planet, a blue ring circling it, yellow stars twinkling, at the edge of the solar system, pink words declaring, "You Are The Moon And Stars To Me!" On the back of an envelope, lady bugs perched on flower petals, red hearts bright on black backs. Above the flower petals appeared "Pig Latin—sort of," the letters themselves, a rainbow of colors—"IA OVELA OUYA!" and "LEASEPA ITEWRA," the translations being "I love you" and "Please write." Occasionally postscripts tattooed backs of envelopes. "P.S.," Eliza wrote early in July, "Caroline in my cabin does several animal noises. She does herds of cows, a hyper Chihuahua, and a beached whale." "P.P.S.," she added to the same letter, "I dreamed last night that I was hiking down a hill when a group of Vikings showed up with five mountain lions in plastic bags. They released them on me, and I kept kicking them off the ledge I was standing on. I wonder what it means."

Down the margins of letters themselves, Eliza drew dragons and orchids, and once a green fish blowing eight blue bubbles. Suspended in each bubble was a letter, the eight reading, "I Love You!" At the bottom of one letter she drew herself, three and a half inches tall. Annotations buzzed about the picture, arrows attaching them to the drawing. Above a moppy head appeared "lighter unkempt hair." At the other end of the drawing an arrow split and pointed at two green feet, the annotation reading, "large feet as always." Beneath a thin, flexed arm hung "slightly more muscle." In contrast calves bulged, the swelling attributed to "hiking trip."

Alford Lake divided the camp summer into halves. While many girls spent seven weeks at camp, others only attended for three and a half, some coming the first session, the rest the second. At the end of three and a half weeks, one group of campers departed, and another group arrived. Gluing the two halves of the summer together was Visitors' Weekend. The camp held a banquet, and the parents of most campers attended, many traveling long distances, from Florida and Ohio, for example. Vicki and I spent banquet day in Beaver River. In a letter Eliza described the festivities. The letter arrived on a rainy morning, and Vicki read it twice. By the end of the second reading, sunlight fell in golden arcs.

"Dear Mommy and Daddy," Eliza began, "I wish you could be here right now. You would laugh so hard, Daddy especially, who loves to make fun of pomposity. First, Abigail and Muffy left on Friday. I must admit that I wasn't all that sad. They were nice, but I wasn't close to them. Of course Caroline was positively salivating over Abigail's twin brother, Peter. I wasn't at my best. It was hot, and I was suffering from a moderate dose of homesickness. Everyone was leaving, and I was so tired from the previous day of inactivity that I wanted to go, too. But I recovered enough to practice my French horn."

"Visitors' Weekend was scheduled to start at five. Over half the camp had left, being only first session, but every remaining camper except ten of us had visitors coming. Caroline's parents drove all the way from Virginia! I think that it was pointless to spend money to visit her when she didn't even want them to come. Anyway, I moseyed up to the front of the farmhouse a little after five. Lots of parents were already there, *and they looked exactly like the people at Princeton*. All the women wore some kind of khaki bottom, a black top, and gold earrings. The men wore faintly Hawaiian shirts. It was an unspoken dress code. I wish you could have been there. Mommy could have shown the women a thing or two about style, and Daddy would have been the life of the party in his chartreuse jacket and bug shirts. I was introduced to Elizabeth's parents, and (I am not joking) their names were Chip and Connie. Can you believe it?"

"Since I felt like a sore thumb, unwanted by other people's parents, I started back to the tent glumly. But I found something that made me feel great. I saw a dead snake. It was very small, less than a foot long, and had obviously died from heatstroke while crossing the field. It had been dead about a day. Its eyes were shriveled, and its tail was beginning to dry. Its mouth was open, and its tongue resembled dried seaweed. I was so excited that I immediately picked it up and ran to the Outdoor Explorations building, where using *A Field Guide to Reptiles and Amphibians of Eastern and Central North America,* I identified it as an Eastern Garter, *Thamnophis sirtalis sirtalis.* Eastern Garters vary greatly in coloring and pattern. This one was olive green with very faint yellowish stripes. It had been in the process of molting, and I could see shiny scales beneath the outer layer of its skin. The snake cheered me, and I brought it back to my cabin, and to the horror of my citified tent mates, kept it in my trunk overnight. Their parents made remarks, saying, 'the only good snakes are dead ones.' The next day I took it out. I wanted to preserve it, but no formaldehyde being handy, I decided to let the flesh decay and keep the skeleton. Since I didn't want animals to take it, I placed it on a bark ledge on a tree. I crushed pine needles to disguise the scent and covered it with dry leaves. However upon reconsideration, I believe I may have taken the wrong approach. Dirt probably contains elements essential to decomposition, so I may bury it. I know my fascination with this snake seems odd, but I haven't had much to do recently. We've pretty much sat around for four days, waiting for old campers to leave and new campers to arrive."

"Anyway back to Visitors' Weekend, I went up for a buffet dinner on Friday and could not believe my eyes. I felt as though I was at the Ritz! There were three white awnings and tents set up. Under one was the drink table. There were two silver tureens with blue lemonade, pineapple slices, and purple orchids floating in them. In the middle was an elaborate silver fountain in which flowed more lemonade. Under the next tent were the hors d'oeuvres. There were plates of cream puff things, small pastries, crackers, and some goopy cheese, a loaf of multicolored stuff, and a waterfall of blue ice on which reposed many shrimp. Finally under the last tent were the desserts. There were five different kinds of artery-clogging cakes and champagne glasses filled with chocolate mousse and raspberries. It was amazing! The cooks wore linen chef hats and coats, and the garbage cans were covered with shiny white paper and had black bow ties around them. Oh, I forgot to tell you that I ate a shrimp. It was rather chewy, but I'm not adverse to trying one again."

"Sarah and I had our eating plan all worked out. We got in line at precisely the right moment. After allowing a suitable number of parents by, I had a little of everything: roast potato salad, rice, broccoli, and cauliflower salad, vegetable stir fry, French bread, and seasoned chicken. I then had a piece of the thickest, richest chocolate cake ever. My piece weighed at least a pound. Instead of having a little bit of frosting in the middle, it had a little bit of cake, sandwiched between two huge slabs of frosting. It was delicious. Sarah had a chocolate cheesecake. We both then had a mousse glass. I felt like a brick. After dinner we had a campfire. My tent sat on the porch of the laundry house. We read an incredibly sappy poem Elizabeth had written for Kelly. Tina and Ali performed an African dance, and counselors sang a few nice songs."

"The next day we went to see the horse show in the morning. There were snacks out, more cream puffs, and pastries filled with strawberry jam. I ate lunch with Caroline and her parents. The night before, they asked me what I wanted and generously bought me lunch. I had a delicious deli-made turkey sandwich, potato salad, a Pepsi, and a whole Hershey's milk chocolate bar. It was awfully nice of them. I went swimming later. Everyone thinks the bottom of the lake is disgusting, but I love it. I weave through the reeds, exploring. The other day I found a mussel that snapped shut when I touched it. We also went to Scrub Beach where we washed our hair in the lake. Alford Lake is the second cleanest lake in Maine. Last Saturday morning I got up at six o'clock to participate in the annual loon count. The camp is responsible for keeping track of the loons on the lake. Thirty of us paddled silently into the middle of the lake. The morning was beautiful. The lake was still as a sheet of glass. My canoe spotted four loons. They dove under the water and popped up three minutes later all the way across the lake. I love their calls. They are so ghostly. Are the calls territorial or are they mating calls? I'd like to know."

A garter snake twisted across the bottom of Eliza's letter, its red forked tongue extended, feeling for warmth. Above the snake hung a line of endings, "I love you so much! I miss you! Please write! I love you!!!!!!" Words, Vicki said, to warm fond parents. Vicki started to make soup, and I walked down to George's Field. In the high grass around the field, purple fringed orchis bloomed, the petals flaring cut like skirts of gay party dresses. In low damp near the woods, wild mint grew knee-high, blossoms surrounding stems in blue muffs, three or four muffs blooming at the same time. I walked back to the house. A garter snake stuck its head through a hole in the side of the barn. Curving upward in order to survey grass around the barn, the snake wrote the first half of its body backwards into an *S*. The flanks and belly of the snake were bright yellow. "Gosh," I thought, "I'll have to write Eliza about this." ❖

August

August in Nova Scotia is silent. Words slip from days, reducing idea to twig. In September when school begins, talk buds then during winter blooms, turning cold into seasonal chatter. This summer August stabilized the fibrillation of the academic year. Instead of hankering for lively event, I roamed graveyards, thoughts of the past rather than the future quickening hours. In the Beaver River cemetery, wreathes of eyebright and yarrow curved across paths. From Churchill Lake a loon mourned, and in a cat spruce, a raven ground song into gravel. On tombstones doves cradled olive branches in their bills. A sickle sliced a sheaf of wheat, and an anchor splashed through granite and hooked a Bible. Atop the grave of Lizzie Crosby, the Gate of Heaven burst open, rays of light beckoning from a crown above the keystone arch. "One precious to our hearts has gone," the inscription explained. "The voice we loved is stilled. And though on earth the body lies. The soul is safe in heaven." Down a slight slope, a stone the size of a loaf of bread marked the grave of Comfort and Minnie Lewis's son, Ervin. The boy lived for two years and four months, and the inscription said, "Our Baby."

I'm not eager, as my friend Josh phrases it, " to chew dandelion roots"—at least not until Eliza enters college. But August is the month of remembrance, provoking melancholy and making me world-weary. I sat on benches in graveyards and talked to Mother and Father. At Chebogue, I told them that Francis entered college in September. "He's never had a blister, but he is a good boy," I said. "You'd love him." I described Edward's dark moods. I told my parents that I wished that they hadn't moved from Nashville so he could visit. "I'm sorry," I said, "that the babies came late, and you missed them." Later, I read stones and watched gulls wheel above the salt marsh. On March 16, 1859, Sarah Maria, the wife of Captain George Clements, died. She was twenty-two. "Oh! Maria dear," her marker read, "So Beautiful, So Young to Die / So Many a Fond and Foolish Hope / Upon thy Grave Shall Lie." Eleazer and Hannah Johnson had two sons. The older, James Albert, died before his sixth birthday. The younger, Evelyn Lorenzo, was "lost at sea" during his seventeenth year. The boys shared a stone. Carved on it was a quatrain.

> They have left the dear place of their childhood forever.
> To be of that band which cannot sever.
> They have gone in the home of the redeemed ones
>   to dwell.
> Though fondly we loved them, may we say "It is well."

The next day I received a letter from Ann Brothers, a childhood friend. Ann and John, her husband, were moving into a smaller house. While emptying a chest, Ann found a letter I mailed her on October 3, 1963, written the day after I arrived at Cambridge. I sailed to Britain on the *United States.* When I boarded the ship, a steward handed me a telegram from Ann, wishing me a romantic voyage. Joy and optimism fizzed from my response. "Dear Ann," I began, "I certainly appreciated your telegram and tried my best to live up to its instructions. I maneuvered the best I could with one date until 4:00 A.M. then another from four to eight. Alas, I made a mistake, one I've never made before. I fell for a girl. The falling was not mutual. I fell hard. She slipped softly." After informing Ann that the girl "reminded me a lot of you," I described the boat trip. Every night I danced or stomped, as I elegantly put it, until sunrise. "I even got invited to Kenya for the summer by a wonderful lady who couldn't control a caustic tongue and who downed a case of Scotch."

100   August

My first purchase in Cambridge was a bicycle. "My rear end is sore from the seat which slips up and down," I recounted. "Also I have wrecked twice. Cycling is hell. The English drive on the left, and several times I have found myself pedaling on the right, headed straight for a car. Streets are narrow, and students ride bicycles. What legs I will have in two years!" "Cambridge," I continued enthusiastically, "is quaint and could not exist in America. I really love this place. I have not found any girls to love, though, except a French girl who could not understand English. Anyway the girl I fell for on the boat is living in France. I seem to resemble you, Ann, and fall for one person after another. By the way don't hurry matters with John. You don't realize what an overpowering sex symbol I'm going to be when I return home—either that or an ass. Some say I am already wearing the hide of the latter."

I liked the boy who wrote Ann. He rushed into the future heart pounding and arms spread. The boarding house in which I roomed was damp, but that did not blight enthusiasm. "I have made friends with the house cat," I said, "and the creature has already consented to sleep on my feet at night." Ann taught at Ensworth School in Nashville, and I asked if she enjoyed her classes. Then I urged her to write, drawing thirty-three stars around the request, saying, "you can't believe how long it took me to draw those stars. It was mighty hard." I noted that deodorant had "not gone over in Europe." "Some Frenchie on the boat," I recounted, "didn't use a deodorant, so I ended up with his escort. I call that my D. D.— deodorant date. What a pleasant subject!" I closed the letter, saying I had to pedal to college for dinner, two and a half miles in a drizzle. "Blazes," I exclaimed, "don't tell mother. She will have me in a pine box." I signed the letter, "Love, Sammy—soon to be prime minister."

Eliza read the letter. "Daddy," she said, "you were a bird. Did you always enjoy Cambridge?" "Yes," I said, thinking that although age had pruned feathers and clipped spirits, "great experiences," as I told Ann, still made me chirp. No longer do I sign myself "prime minister." Now instead of hitching close to "a fine girl," I embrace place. Much as expectation of the future entangled youth, the middle-aged me ferrets through the present, the invitation to Kenya satisfactorily transformed into safari down the lane, past the blueberry field and out to the drumlin, steep above the Bay of Fundy. Instead of bounding from topic to topic, I amble. As a result observation rolls slowly, green with stem and bud rather than boyish exuberance. This August I studied plants bordering the lane, in the sun, bay, alder, meadowsweet, sheep laurel, Indian pear, chokeberry, wild rose, and winterberry. In the low damp, spears of soft rush sliced through horsetail, behind them, cinnamon ferns, leaves spraying up from rootstocks like water through nozzles. Farther along the lane appeared high bush blueberry and mountain holly, the berries of this last, soft red bulbs on slender claret stems. In low spots white spruce rotted, green lichens flaking scabby from branches. Near the headland spruce spread into healthy triangles. In the morning yellow jackets gleaned twigs for spiders. Fragrances eddied across the lane, in sunlight, rose potpourri; in mossy wet spots, sour wine; and near the headland, a dry swell of resin. During the day, aromas changed. When fog soughed off the water, air became mothy. Throughout the day air rained along the lane; sometimes currents seemed dry and crunchy; other times, air drizzled and ticked.

I dawdled. On red maple, wood lice lurked under fists of moss. Sixteen tarnished plant bugs nested in an alder envelope. Cat's ears bloomed in George's Field, the flowers yellow constellations pasted to a grassy green sky. Amid the stars, blossoms whirled around plantain, anthers on filaments creamy and shaped like hearts, yellow seams glowing in the middles. When I brushed the flowers, they shed thin cirrus clouds of pollen. Fireweed grew near the highway. At the end of August rain fell for four days. The fifth day was sunny. At noon pods spilled seed like milk. For two days seeds surfed the air, turning breezes frothy. While many seeds washed up on shrubs and trees, spider webs flossed others out of flight.

My August differed from that of the children. One morning while running the path atop the drumlin, Francis surprised a couple disporting themselves. Francis did not notice the festivities until he was amid them. All he could do was hop, skip, and jump high. In a posture better suited to seeing Francis than her companion, the woman said, "Jesus." "Not Jesus, but François," my son said as he gallivanted down the path. Unlike me, the children toyed with ideas. "Daddy, money once freed people to be individuals," Eliza said at breakfast. "Now money turns people into conformists who buy brand name clothes and cars and who take conventional exotic vacations. Money reduces life to platitude."

"Interesting," I said and ambled out to George's Field. At the bottom of the field behind a hedge of rose and winterberry, the cow pond gapped like a cavity. The pond was the size of our kitchen. Humic acid shadowed the water, making it appear brown, purple, and yellow depending on how light shifted and shuttered. Four green frogs lounged on pond weed. Around the pond, wool grass tumbled loosely, and bog rush shred into nutlets. Bumblebees dug pollen out of pickerel weed, and warblers hopped through alders. A redstart hunted insects, and a dragonfly stammered over the water. "Eliza is right," I mumbled as I stared at old man's beard rheumy under a shadow. "Money binds people to convention."

Not obligation or appointment but a flight of orange crescents and the hatching of American ear moths marked the August calendar. At the end of the month flat-topped asters and goldenrod spattered the blueberry field. Ladies tresses bloomed on the bluff, and by the stonewall west of the house, blackberry canes curved gibbous, waxing heavy with fruit. Picking blackberries is red work, and for a fortnight my fingers resembled pincushions. Often after breakfast I sat on the kitchen porch and listened to hummingbirds throb the air. Two pellucid wasps kited across the meadow, abdomens blowing like tails. Wolf spiders hatched; one morning I counted fifty-four on the wall behind my chair. The red maple sprouting amid rugosa roses suddenly wilted. Some time earlier a porcupine gnawed abrasions into the bark, and colonizing the sapwood, a canker girdled the trunk, the fruit bodies of the canker spotting bark brown and measly.

During August I roam days. Only afterward do I force random observation into paragraphs, creating the illusion of unity. After lighting the stove one morning, I hunkered in George's Field and watched crows forage high grass for insects. Pink-edged-sulfurs wafted over chokeberry, trembling like small yellow leaves. A blue damselfly lit on my left arm. For a moment I imagined that I'd slipped seamlessly into the pasture. Perched on winterberry, an olive-sided flycatcher scanned scrub for insects. A mouse sat on the branch of a spruce, peeling seeds from a cone. Beside the lane ants swarmed from the ground and swirled yeasty into the air, rolling hot over each other in a mating frenzy. A kestrel swept across the abandoned pasture east along the bluff, its red tail flaring. At the bottom of the bluff, metallic bees worked sow thistle. A garter snake lay motionless in the lane, swallowing a toad. I didn't see the snake, and when I trod close, the snake spit out the toad and opening grass into a seam, vanished. The toad wasn't dead. I picked it up and wrapped it in a fold of my shirt. By the time I reached the side meadow, the toad had recovered, and I turned it loose under a larch. Only rarely, and usually inadvertently, do I rescue one creature from another. Still, occasionally I can't resist meddling. One afternoon I noticed a green caterpillar on a willow twig. Atop the caterpillar stood four white egg cases shaped like funeral urns. The cases contained grubs of a parasite, probably those of a chalcis fly. Eventually the grubs would burrow into the caterpillar and chew life away. Then the caterpillar would lose body, and slumping into folds look like a threadbare jacket sagging on a cardboard hanger. After pausing for a moment, I flicked the egg cases off the caterpillar.

The last week in August amid concertina wires of blackberry canes, I discovered a cecropia moth caterpillar fattening on meadowsweet. Close by a tachnid fly rested on an alder. Tachnid flies parasitize caterpillars by laying eggs on stems. I shook the alder, and the fly vanished. Next I removed the caterpillar, and for two days fed it in the study. Afterward I returned it to the blackberries and watched it swell like a sausage.

Occasionally I left the farm. Rarely, however, did I travel far from plant or animal. One Saturday Vicki, Francis, and I attended the "Flower Show and Tea," sponsored by the Yarmouth Garden

Club. Francis wore a shirt purchased at the Tennessee Aquarium in Chattanooga. Three fish swam across the front of the shirt, a lake sturgeon, a paddlefish, and an alligator gar. At times the show reminded me of a coral reef. While dahlias and lemon puffs opened like anemones, gladiolas and gooseneck loosestrife waved like blades of seaweed. Love-lies-bleeding washed from arrangements and swept across the floor like cord weed. Here and there roses squatted immobile, their thorns sharp pincers. Instead of fish, Vicki, Francis, and I resembled shore birds, ruddy turnstones darting from vase to vase. Clucking, we drank tea and ate sandwiches stuffed with asparagus and cream cheese chunky with maraschino cherries.

The next Saturday we attended the Western Nova Scotia Exhibition. I ate a ginger ice cream cone and coveted a New Holland tractor, its blue parts exposed, an alluring motherboard of pipe and piston. At the cattle auction, the champion steer sold for $2.35 a pound and the reserve champion for $2.15, bidders being local stores, Kent Hardware, Sobey's, Canadian Tire, and Foodland. I sat in the cattle barn, the batter of cud, hay, and manure more soothing than words. Color rippled across cattle like muscle, plumes of red guttering shorthorns, blond floating over Simmentals.

In August I gathered, preparing for September work. After a hundred and thirty years, floorboards in the barn rotted. Walking the barn risked ankles, and I decided to replace the wood with concrete. "The old boards are almost human," Vicki said. "They cough, groan, and if a person listens, tell stories. Next year the barn will be silent." Although the new floor has not yet been poured, it has already swept away much of the past. To prepare for the concrete, Francis and I cleared the barn. From a stall Francis removed a hundred and forty-one pounds of rocks. A decade ago, he hauled the stones up from the beach. "My collection," he called them. This summer he put the rocks into buckets, loaded them into the car, and drove to the Beaver River outlet where he dumped them on the shore. Afterward whenever I walked to Beaver River, I studied the stones. Tides slowly rolled them from sight, "scrubbing away clutter," Vicki said, "the stuff of memory, and love."

Cleaning the barn took four days. First, I raked then shoveled porcupine droppings. In stalls the droppings were six and a half inches deep. Swallows built nests on beams, and eggshells speckled the loft. Near the door I raised a dump of trash, containing, among other things: lumber enough for a tool shed; three sinks; a toilet; a green plastic fish net bulging with forty-two buoys, children's treasure from summers past; eleven wooden picture frames; three hundred and eighty-six red bricks; nine soup cans filled with rusty nails and screws; six grates from wood stoves; a cigar box containing gears and pendulums for gable clocks; a sheaf of iron spikes, all eighteen inches long; thirty-two feet of stove pipe; eight broken chairs; a wooden rake with spaces for twenty-four teeth, six of the teeth missing; one tire; five deflated inner tubes; two bird houses; a mirror for a dresser; a sway-backed saw horse; six windows, most panes broken; three lawn mowers, the sort in which oil and gas are blended; two steamer trunks; fifteen feet of thick fire hose, the iron connection to the hydrant five inches in diameter; four mattresses stuffed with chicken feathers; a fire screen; three tea kettles; two cracked ironstone washbowls; and webs of driftwood, balsa for children's construction projects.

Efficiency does not matter in August. Often I examined contents of the barn. On a shelf hammered into the back wall sat a dish manufactured in Nova Scotia at the turn of the century. The design on the dish was raspberry, the fruit, six round humps of glass surrounding a seventh hump. Two circles of fruit decorated the lip of the dish, the inner circle containing fourteen berries, the outer heavy with twenty-eight. Two glass handles resembling palms stuck out from opposite sides of the dish, each palm holding a pair of raspberries. In a chair lay a red "Gilbert Big Boy Tool Chest." The chest contained nails, half a screwdriver, and a sprung door latch. Two boys appeared on the lid of the box. Both wore shirts with collars, one shirt green, the other blue, sleeves neatly rolled above elbows. While the boy on the right held a hammer, the one on the left admired their handiwork, a small bookcase. Each boy wore a starched work apron, "Gilbert Big Boy" stamped on the apron of the boy standing on the right. Both boys smiled. Their teeth were white and straight. Both had brown hair, parted on the left side of their heads and brushed high off their foreheads. The haircuts tapered, and the boys had side-burns. I kept the dish and toolbox, storing them in the backhouse next to crab shells Eliza painted eight summers ago.

At the bottom of a fish box lay two bug sprays, the smaller one Black Flag, the larger Flit. Printed on the plunger of the Black Flag was the warning "Caution—Do Not Spray In Or Near An Open Flame." A dozen soldiers marched through rust eating the pump of the Flit sprayer. The soldiers wore black hats, red coats, and white bell-bottom trousers. Black packs clung to their shoulders, held in place by yellow and white bandoliers, the yellow band strapped tight across the left side of their chests, the white across the right. Flit, directions stated, skirmished effectively against "Flies, Mosquitoes, Moths, Bed Bugs, Ants, Cockroaches."

In the August of life I don't expect to discover unity or mean-ing. Bits satisfy me, however. In a trunk lay a certificate issued by the Shelburne Juvenile Temperance Society on September 12, 1858. That day Issachar MacKenzie joined the Band of Hope. "I do voluntarily promise," Issachar declared, "that I will abstain from Ale, Porter, Wine, Ardent Spirits, and all intoxicating Liquors as beverages and will not give nor offer them to others." Beneath Issachar's signature was a woodcut depicting "Religion and Temperance Guarding Youth from Evil." A child stood between two women dressed in white robes. The woman to the right of the child grasped the boy's right hand in her left, her own right hand raised, her index finger pointing upward. On the other side of the boy, Temperance held the child's left hand. Cradled in her left arm was a shield, a black cross quartering the front, and running diag-onally from the upper right to the lower left a banner reading TEM-PERANCE. Just beyond the shield four snakes stood on their tails, curling like breaking waves, fangs splattering venom.

When I first taught, I forged links between things. Eventually age exposed the smelting. Still, habit lingers, and soldering frag-ments together satisfies. Also in the trunk lay MacKenzie's coffin plate. Before burials undertakers removed the plates from coffins and gave them to relatives who displayed them in parlors, often attaching them to walls above mantles. Issachar MacKenzie died December 1, 1881. He lived thirty-five years, two months, and twenty-eight days, joining the Temperance Society the day before his twelfth birthday.

Eighteen inches high and twelve wide, the coffin plate was tin. Painted black with Issachar's name and the dates of his life in gold, the plate resembled a shield. Lobes stuck out embossed at both sides and at the top and bottom. Pressed into each side lobe was an angel. Both angels were female, the outside breast of each bare, arms nearest the center of the plate cradling sheaves of wheat. Atop the upper lobe appeared a six-pointed crown, a star shining above each point. Over the stars frolicked a host of rotund naked boys. Painted in gold around the base of the crown was the word "GLORIA." Below the crown a dove beat through the black, an olive branch in its beak. Swirls decorated the lower lobe of the plate, looking like vines blowing from a lattice.

Purpose determined reading when I was young. Nowadays I read randomly. Lining the middle drawer of a dresser in the loft was the Friday, March 10, 1916, number of *The Yarmouth Telegraph.* Distributed to subscribers of *The Yarmouth Herald,* the *Telegraph* contained four pages of local and national news. I spent a morning reading the *Telegraph,* sitting in the loft, my back against a beam, left leg dangling over the lip of the floor. The parochial appeals to me more than the national or the international, and I first read local news. E. Chesley Allen, principal of the South End School, accepted a position as Supervisor of the Truro Schools and Principal of Colchester Academy. The paper implied that finding a replacement for Allen would be difficult. A "gifted" naturalist, Allen studied birds as well as children, and during the past year "issued" a booklet "devoted to the identification of native birds." On "Saturday last," Miss Grace Fulton returned home after spending "several weeks in Halifax with friends." C. F. Jamison, "formerly of Yarmouth," moved from Medicine Hat to Lethbridge in order to enter "the law office of C. F. Harris, the famous criminal lawyer."

In Truro, Mr. and Mrs. John Pratt, their thirteen-year-old daughter, and two grandchildren "burned to death." Mr. Pratt "was found near the front entrance" of his house "with one of his grandchildren in his arms." Among the bequests of Kenneth Dawson of Bridgewater was a thousand dollars to the Rev. Robert W. Norwood "for the education" of Norwood's son Robert. To both the Infants Home and the Children's Hospital, two institutions located in Halifax, Dawson left a thousand dollars. Dawson's will was admirable. After providing handsomely for his wife and daughter, he left large bequests to a cousin, an aunt, and a sister. To his brother Robert he bequeathed "the old Grandfather clock." Lastly he deeded land for a hospital to Bridgewater. To spur construction he left the city twenty thousand dollars, contingent upon town's matching the amount in five years.

War news filled columns of the *Telegraph*. Beatrice Caneshire, a nurse at a military hospital in London, wrote Jacob Foshes, assuring him that Andrew, his son who had been wounded in the left arm at Etables, was "progressing favorably." Ernest Monroe, "previously reported as killed in action," was, the paper stated, "officially reported as wounded in the right foot." Admitted to a hospital at Boeschepe on February 8, he had so improved that he "would be able to go to the front again soon."

Five columns composed the front page of the *Telegraph*. The middle column described an inspirational film, "Canada's Fighting Forces," produced under the "direction" of the government in order "to show the people of the Dominion the actual life of the brave Canadian boys who go overseas to fight for King and Canada." On Tuesday, March 14, the film was going to be shown in Yarmouth at the Royal Opera House. Ground seats cost twenty-five cents; Balcony, fifteen; and Gallery, ten. People with "red Maple leaf blood" coursing their veins, the article stated, "will want to attend and see how our boys in khaki are making history." Corporal White, "hero of Ypres and St. Julien" and winner of the "Distinguished Conduct Medal for rescuing wounded comrades under fire," was booked to speak. The corporal presents, the account declared, "a most thrilling and inspiring story of the actual life of the soldier boys, the perils they have to face, the comradeship of the trenches, and how they are to the last man resolved to carry the struggle through to victory."

Exhibited on Friday and Saturday at the People's Theatre were pictures of the 85th Overseas Battalion, Nova Scotia Highlanders. Making war never stops. Still, diversion was available. Along with pictures of the Highlanders, People's was showing the "5 reel Gold Rooster Feature" *Little Mary Sunshine.* Sunlight, not the roar of cannons, shone through the only poem in the *Telegraph,* Teresa Houley's "Spring Gold." "Crocus, Coltsfoot, Celandine, / Dandelion, Daffodil," the first stanza read,

> Who the secret can unfold
> Why the earliest flowers that shine
> In the meadow by the rill,
> Always, always are of gold?

Recruiters scoured western Nova Scotia. Cape Island, an account from Clark's Harbor reported, "noted for its breed of strong, steadfast and robust men, men whose life calling involves almost daily contact with the dangers of the deep, has answered right loyally to the call for men for the 85th Overseas Battalion." "Fifty sturdy sons on Cape Island now have enlisted for the Shelburne County Company of the 219th Battalion of the Brigade." Accompanied by a band, a recruiting party visited the island. Among the recruiters was D. Cutten, "president of Acadia University and now of the Highland Brigade." Cutten "spoke of the work that the women are called upon to do in this war, that they should encourage men to enlist, and neither hinder them from doing so, or say, 'well, if you must go, you must.' He pointed out what this war meant to women, and drew a clear line of distinction between the German and British conception of what it was to the weaker sex, and appealed to every woman in the audience to do all she could to induce the men, if of recruitable age, to go."

Throughout the paper, short, enthusiastic paragraphs described the war. "With blasting hurricanes of shell fire and furious infantry fighting the battle for Verdun is now entering the third and what may be the final phase," a report from Paris stated. "All military experts here are united in the belief that Germany is prepared to make sacrifices unequaled in this war. French commanders are without semblance of fear as to the final outcome." Because Yarmouth was a port, much news described war at sea. "Two British Torpedo Boats Sunk by Mines," a headline recounted. "Portuguese Seize Four Large German Steamers and Intern 400 Officers and Men," another headline reported. An article noted that two German commerce raiders had begun cruising the North Atlantic. "Rumors that several merchantmen have been captured, stripped of valuables and crews by the raiders, and abandoned in a sinking condition, are persistent, but the names of the Germans or what disguise they have effected in order to slip upon commerce ships or other details are lacking." War affected the contents of almost every column, even "Religious Matters." At the Tabernacle on Friday evening at seven, the Rev. Wm. J. D. Gibson was slated to preach a sermon entitled "Why I Enlisted." Dr. A. R. Campbell, declared a notice inserted by Landry and Cameron, barristers in Yarmouth, "who has enlisted for overseas service, has left his accounts with the undersigned for collection. Parties indebted to him will please make payment to us."

Buying and selling may be more eternal than fighting. The Saturday special at Giannou's was Cream Mints and Checkerberry at nineteen cents a pound. Two tins of Golden Syrup cost twenty-five cents at Cain Brothers. "Now is the best time to have your bike put in first class shape for the coming season," Yarmouth Cycle advised. "One of the best Bicycle Repair Men in Canada has charge of this department." W. D. Ross urged readers to buy hosiery for 1916, warning, "NEW STOCKINGS will be high in price, poor in quality, uncertain in color." "On account of the inclemency of the weather," M. P. Cook extended the previous weekend's sale. Stamped in thick type above the advertisement for Orrine, a patent medicine, was the announcement "DRUNKARDS SAVED." "This offer," the advertisement stated, "gives the wives and mothers of those who drink to excess an opportunity to try the ORRINE treatment." Priced at a dollar a box, Orrine came into two forms, in pills "for those who desire to take voluntary treatment" and in powder for "secret treatment."

"Wanted," Mrs. E. C. Killam on South Park Street advertised, "a capable girl for general housework." After reading the notice, I put the paper down, got up and stretched, and returned to cleaning. I finished just before dusk and walked to the headland. Thin spindles of waves turned toward the shore where they unraveled into white yarn. In August I often stood on the bluff and watched the sun set. Colors pooled damply then dried black. Some evenings light beat pink and purple across the bottom of anvil clouds. Other times fog lay loose and frosted across the distance, and the horizon glowed fluorescent, slats of yellow and blue shuddering toward the shore. Often I watched the moon, its moldy seas spreading like spores.

I hoarded observation. At Black Point I studied birds, knowing that September would clip roaming into topiary. I imagined sound beating like merlins or soaring like blue herons until their necks unrolled, and raising their heads, the birds lifted out of ease into sharp thought. Sanderlings and least sandpipers foraged wrack. Semi-palmated plovers churred while turnstones pecked through barnacles. In the distance cormorants sunned, wings metallic in the light. Behind the point a marsh hawk dawdled the breeze, and a red-eyed vireo clung to a spruce, the black and white lines above its eyes giving the bird a pedantic expression.

Other days I ambled over the drumlin to Beaver River. A spotted sandpiper hunted through rushes bordering the marsh behind the inlet. A red eft lay dying in gravel. Sparrows foraged nearby. Perhaps a fledgling pecked the salamander, not knowing red efts were poisonous. Beside the road Queen Anne's lace raised parasols; green drained out of goutweed; and tortoise shell beetles stapled holes through hedge bindweed. On the way home from Beaver River, I often meandered the boggy wood behind Ma's Property. At times the wood resembled the sea. Hummocks of moss slipped across the ground like sand. Above trees, birds paddled the wind. Between branches a krill of insects floated through bars of light. A spotted salamander hid under a reefy log. Now and then currents of air swept through the wood turning cinnamon ferns like kelp. Mushrooms bloomed in the woods like shells: amanitas, yellow, red, and gray, caps crusty and barnacled; chanterelles, gills splitting and wavering down stalks; and red waxy caps, round as limpets. Small mycena floated above the moss like fairy shrimp, and winter slippery caps clumped together like snails, green sticking viscous to my fingers when I touched them. At the edge of the field three sheathed stalks bumped each other, the caps bleached like crab shells stranded above high tide. Spruce stretched sideways, blown down throughout the wood. In falling, spruce pushed over other trees, creating sunny open pools. Brambles colonized the pools, their canes, forests of coral. Jewelweed grew in banks, orange flowers trembling in the breeze like minnows. Panicles of rattlesnake grass dangled in tentacles, and the mottled leaves of buttercups grew low atop moss like algae.

As days shortened, I took longer walks. White pennants of tawny cotton grass waved amid peat above Bear Cove. A green snake wound rings around my fingers. A mourning cloak butterfly clutched a root beneath a toppled spruce. When the butterfly pinched its wings together, it looked like a wood chip, lichens growing around the edges. Several times in August I tried to stamp method upon observation, determining to study caterpillars. Many caterpillars feed at night. To collect them one spreads a sheet under a shrub and dislodges caterpillars by whacking branches with a stick. I am no longer a night roamer. Sheets bring sleep, not caterpillar hunting, to mind. Moreover because caterpillars molt, usually progressing through five or so larval stages, identification is difficult.

This August was, however, the month of the white-marked tussock moth caterpillar. I found caterpillars crawling on front and side porches, my neck, on witherod, willow, Indian pear, poplar, red maple, hawthorn, golden chain tree, paper birch, red oak, alder, apple, winterberry, and mountain ash—almost every tree and shrub except the black ash at the edge of the kitchen meadow. Other tussock moth caterpillars thrived during August, the definite-marked and yellow-based on alders, the former bright yellow, the latter with sooty black tufts of hair along its back, long black lashes at the head and rear of its body, sweeps of white hair in between. Eight black tufts formed a ridge down the back of the hickory tussock moth caterpillar, a snow of white hair sloping under and away from them. Small purplish grays fed on Indian pear. A black stripe stretched the length of the caterpillar, dividing the dark purple upper two-thirds of its body from the lower, lighter, almost green, bottom third. Sometimes grays curled on leaves in Ss, looking like bird droppings. Other times they rolled into tight knots and resembled snails. A yellow bear grazed on alder; a juniper twig inchworm hitched over black and green lichens; and an orange humped maple worm chewed leaves. The caterpillar of a Polyphemus moth crawled through grass beneath an oak. The caterpillar was big as my thumb. A yellow ring circled its head, and yellow lines trailed down its sides, red knobs sticking up like bright bulbs. Green radiated from the caterpillar, so much so that Eliza named it "Jamaica."

Observing caterpillars is tonic for character. More often than not I failed to identify caterpillars. Soon simply finding an insect satisfied me. The person who has grown comfortable with fractions of things is more likely to enjoy life than someone who views bits and pieces as emblems of failure. A caterpillar striped like a tiger crawled atop a leaf. Ten bands of orange hair circled the caterpillar's body. Between the bands gleamed fleshly black rings. The insect's head was black and looked like a polished seed. Spilling over the head and the rear of the caterpillar were cowlicks of white and yellow hair. "Call it Tiger Bright and be content," Eliza said.

I did better by a minute rusty caterpillar that hunched itself into twig and leaf scar on an alder. With a lumpy head and sharp flanges extending from its sides, the caterpillar was a *nemoria*. For two days I confined the caterpillar of a sphinx moth in a jar, during which time I tried and failed to identify the species. Pale blue along the sides and white underneath, the insect's dorsal horn curved into a yellow tip. Like a scythe, white slashed the green along the caterpillar's sides. Surrounded by white sashes, the insect's spiracles glowed red. In hope of identifying the caterpillar, I studied its droppings. The droppings looked like small bales of cotton wrapped in burlap and cinched bulging by twine. Six stacks of frass, four to a stack, composed each dropping. "Knowing the caterpillar will become a sphinx moth is enough," I eventually told Vicki. Of course vast numbers of caterpillars do not become moths. On a golden elder a parasitic wasp held a green inchworm. The worm curved beneath the wasp in an immobile half-moon. The wasp faced the rear of the worm, its front and back legs a sling. The skin immediately behind the worm's head was rough and broken. A line of silk attached the worm to the elder. When the wasp flew off, the worm dangled motionless for a moment. Then abruptly it wriggled and started hauling itself into the tree, carrying the wasp's egg behind its head.

Although August lends itself to meandering, people who meander rarely stray far from the familiar. After camp ended in August, Eliza came to Nova Scotia. In shop at camp, she made me a present, a bright green stool, on the top of which she drew two moths, a cecropia and a tulip tree silk moth. The moths fluttered through intricate oranges and browns, the wingspan of the cecropia five and a half inches, that of the silk moth five inches. "I thought you'd like the pictures," Eliza said. "Moths and caterpillars have always interested you." "Not just during this summer?" I asked. "No, Daddy," Eliza said. "Caterpillars have molted through your conversation for years." ❖

September Rain

July and August were dry. In Carthage, Ben Meadows walked from his cornfield to the Tabernacle of Love, the first time he'd entered a church in a decade. "Lord," he prayed, "I've not been in the habit of calling on you. I know the world keeps you mighty busy. This being August, I reckon you must be on vacation, and I hate to disturb your holiday. But if you'll spill a little rain over Carthage, I won't trouble you again, and you can go back to stretching out on the old cumulus and sipping milk and honey."

The drought broke in September. In Storrs the first rains didn't fall from the sky but welled up from life. The Tuesday after Labor Day, Eliza entered high school. She wore new penny loafers, white stockings, a black skirt, and a white blouse with a bouquet of pink roses embroidered on the collar. The previous Saturday she had her hair bobbed, and she looked sweeter than a hillside green with butter and sugar corn. I walked her to school, shouldering her backpack, the first time I'd ever carried a girl's books. At the corner of Bolton Road and Route 195, I kissed her goodbye. As she crossed the lawn to the door of the school, I felt weary and unutterably sad. Tears slipped down my face. "No good will come from high school," I muttered, turning toward home, chin pressed into my chest to prevent passersby from seeing me as the foolish, fond father that I was.

115

The following Saturday I drove Francis to college, eighteen years, three months, and twenty-seven days after his birth. After hugging Edward and kissing Eliza and Vicki, Francis got into the car. For seven miles he stared out the side window. Not until we reached the interstate did he square around in his seat. "Gosh," he said, rubbing his hands over his cheeks, "I'm going to miss home." "We'll miss you," I said, gripping the steering wheel. For a while Francis was silent. Youth is sunny, however, and clouds soon drifted from Francis's mind. "Daddy," he said, "we are the slowest car on the highway. Drive faster." "No," I said.

At Princeton I helped Francis unpack. At four-thirty that afternoon I started back to Connecticut, bringing Vicki a Sacher Torte from Chez Alice, a bakery. I got home at 8:40. Later, as Vicki and I sat in the kitchen eating the torte, we talked about Francis. In June he'd signed up for a freshman trip, hoping to kayak the Delaware River in Pennsylvania. The morning after I left him in New Jersey, he returned to Connecticut to hike the Appalachian Trail. That afternoon thunderstorms rolled across the state, ringing like heavy steel curtains. Black rain fell for the next six days. "Somewhere on the Appalachian Trail is a clearing," Vicki said the following weekend. "In the middle is a clump of mushrooms, Francis being the one with huge feet at the end of the stalk."

Clear skies did not bring sunshine to the house. Last spring squalls gusted through Edward's days, and he quit high-school sports. "I hate organized athletics," he said, adding that he was failing two courses. In fall he had been an eager student and athlete, playing quarterback on the football team and starting French. "French will compliment Latin," he said. The class progressed so slowly, however, that Edward lost interest. Instead of studying or playing baseball in the spring, he shut himself in his room and read Fitzgerald and Hemingway. I'm Mama Bear. I worry about my cubs. Rather than letting mood ebb away, I rear. I thought that changing Edward's exterior environment might change his interior mood. Consequently I pushed him into applying to Loomis-Chaffee, a private school in South Windsor, thirty-two miles away. To hold Edward's place I sent the school $1,800

September Rain   **117**

in May then $9,300 in June, a gully washer of cash, Vicki said. In July E. O. Smith high school mailed Edward's grades to Nova Scotia. He hadn't failed anything, receiving four A's, a B+, and then a C in fourth-year mathematics. On the national test for third-year Latin students, he made a perfect score. After finishing the sophomore course in American History, he took the Advanced Placement Examination and made four, five being the highest possible. "Now what?" Vicki said.

I'd acted precipitously. Night after night microbursts of worry awakened me. "You have ruined high school for him," Vicki said. "But you are addicted to worry. If you weren't fretting about Edward, you'd worry about Eliza or Francis and wreck their lives." In June Edward said he'd play football at Loomis. At the end of August he changed his mind and, closeting himself in the study, read Salinger.

After Edward refused to play, I slept poorly. Worry clouded days, and acquaintances said I looked badly. "That's because I suffered four nervous breakdowns before breakfast," I said one morning. In May I ignored the distance between Storrs and South Windsor. Once Loomis opened, both Edward and I slept less. Driving Edward to class took between forty-two and fifty-four minutes. After leaving Edward at school, I returned to Storrs and taught. Late in the afternoon I fetched Edward, the two round trips usually taking 192 minutes or three hours and twelve minutes.

Early in September, Hurricane Floyd banged into Connecticut, and rain rumbled across the state in grates. That afternoon driving to Loomis took an hour and eighteen minutes. "School has washed away your life," Vicki said. Suddenly the story of a farmer who refused to attend church came to mind. In berating the man for neglecting the Sabbath, a preacher pointed at the farmer's dog Trout and said, "you are man with a soul, not an animal like that hound." "Trout barks, eats, sleeps, and chases cats and rabbits," the farmer answered. "He never works. In four years he'll die, and that will end everything for him. I get up at three-thirty in the morning to milk cows. During the day I plough and do chores. I don't play. My troubles never end. Rats get in the corncrib. A groundhog falls down the well, and lightning strikes the dairy. When I die, I'll go to Hell. I wish I'd been born a dog."

That night I encouraged Edward to return to E. O. Smith. "No," he said. "I haven't made friends at Loomis, but the courses are hard, and I like difficulty." Saturday Dorothy Dorr suggested that Edward ride to school with her son Geoff, the only other student at Loomis from Storrs. Geoff persuaded Edward to run cross-country, and melancholy began to lift. At the university bookstore I bought *Harry Potter and the Sorcerer's Stone,* a novel describing the adventures of an eleven-year-old whose overcast life suddenly cleared when he discovered he was a wizard. Even the mail turned sunny. A man wrote me from Missouri. He had just read *Deprived of Unhappiness,* a collection of my essays. "Your pieces are quirky," the man wrote, "and they inspired me to write an essay. I call it 'On Quirkiness.'" "Quirkiness stems from two causes," the essay began. "The first is inherited character which medical doctors say comes from genes. The second cause is environment. Sociological doctors believe environment can cause quirkiness as San Francisco did in the Hippie Days. Quirkiness can take two forms, either in speech or action. Speech involves words, and action means doing things. Quirky actions are strange actions, and quirky speech is strange speech. To be quirky can be good, or it can be bad. Sometimes being quirky is neither. Then it is neutral, and some might say not real quirkiness." At this point I leapt back into *Harry Potter* and soon was studying at Hogwarts, the school for aspiring wizards.

I finished the novel after dinner. I slept well. Not once did thoughts educational turn the night into damp perspiring insomnia. The next morning I went for a walk, the first I had taken since returning to Storrs from Nova Scotia. Mood influences appreciation, and hill and field seemed magical. Blue jays piped from woods bordering the cut for the power line. A hawk sliced through scrub atop a ridge, his tail feathers sharp and white in the shade. I walked over the lip of the ridge, and a grouse exploded from a patch of sunlight. Color had begun to leach from season. Behind the beaver pond ferns sagged, and spadixes of skunk cabbage sank hard into the ground. Only clearweed flourished, and even its stems had begun to loosen into curves. In the Ogushwitz meadow most goldenrod had gone to kernel. Here and there, though, clumps of late goldenrod dappled the field. Locust borers busied themselves atop blossoms, their backs black and orange, stripes wavering, creating the impression of heat. A hister beetle squatted on milkweed. Crickets sang in the grass, and bees transformed small white asters into bushy hives. A praying mantis flew past, wings waving like silk. From the sharp tips of milkweed pods, seed spilled and rolled into loose silver balls. While a great spangled fritillary trembled like a worn leaf, monarchs glided effortlessly fresh and orange. On the walk I shed pinching responsibility. When I returned home, I noticed a spotted apatelodes caterpillar clinging to a peony. Yellow swept brushed over the caterpillar. Along the insect's back pencils of hair stuck up startled, the bodies of the pencils green, the ends black, making the clumps of hair look like dry stems. "Edward, look at this caterpillar," I shouted. "Not now, Daddy," he said. "I'm reading the *Aeneid.*" "Oh," I said, "oh, yes! Let the rains come, no matter whether they batter afternoons gray or drizzle blue through nights." ❖

Road Warrior

At six-thirty I dropped Edward at the Dorrs' driveway so he could ride to Loomis-Chaffee with his friend Geoff. The Gurleyville Road curved around Valentine Meadow like a hard rib. In the meadow fog pillowed fatty, near the lip blowing in straps. Along Route 44 fog whitened hollows, forcing me to drive slowly. Not that I drove fast—my flight to Baltimore didn't leave until 10:15. More than highway lost itself in haze, however. I was starting a book tour, promoting my new collection of essays, *A Little Fling,* traveling initially to Greensboro then to Knoxville, Sewanee, Chattanooga, Savannah, and Nashville. Not only was the tour my first, but it was also the first sponsored by the University of Tennessee Press. In June the publicity director of the press resigned and went to work for AT&T. Overnight the tour tumbled on to the desk of an intern, an undergraduate unaccustomed to brassy hawking and selling. She worked hard, mailing sheaves of letters to radio and television stations urging them to interview me. Her tone was differential, however, that of a student begging favors from a crusty professor. "We feel that this book would be of interest to your listeners and hope that you will consider publicizing his appearance," read a note to the program director of Nashville Public Radio.

The program director ignored me. Before I left Storrs, though, three reporters telephoned. "I want to tell you up front that I haven't read a word you have written," a man stated at the beginning of an interview. "In fact I've never heard of you." "Now, how do you spell your name?" another reporter said before asking, "have you ever written anything?" "Well," I said, "I am going on a book tour." "Oh, yeah, that's right," the reporter said, "I scribble lots of stuff, and I forget things." The third reporter sounded like a child, and I asked if I should address her as *Miss* or *Mrs.* "At two-thirty this afternoon," she said, "I will have been married nine whole months." "That's wonderful," I said. "I do hope your husband's a nice fellow." "Oh, yes," she answered, "he's a good Christian man."

Finances of the tour smacked of autumn, change falling from my wallet like leaves. The press paid for my room in Greensboro, $112 at the Koury Convention Center at the Holiday Inn; two plane flights, the first from Providence to Greensboro, the second from Nashville to Providence; and then for a car, a blue Chevrolet Malibu I rented from Avis at the Knoxville airport at nine o'clock the night of October 3 and which I left at the Chattanooga airport at 7:15 the morning of October 7. I drove the car three hundred and five miles, initially around Knoxville then to Sewanee by way of Chattanooga, the next morning returning to Chattanooga. The car cost $347.73. Early in September, the intern scheduled a book signing at six in the evening in Memphis, planning for me to spend a day driving from Sewanee, some three hundred and ten miles away, ninety miles from Sewanee to Nashville then two hundred and twenty more miles to Memphis. I'd never been in Memphis, and I would have arrived as afternoon traffic clogged streets. I changed the plan, noting that at most I would sign six books. Instead of grinding back and brain to gravel, pounding the interstate, I suggested spending the day in Chattanooga.

I kept the press's expenses low. Flights from Providence were cheaper than from Hartford. Although Bradley Airport is only thirty-five minutes from my house and driving to T. H. Green in Rhode Island takes an hour and fifteen minutes, I flew from Providence. The flight to Greensboro and the return from Nashville only cost the press $252. In fact flying from Providence cost me money. I left my

Toyota at Thrifty Valet Parking on Post Road early on October 2, retrieving it at 6:24 the evening of October 10. While parking at Thrifty cost $63.82, as a state employee on "literary business," I could have parked free at Bradley. For the tour I was $679.34 out of pocket, big items being rooms: two nights at the Fairfield Inn on Alcoa Highway across from McGee Tyson Airport in Knoxville at $132.46, and two nights in Nashville at the Marriott on Fourth Avenue costing $249.88.

The other major expense was $80.11 for two pairs of orange and white athletic warm-up trousers, purchased as presents for Eliza and Edward at the University Book and Supply Store in Knoxville. Eliza liked the trousers and wore them to volleyball practice two days after my return. Edward's trousers were too big, and after trying them on, he dumped them in the upstairs hall atop a heap of dirty clothes. During the tour I taught a class at the University of Tennessee and gave evening talks at Sewanee and the University of Tennessee at Chattanooga. Rarely do I speak for less than $1,500. When a talk requires me to fly, I charge at least $2,500 plus expenses. On the tour I spoke for free, "cheapening the wares," Vicki said. Sewanee, however, surprised me, giving me $500, thus reducing the cost of the tour to $179.34. During the tour I sold approximately 172 books. The book was priced at $26, my royalty being 10 percent of the net. After deducting 40 percent of the price for booksellers' profits and another 15 percent for additional discounts, I earned a tenth of $12.48 or $1.248 a book, the royalty thus amounting to $214.656. In short after subtracting expenses, the trip earned $35.31. Or to put the finances another way—I was away from home nine days. Calculated on the basis of an eight-hour working day, a figure that deceives, for I spent more than eight hours each day traveling, visiting, and signing, I earned an hourly wage of $0.49. "But you haven't added in sales on Amazon.com," my friend Josh said when I cited the statistics. Josh was wrong. The figures included Internet sales. Before the tour Amazon had not sold any copies of my book. I have now been home for three weeks and six days, and Amazon's sales have remained zero.

Because the tour lasted nine days and I had to wear a tuxedo in Savannah, I carried two suitcases and a backpack. I crammed tickets, money, eyeglasses, schedules, talks, then a toothbrush and toothpaste into the backpack. At USAir in Providence, I checked the two bags to Greensboro. My first flight was on MetroJet, and I asked the clerk at the counter to describe the airline. "Greyhound of the sky," he said. At the Paradies Shop, an airport bookstore, I bought Patricia Cornwell's *Point of Origin* for $8.55. Butchery flies well, and I read Cornwell on planes. Before buying the book, I skimmed the first chapter. Cornwell's characters reappear in book after book, and I was not sure if I'd read the novel. Still, I bought it, reading eighty-seven pages on the flight to Baltimore.

At Ocean Coffee Roasters I purchased a medium-sized cup of coffee for $1.34 and sitting at a table studied my surroundings. Anton Airfood managed the food court, a group of franchises that shared a kitchen, these including Newport Creamery, Godfather's Pizza, Narragansett Grill, Del's, as well as Ocean Coffee Roasters. Del's peddled fruit juice, especially "soft frozen lemonade," a small glass costing a dollar, a large, two dollars. Pizzas at Godfather's were small, cheese costing three dollars, pepperoni $3.95, and also for $3.95 "breakfast" pizza. Priced at $4.25, the most expensive pizza was Humble Pie, loaded with pepperoni, sausage, onion, and green pepper.

Often during the tour, time stretched like a desert, and I spent hours trudging mirages sandy with small observation. After drinking the coffee, I walked to the departure gate. From Baltimore my plane continued to Orlando. Beside the gate idled a train of wheelchairs, seven cars lumpy with old people. Sitting in rows near the check-in counter were families traveling to Disneyworld. I sat and waited for my flight. On the row behind me a small bear in a red jacket dozed in a valise. A little boy cradled a polar bear, and a khaki elephant curled in the lap of a freckled girl. Seventeen years ago I bought Francis a gray elephant in London. The elephant had a broad white tongue and white tusks two inches long. He wore a blue play suit, across the chest of which chugged a toy train, a red engine pulling two cars, one yellow, the other green, both rolling atop black wheels. Francis named the elephant "Ellie," and although years stuffed Francis's room with a zoo of animals, Ellie remained his favorite. This September Francis entered college. I packed the car and drove Francis to New Jersey. Before leaving Storrs, I asked him if he wanted to take any animals to school, "maybe Ellie," I said wistfully. I knew what Francis would say before he spoke. Yet, when he said *no,* I felt sad. "Damn," I muttered as I looked at the little girl's elephant, "damn." I didn't mutter long. My plane landed, and I watched passengers disembark. A daughter rushed up the gangway and hugged her mother. Large and top-heavy, both women had thin legs and wearing dark trousers, looked like pears standing on black stems. For ninety-two seconds the women hugged. Then they stepped back, looked into each other's eyes, and hugged again. Because a clerk began to bustle passengers onto my flight, I didn't time the second embrace.

On reaching Greensboro, I telephoned the Holiday Inn, and the hotel sent a courtesy van to the airport to fetch me. I checked into the hotel at 2:40, my room being on the twenty-sixth floor, far above the top rung of any fire ladder. On the flight from Baltimore to Greensboro, I refused the peanuts Piedmont Airlines served as a snack. I was hungry, and after dropping my bags in the room, hurried downstairs to the Guildford Ballroom, a forty-thousand-square-foot bowling alley, lit by chandeliers and with a stage at one end. The room housed the trade show of the Southeastern Booksellers Association. Two hundred and eighty-eight exhibitors displayed wares on low, lunch tables, books stacked heavy in columns or leaning akimbo on racks, looking like doors slipping hinges. Before examining books, I rummaged for food, cadging a square of dark chocolate from the University of Alabama Press, two nubs of Swiss cheese from Chariot Victor, then three crackers spread with "Dilly Shrimp Dip," the dip made by a member of the local Junior League. Culinary pickings being slim, at five o'clock I dodged cars in the hotel parking lot, crossed an access road, and for $5.24 bought a chicken teriyaki dinner in the Four Seasons Mall. Salty, the bird rose to my crop, and after the meal I roosted in my room and finished *Point of Origin.*

Earlier that afternoon, I searched the ballroom in hopes of discovering writing friends. Not until the next morning did I see anyone I knew. Then I met Connie May Fowler, author of *Before Women Had Wings* and most recently *Remembering Blue*. Each winter the Jacksonville Public Library sponsors a literary festival. Six years ago Connie May and I participated. After returning to Storrs, I never heard from the festival again. "Sam," Connie May announced, "we are banned from Jacksonville." "What?" I said. "Banned," she said, "and I thought we were having a lovely time." Writers attending the festival stayed in a motel several miles from downtown. A van ferried us to events. Connie May, her husband, Mika, I, and others, including Kaye Gibbons and her husband, sat in the rear of the van and chatted. Another participant at the festival who, so far as I could tell, liked neither men nor women who liked men sat in the front seat next to the driver. Unknown to us, she jotted down our conversations. Later, she sent transcripts to officials of the library, saying we were not people who should participate in literary festivals. "I can't believe that," I said. "Yes," Connie May said, "we are banned from Jacksonville."

While roaming the ballroom, I collected souvenirs: a book bag from Tennessee, on one side a white square, in the middle blue letters declaring "The University of Tennessee Press Advancing Knowledge for 60 Years, 1940–2000"; from the University of Alabama Press, a church fan with a wooden handle shaped like two ice cream spoons glued end to end; then a rack of ballpoint pens, advertising Ingram, Southern Book Service, and Hill Street Press. An editor at Florida gave me a copy of *Florida Wildflowers in Their Natural Communities*. During dark moments on the tour, I opened the book and plucked bouquets bright with red basil, dog hobble, pine lily, and Osceola's plume. Ambling aisles between tables, I studied presses. Because people in the room were strangers, I talked to myself, praising my observation, noting that Peachtree had forsaken Southern literature for children's books and that Longstreet had pitched humor for business and self-help.

In front of the stage stretched a row of tables. Behind the tables sat authors autographing books, ten authors at a time. At eleven Sunday morning I signed. The books were free. An author was not allowed to sign unless his publisher donated a minimum of one hundred books. "Chum to stir waters," explained Gene Adair, marketing manager at Tennessee. Booksellers lined up to receive copies. Most were sharks who sold the books at their stores. People who intended to sell my book asked me not to inscribe the title page, instructing that I only sign my name, sometimes requesting that I date the signature. The greed irritated me, and several times I said, "since you are buying this book free, why don't you send a nickel to charity?" A few booksellers returned to the line for second copies. "Would you inscribe this one," a man said. "I'm not going to sell it. I skimmed the book. I liked the essays, and I want the book for myself." "I'm not taking this to sell," a woman said. "I'm giving it to my daughter for her birthday. She likes essays. Would you write, 'Happy Birthday, Louise. Your Mother never forgets you when she buys books.'" At the end of the show, booksellers packed libraries into cardboard boxes, rolling them out of the Holiday Inn on dollies. Having paid for travel, hotel rooms, and registration, store owners, I suppose, viewed the books as perquisites. And in truth I picked up a handful of books in hopes of finding something to read at night.

After finishing *Point of Origin,* I went to a party sponsored by Algonquin. I arrived just as food ran out. Still, I scooped up a Heineken's beer, a crab cake, three cherry tomatoes, and a biscuit stuffed with ham. I didn't talk to anyone, but I got advance proof of Louis Osteen's *Charleston Cuisine. Recipes from a Low Country Chef.* "For Vicki," Osteen wrote on the title page, "who needs to know about Southern Cooking—Come to Charleston." Since the proof was "uncorrected," I wondered if proportions listed in the recipes were correct. Still, because Southern cooking does not appeal to Vicki, matters of cup and tablespoon were beside the point.

I sleep fitfully in hotels. Later that night I watched *The Twelve Monkeys* starring Bruce Willis, a movie I'd seen in Storrs. In Knoxville the following night I watched Kurt Russell in *Soldier*, a film about space soldiers. I thought I would watch a movie every night. My room in Sewanee did not contain a television, however, and after the visit to Sewanee I was too weary to keep abreast of plot. At the Koury Center, the Fairfield Inn, and the Marriott, mirrors papered bathroom walls. The cheaper the room, the more mirrors in the lavatory. The more mirrors the less I sleep. Moreover I loathe walking into a bathroom and no matter where I turn seeing my saggy self, meat swaying from me in dewlaps.

At the start of the tour, cadging food became a game. At eight the first morning in Greensboro, I attended the Millennium Breakfast sponsored by a gaggle of publishers. I didn't have a ticket to the breakfast. A woman collected tickets at the entrance to the dining room. I told her I left my ticket in my room on the twenty-sixth floor. Before she spoke, I strode into the room. Food was dreadful. I drank three cups of coffee, buttered a cold croissant, and munched red grapes, fingerprints of waitresses clear on the damp skins of the fruit. I joined eight booksellers at a round table. Sitting with us was a writer, her plate and coffee resting on a glass-bottomed tray, a raised wicker edge surrounding it. Before coffee appeared, she listed the virtues of her new book. For five minutes she spoke without stopping, after which a woman at a nearby table stood and shouted, "Change tables." Quickly the writer vanished, and another author appeared, tray in hand and mouth full of words. One visitor to the table said she would sign her book at any bookstore in the country, this despite living in New York. "Signings thrill me," she gushed, "and I love book stores. The people who own them are just my favorites." "What a nice woman," an owner said after the writer shifted to another table.

Early Sunday afternoon Gene dismantled the Tennessee exhibit, and he, his wife Leslie, and I left for Knoxville in gray van. Gene drove. I sat next to him on the front seat, and Leslie sat on the seat behind. The trip took six and a half hours. So that Leslie was part of conversation, I turned sideways, in the process so corkscrewing my back that for the rest of the tour sitting caused pain to jangle up my spine. Before entering the interstate, we stopped at Chili's, a chain restaurant. Leslie and I ordered Cajun chicken sandwiches, for a fifty-cent charge substituting a salad for

French fries. On the plates a boy fetched from the kitchen were lumberyards of potatoes. "These people didn't order those fries," the waitress said brusquely, jerking the plates off the table. When she returned, the potatoes had vanished, and my sandwich had been bashed out of its roll, the contents scattered across the dish like feathers. "I've never seen a waitress behave like that," Leslie said. On the tour I expected to blow past people like a freight rumbling through whistle stops. But I grew fond of Gene and Leslie, seeing them in Greensboro, Knoxville, and later Nashville, the affection saddening, emphasizing the fleeting nature of acquaintance, even of family and love.

The drive to Knoxville exhausted me. Signs splotched the highway proud as acne, and trucks rumbled past abrasive and unshaven, reducing day to shadow. Only rarely did I notice sunlight breaking green through the Smoky Mountains. When I picked up my car in Knoxville, I was too tired to explore mazes of knobs and handles. Not until the next morning did the handle that locked the Malibu leap to hand. After parking the car and leaving my bags at the Inn, I trudged the shoulder of the Alcoa Highway to Wendy's. For $2.91, I bought a Kid's Meal. "You look tired," the manager said, staring at me. "Give him a big Frosty and a large coke, and toss in three orders of fries," the man said, addressing a boy in the kitchen. "We've got to perk you up," the manager said, turning back toward me. "Thank you," I said.

At lunch Gene had handed me a packet put together by the intern at the press. The next afternoon I was scheduled to teach writing at the university. Later I appeared on WBIR television, on a program called "Live at Five," after which I read and signed books at Davis-Kidd bookstore. In the packet was a map of Knoxville. The distance between bookstore and television station was fourteen and a half inches, as the ruler measured. Seven lines of directions steered me from the university to the station. "Gene," I began. "Sam," he said, reading my expression, "I'll navigate. Even I'm not sure what's the best route across town."

My room at the Fairfield Inn was a box within a box, the only window looking down at an enclosed pool. I slept poorly. At seven the next morning, I ate breakfast in the lounge on the first floor: a bowl of corn flakes, two slices of toast, and two and a half cups of coffee. A television tilted down into the lounge from a nook in the ceiling. While I ate, a blond woman babbled on screen, her voice rising and falling, a smile slicing her jaw. Four business travelers sat at a table to my left. They wore dark trousers and white shiny shirts, creases stamped into leg and arm. I overheard snatches of conversation: "when the rubber hits the road," "our two key points," "offer different opinions," and "it's the money after the fact. That's the problem." The men depressed me. How sad it would be, I thought, if my children had such jobs, staying at airport motels, televisions drizzling words on them at breakfast, their conversations flat as asphalt.

Although I didn't teach until much later, I drove to the Tennessee campus after breakfast, parking in "Area 9" across from the football stadium. Streets along the river had been named for coaches and athletes, Phillip Fulmer Way for the football coach, Pat Head Summitt Street for the women's basketball coach, and for a woman basketball player Chamique Holdsclaw Drive. "The people who run the University of Tennessee," I thought, "must be long-necked, google-eyed peckerwoods. How embarrassing."

Throughout the campus Gideons stood on corners, distributing small volumes containing Psalms, Proverbs, and The New Testament. Ahead of me lay two hundred and ten empty minutes, so I talked to the Gideons. Seventy Gideons spent the morning handing out books. "We could use ten more people," a man told me. I assumed Gideons came from the lower middle class, at least financially. I was mistaken. I chatted with six Gideons: a retired electrical engineer, the owner of a medical equipment store, a pediatrician, a certified public accountant, an entomologist, and the owner of Wildwood Cabinets, a manufacturing firm in Maryville, Tennessee. This last man founded Wildwood thirty years ago. "I'm retiring this year," he said. "I am selling the company to my employees. They helped make the business, and they should own it." In the right lapel of his jacket, the man wore a pin, two small silver feet, the heels pressed together, balls spread slightly forming a minute V. The pin, the man explained, represented the feet of a six-week old fetus. "I'm against abortion," he continued. "But that's not a Gideon stance. It's just my view." "I'm on the other side," I said. "That's all right," he said. "People differ." "Gideons are not confrontational," the accountant said later. I talked for a long time with the entomologist. He had worked for the Tennessee Department of Agriculture for thirty years. We discussed hemlock and balsam woolly adelgids, fire ants, deer ticks, and gypsy moths. "Don't do anything if gypsy moths appear," I advised. "Spraying does more harm than good." "That's what I have heard," the man said. "I have been told," the doctor said, "that people spit on Gideons up North in Maryland and New Jersey." "That's not true," I said. "I live in Connecticut. People in the North are just as nice as they are in the South."

After talking to the Gideons, I explored Hodges Library. The university owned a dozen of my books. "Gideons are everywhere," I said to a reference librarian. "That's because Southerners go to church," she said. Offices of the English Department were in McClung Tower, a stobby, functional building. Chalked on the building's brick facing was "What's SHAKEN? Romans 15:13," *shaken* being slang for *happening*. On nearby steps lay a Gideon New Testament. I looked up the verse. "Now the God of hope fill you with all joy and peace in believing, that ye may abound in hope, through the power of the Holy Ghost."

Not sure where to eat lunch, I explored the building, trusting to happenstance. In a cramped room on the third floor, a representative of Longman's and Addison-Wesley publishers exhibited textbooks. "Eat with me," he said. "Coke and pizza are going to arrive any minute." I drank two cups of Coke and ate two slices of pizza, one plain, the other measly with pepperoni. After teaching, I roamed the campus again. I listened to a mockingbird singing atop a dawn redwood. A ladybug lit on the back of my hand, crawled to the tip of my index finger, and launched herself into the air. At "The Daily Grind" in The Presidential Court, I ordered a small coffee and a piece of chocolate cake. "You look beat," the woman said who took my order. "I'm going to give you a large coffee and two pieces of cake for the price of one."

At four o'clock Gene and I drove to the television station. Outside the studio grew a tulip tree with leaves big as fire shovels. "From what tree does this come?" I asked the receptionist, holding a leaf in my right hand. "I don't know. A maple?" she said, adding, "who are you?" "I'm the love doctor," I said. Several guests appeared on "Live at Five," the nun who inspired the film *Dead Man Walking,* and from Dollywood—the theme park underwritten by Dolly Parton, a country music singer—two men, the food manager and a cobbler who made pegged shoes. Each fall the cobbler worked a month at Dollywood. During the rest of the year he made Civil War reproductions. "Ninety percent of Civil War antiques are fake," he said. "Don't buy any." The food manager cooked buffalo burgers. I ate one, wrapping it in lettuce and tomato. The last person interviewed, I sat through news, weather, sports, and bubbly chatter read from a monitor. The "Big Question" of the day was, "What is the largest number of clothing changes ever made in a movie?" The answer was eighty-five, the record set by Madonna in *Evita.* A chubby man and a blond woman interviewed me. We sat on couches in front of false windows, eighteen panes to a window. Outside the panes a street reached like a forearm up to a white steeple. Shops lined the street, trees green before them, leaves heart-shaped. On a shelf in front of the window stood nine empty leather magazine cases, all labeled to contain issues of *The National Geographic.* The case for numbers published from January through June 1983, stood upside down. "Did you know that one of the cases in the window is upside down?" I said to the woman during the interview. "No," she said. My interview ended the show. Afterward the hosts stood, removed their microphones, and without saying a word hurried off the set. Gene and I got in the car and headed for Davis-Kidd.

At the bookstore, Barbara, a friend from childhood, met me. "Howdy and I saw you on the news, and we had to say hello." Also in the store was Townsend, a classmate at Sewanee whom I had not seen for thirty-seven years. Once a superb golfer, Townsend had aged into a rock gardener. "Flowers are wonderful," he said. After the reading, Townsend treated me to barbecue. A woman's book club met at the store. On my starting to read, they suspended

132 Road Warrior

their discussion and listened. "What fun," one of them said later. None of the women, however, bought my book. I inscribed a dozen books then signed thirty more for the store manager. "Don't worry," he said. "I'll sell them."

During the reading Gene went home, Townsend having assured him he would direct me back to the Alcoa Highway. I checked out of the Fairfield Inn at eight the next morning. I'd been on the road three days. "Was your room all right?" the woman behind the desk asked. "Yes," I said. "Next time you are here," she said, "y'all come back to see us." "Well," I said, "if I'm ever on another book tour, I'll come back. Right now I am a bit too weary to think about returning." "Oh, me. Bless your heart," she said. "You get some rest."

From Knoxville I drove south on Interstate 75 for 113 miles. Then I turned north for 51 miles to Sewanee. Trucks swept along 75, pushing cars beyond the speed limit. Once I stopped and drank a Pepsi to knit frayed nerves. At Sewanee, George Core, editor of *The Sewanee Review* and godfather of Edward, my second son, met me. I stayed in the Chancellor's Suite at Rebel's Rest, the university guesthouse. On my arrival George handed me a stack of books to review, most reprints of rollicking sea stores, among others, Frederick Marryat's *Percival Keene* (1842) and Michael Scott's *Tom Cringle's Log* (1834). Three years ago I visited Sewanee and stayed in Rebel's Rest. Unable to sleep, I strolled into the dining room and from a shelf removed a mystery, E. Phillips Oppenheim's *The Last Ambassador or, The Search for the Missing Delora.* I didn't finish the book that night, so the next morning the *Delora* became airplane reading, going missing in my backpack. The ship novels were frigates, heavy as hearts of oak. Lowering them into the holes of my suitcases forced me to lighten the load, and I jettisoned five books I'd carted away from Greensboro. Although paperbacks, the books were autographed, a good swap for the *Delora*. In the dining room I stood Fred Bonnie's *Detecting Metal* beside Margaret Maron's *Storm Track,* the title pages autographed but not inscribed. Writers inscribed the three remaining volumes. "For Sam Pickering," Tom Corcoran wrote in *Gumbo Limbo,* "Can't Put It Down." "To Sam, who probably lived his version of this time," Nanci Kincaid wrote in *Crossing Blood*, an account of growing up in the South. On *Mr. Spaceman,* Robert Olen Butler wrote, "For Sam. It was great meeting you."

I spent the afternoon at the Sewanee Book Store, chatting with students and signing thirteen books. I also signed books after my talk that night then again the next morning at the book store. The manager of the store coached rowing at the college, and he gave me a white cap with "Sewanee Crew" stitched across the back, and two tee-shirts, one purple with white letters stamped on the chest, the other white with purple letters, both shirts reading "SEWANEE CREW."

That evening George and Susan Core took me to dinner at Pearl's, a restaurant mid-way between Sewanee and Monteagle. I ate fried green tomatoes and crab cakes. The dean of the college and his wife ate with us. They did not attend the talk. I spoke to two hundred people in Convocation Hall, not one a member of the college administration, a slight that irritated since Sewanee touted me on the school's web site. After the talk an older woman said, "I want to thank you." Her father died slowly and painfully. While bedridden, he read my books. "They made him laugh, great belly laughs, and cheered his final days. Thank you." The woman did not purchase my new book. "What would she have done with it?" Josh said later in Storrs. "Plant it on her father's grave? Dead people aren't great readers. In fact most of them, even graduates of Harvard and Yale, are illiterate."

The next morning after eating patty sausage with George at the Smokehouse Restaurant and listening to flickers yelp through oaks in front of Rebel's Rest, I drove to the University of Tennessee at Chattanooga. Much as George managed my time at Sewanee, so Bill Berry, provost at Chattanooga and a friend from graduate school, organized my visit to Chattanooga. I stayed at the Adams Hilborne Mansion on Vine Street, a bed and breakfast set on a hill overlooking the university. Once the mayor's residence then later a funeral home, the house was, as a journalist put it, "one of the best inns in the South." I stayed in the Presidential Suite, so named because a signed picture of Lyndon Johnson hung on the

134 Road Warrior

wall. The owner's father served as Ambassador to Pakistan. A silver sheet hung above an end table, letters pressed into the metal. "To Ambassador Benjamin H. Oehlert, Jr.," the sheet read, "We, the members of the official American Mission in Pakistan at Rawalpindi, Dacca, Karrachi, Lahore, and Peshawar, wish to express our appreciation for the privilege of serving under your inspiring leadership since August 15, 1967. Our admiration is heartfelt. We offer our warmest and best wishes to you and Mrs. Oehlert upon your departure from Pakistan."

Across the room on the opposite wall was the photograph of President Johnson. In short sleeves with his collar open and the top and second buttons of his shirt undone, Johnson stood at the entrance of a stone building, weight teasing mortar from between blocks and wood framing a doorway white. Before the president was a dark wooden lectern, the seal of the United States pasted on the front and three microphones twisting upward like snakes. I studied Johnson's handwriting. He wrote hurriedly, the signature one line, the *n* at the conclusion of *Lyndon* sweeping up slanted to the right joining the top of Johnson's middle initial, the circle at the bottom of the *b* then rising up in a scoop to the top of *J*.

The concierge told me my room rented for $225 but that the university paid the corporate rate, $125. That night I spoke to two hundred people. In the talk I said the price embarrassed me. "'A hundred and twenty-five, 225, my friend Sam,' Bill should have said, 'is a $350 man at the minimum. To pay less for his room would insult not just Sam but the whole academic profession.'"

The furnishings of the room were originally purple, but sunlight had baked them brown. Not until I glanced into the bathroom did I feel presidential. The second biggest tub I'd ever seen filled half the room. Although I showered at Sewanee that morning, I decided to bathe, clambering into the tub at 1:50 in the afternoon. The sides of the tub were pink and high, and I climbed in carefully. Inside, I sank and stretched out, shoals of chest and belly rippling unappealingly in front of my chin. That night during the talk I described the bathroom. Later a woman said, "you should share the tub and a bottle of champagne with a new friend." Thinking such activity would smack of domestic and thus ordinary, not imported, pleasure, I said, "I'm not the lad I used to be. No longer can I manage more than two baths a day."

Bathing invigorated me. Afterward I ambled down Vine Street to the university bookstore. I sat in a rocking chair opposite the front door behind a portcullis of books. Few people broached the barrier, and I signed seven copies, all for faculty members. On the way to the store I visited Lupton Library to see how many of my books the university owned—two, both scholarly, not collections of essays. Chalked across a terrace below the library was "LAUREN TURNER U ARE OWLSOME," the *Owlsome* blue, the other words yellow. An owl, a student in the bookstore informed me, was the mascot of Chi Omega sorority. Lauren Turner pledged Chi Omega. "I'm a Chi Omega," the girl said, "and Lauren is really nice."

The tour provided little opportunity for exercise. In hopes of loosening the binding around a bale or two of cellulite, I sauntered Vine Street. The neighborhood had once been Chattanooga's best. The street clung to the side of a hill, houses on the river and lower side of the hill dropping off behind, their backs pounded into the slope. On the opposite side of the street and the upper side of the hill, walls supported lawns and porches behind bulging trusses of stone and cement. Businesses were moving into the neighborhood, lawyers having recently paid $450,000 for the house across the street from the Mansion. The day was warm; yet smoke billowed from a chimney. "The home of an old person burning coal. The next house to be sold," I thought. A woman walked a ratty dog on a leash. I asked her about real estate and discovered she was a member of the Board of Trustees at Sewanee. In June an alumnus nominated me for the presidency of Sewanee. Before the tour I cantered out of the race, pleading intellectual spavins.

I ate dinner with the English Department at the faculty club. The main course was Chicken Kiev. Stains displease Vicki. Because Chicken Kiev squirts butter and garlic like a water pistol, I slung my necktie over my right shoulder and down my back. Bill Berry was wearing a new tie, and he did the same, explaining that we belonged to a secret society, draping ties over right shoulders being part of the society's culinary hocus-pocus. Later my speech went so well that I was foolishly ebullient. John a classmate from Sewanee attended. John is now a circuit judge. As a result when I signed a book for him, I didn't write what I really thought, "John, I am proud of you, and I love you." Instead I scribbled, "I'm glad the payment took care of things. If you ever need a little something special, just mention my name to Tiffany." At the signing following the talk, a man gave me a cigarette lighter. A metal band circled the lighter; stamped on the band was the face of Jesus and the capital letters WWJD, standing, the man explained, for "What would Jesus do?" I had not seen the abbreviation before, but from henceforth, it appeared throughout the tour: on a bumper sticker glued to a black Mercedes in Savannah, on a yellow wristband worn by a burly man flying from Atlanta to Nashville, and scrawled across the sidewalk in front of the Bennie Dillon Building in Nashville.

On the seventh I was scheduled to fly from Chattanooga to Atlanta at 10:15 and from there to Savannah. Nervous that morning traffic would make me miss my plane, I got up early and drove to the airport, so early that after returning the rental car, I caught the 7:35 flight to Atlanta. Savannah wasn't strictly part of the tour. Last April I agreed to address the thirty-fifth anniversary dinner of the German Heritage Society, a gathering of four hundred men, one hundred and fifty members and two hundred and fifty guests. The Society paid my way to Savannah from Chattanooga then from Savannah to Nashville. I also received a $2,750 honorarium, the last two hundred and fifty dollars tacked on to the fee to cover the cost of a tuxedo.

I stayed in the State Suite in the DeSoto Hilton. Furnishing the suite were eleven chairs, eleven tables, two television sets, three bathrooms, four hair dryers, seven lamps and one chandelier, three sofas, eight hand towels, nine bath towels, then twelve toilet bottles containing things such as shampoo and mouthwash. I stuffed the bottles into my overnight kit and carted them away when I left Savannah the next morning. On my arrival I filched an apple from a bowl in the lobby, the first fruit I'd eaten on the tour. After depositing my bags in the suite, I roamed Savannah for an hour, circling squares near the hotel: Chippewa, Orleans, Pulaski, Chatham, Monterey, Calhoun, and Lafayette. Spanish moss draped from trees, but I was too tired to notice much. "Some day," I thought, "I'd like to return and see this town." The apple not proving breakfast and lunch enough, I snacked in Cleary's Restaurant. I asked the waitress if spinach salad was tasty. "I ain't never had it, but some have," she said. I should have ordered what the waitress ate. The salad was terrible.

Until the speech in Savannah, I'd never made a talk that pancaked. "Don't tell me about it," Vicki said when I returned to Storrs. "Didn't you feel terrible while you were speaking?" she asked. "You bet," I said. I began at ten in the evening. The audience was male, most middle-aged or older and, if they resembled me, used to being in bed by nine-thirty. Before I spoke, they had pledged allegiance to the "Flag of the United States of America" and sung "The Star-Spangled Banner," "Dixie," "Edelweiss," and "The National Anthem of the Federal Republic of Germany." They'd consumed "Paprika Cod" on vegetables, "Oat Dumpling Soup," loaves of buttered pumpernickel bread, Hearts of Palm Salad, Lemon Sorbet, "Herb Stuffed Pork Loin with Chanterelle Sauce, Spaetzle, Braised Red Cabbage," and lastly a six inch beer mug made from chocolate and frothy with "Berry Mousse." Most had drinks before the meal. During they meal they drank two wines, a Lieberfraumilch and a Schwartz Katz; a stein of beer, and a peach schnapps. I stood behind a lectern along one wall, the ballroom extending almost beyond my peripheral vision to the left and right. Even worse, the program labeled me a "Humorist." What started out as a forty-minute address collapsed into twenty-five. Stories that never failed to stir tempests of laughter provoked doldrums, bringing a rain of perspiration from my forehead. At the end of the speech two people said they enjoyed the talk. I fled the ballroom and hid behind an ornamental pillar close to a block of elevators. Sitting nearby was an old man. He had attended the banquet, but he didn't recognize me. The man had a game leg and was waiting for the lobby to empty before he took an elevator to his room. Under the guise of Good Samaritan, I waited with him.

138 Road Warrior

Once the lobby was clear, I helped him, and myself, creep into an empty elevator. My flight left Savannah at seven-thirty the next morning. I arrived at the airport at 6:15, sneaking out of the hotel before anyone who attended the banquet got up.

I changed planes in Atlanta. In Terminal A, my spirits revived. At the Country Western Bar opposite Gate 27, I bought a cup of coffee. No cream being visible on the counter, I asked for milk. "You'll have to buy it," the woman at the cash register said. "We don't provide milk for coffee." The woman pointed at a plastic glass containing packets of "Coffee Rich." Circling the lid of each packet were two lines of minute type, listing the ingredients of Coffee Rich. "If I dumped this powder in my cup, I'd fail urinalysis and be banned from next year's Olympics," I said. "What?" the cashier said. "He means," the woman standing behind me said, "that he's not turning his mouth into a landfill. Neither am I. I'm buying coffee elsewhere."

I sat down to wait for my flight. Across from me were four women, volunteers who helped cancer patients. The women were flying from Jackson, Mississippi, to Nashville for a meeting at Opryland. A smiling woman gave me a brass pin, the word "Mississippi" stretching across it. Never again, I decided, would I speak to an all-male group. Middle-aged men are not so lively as middle-aged women. Women hear better than men, and they buy more books. Two nights earlier, the husband of one of the women baked chicken. "The bird only had one arm," he told his wife when she came home from work. "I looked in the oven," she recounted, "and sure enough the chicken had one arm." "The other arm did not flutter into sight," she continued, "until we sat down at the dinner table and I poured ice tea. The arm was swimming in the bottom of the pitcher." The women were peppy. Instead of speaking to the Southern Festival of Books, they suggested I address their meeting. "We'd be a terrific audience," they said.

A festival volunteer met me at the Nashville airport. After checking into the Marriott and autographing a program for the desk clerk, I walked four blocks to the Hermitage Hotel where the Festival hosted a Hospitality Room on the second floor. In the room I ate lunch: a croissant, coffee, green grapes, and two hunks of chocolate cheesecake. Afterward I buckled on cheerfulness and visited publishers crowding the War Memorial Plaza. Sixty presses set up booths, many exhibitors familiar from Greensboro. I talked to Gene and Leslie at the Tennessee exhibit. My book stood on a stand. "In Nashville," I said, "I will sell the copies you brought and more." Next day proved me right. After my talk, Gene quickly ran out of copies. Two years ago the University of Georgia Press published one of my books, and I talked to Mary Beth, the press's marketing manager. That evening Reynolds Price gave the Robert Penn Warren Lecture on Southern Letters. A ticket to the lecture and the meal beforehand cost fifty dollars, not something for which I budgeted. "Sam," Mary Beth said, "I have an extra ticket. Would you like to attend as Georgia's guest? The food will be filling, and you look like you could use a big meal."

After wandering exhibits for two hours, I returned to the Marriott to shower and change clothes. I telephoned Vicki from the hotel using a calling card for the first time. Since June Eliza had lost twenty pounds. When I left Storrs, she was five feet nine inches tall and weighed ninety-eight pounds. Eliza ate well and was fit, playing on the junior varsity volleyball team at high school and running on weekends. Weight had slipped from her mysteriously. The morning I arrived in Nashville, Vicki took Eliza to Dr. Dardick. "Things don't look good," Vicki said on the telephone. "Ken found proteins in Eliza's urine. He is running more tests, but there is a chance her kidneys are failing." I did not reply. Before I went on the tour, Eliza cut two hearts out of red paper. On them she wrote, "Have A Good Trip!" and "Good Luck," signing them "Love, Eliza." She buried the hearts beneath clothes in my suitcases. I discovered them when I unpacked. Eliza is the only family member who likes me. Before going to sleep, she kisses me goodnight and says, "I love you, Daddy." Neither the boys nor Vicki show affection. Busy at college, Francis has shunted me onto the every-other-Sunday family email schedule. As for Edward, I so disrupted his days by pushing him into private school that he hasn't spoken to me in three weeks, this despite my driving him to and from school several times each week. And Vicki? Twenty years of marriage have changed her affection to tolerance at best, and at worst, minor irritation.

Scribbling essays colors my days, transforming straight lines into loops. If Eliza were to become terribly sick, not only would I stop erasing and distorting, but I'd also put a period to myself. Sitting on the bed after talking to Vicki, I remembered a tale that appeared in *Early Piety,* a children's book written by George Burder and published in 1806. In September I read the story to students. A hermit, Burder recounted, set out to discover if Providence guided men's lives. A "beautiful youth" joined the hermit on the pilgrimage. The two spent a night at the home of a benevolent old man who was the father of a baby boy. After dinner, the youth and the two men discussed religion. The next morning before he and the hermit departed, the youth "went to the cradle, in which was a pretty infant, (the pride of its aged father) and broke its neck." After witnessing the youth's cruelty, the hermit fled. The youth pursued the hermit, and after catching him on the road turned into an angel and justified his action. "The child of our pious friend," the angel explained, "had almost weaned his affection from God; but to teach him better, the Lord, to save the father has taken the child. To all but us, he seemed to go off in fits, and I was ordained to call him hence—the poor father now humbled in tears, owns that the punishment was just." "Horseshit," I said aloud. To escape melancholy I went to the dinner early and bought a glass of red wine for $4.50, the first wine I sipped on the tour. The dinner slipped quickly past. A man in a brown suit introduced Price. The next thing I heard was applause. I had fallen asleep and missed the lecture.

The next morning was rainy. I didn't want to pay eight dollars for breakfast in the hotel, so I put on wrinkled khakis and a worn shirt and walked streets, searching for a place to eat. Because the day was Saturday, restaurants downtown were closed. Eventually I walked down Fourth Avenue to Broad Street. A group of men gathered outside Robert's Western Café, waiting for the door to open at nine o'clock. I joined the group. All smoked and had lived rough, their faces red and pocked, clothes gritty, in places worn shining from losing their grips on Life. The men addressed me as "Sir." After unlocking the door, the owner of the café jabbed his right hand at a man with watery eyes and commanded, "You! Leave!" The man obeyed. The restaurant was long and narrow, resembling a hall. To the left of the front door was a small, elevated bandstand. A shelf ran the length of the room, pairs of cowboy boots lining it like books, toes pointed outward. Tacked above the bar were dollar bills, all signed. I ordered sausage and eggs sunny side up. When the waitress poured my coffee, she handed me a packet of Coffee Rich. I didn't ask for milk. A man in a blue jacket sat next to me. Many years ago in Indiana, he began, a dispute over parking turned violent. A drunk attacked him and his brother, shooting the brother with a twenty-gauge shotgun. The drunk fired three times then his gun jammed. The brother raised himself off the ground, blood pooling over him, pulled out a forty-five magnum, shouted "now, it's my turn," and killed the man. The brother, himself, almost died, spending fourteen days in intensive care. "The man with the shotgun was crazy," my breakfast companion said. "We tried to reason with him. We told him to put the gun away. I told him we kept a pistol in our truck. But he wouldn't listen. If my brother hadn't shot him, I'd be dead. What else could my brother have done?" "Nothing," I said. "He didn't have a choice. He did the right thing."

After breakfast I walked back to the hotel to change clothes. A beggar hunched in a doorway, his body reedy and alcoholic. He wore an orange jacket, "Volunteers," the nickname of athletic teams at the University of Tennessee sewed on the back in white. The man begged change. I said that I had none and climbed the hill. Seventy-five yards later, I turned around. The man had stood, and drifting around a parking lot, searched for cigarette butts. I hurried back down the street. "Here," I said, giving him five dollars, "get breakfast," thinking all the while, "maybe this will help Eliza." "Thank you, sir," the man said.

142   Road Warrior

At one o'clock that afternoon I gave my final talk, speaking in the Senate Chambers in the Capitol Building. The room was spacious. The ceiling was forty feet high, and a dozen red columns supported a gallery. As I waited outside the chamber, I thought about Eliza, and wondered how I'd perform. But then Elizabeth Proctor, the eighty-two-year-old mother of Bill Weaver, my oldest friend appeared. "I couldn't miss you," Mrs. Proctor said. "I love you." I pressed worry into the back of my mind, and the talk succeeded.

I began eleven minutes late, the moderator of the previous session having lost track of time. C-SPAN, the television channel, filmed my presentation. The producer instructed me to wait ten minutes before beginning. "No," I said, "enough time has been wasted. I'll speak for eight minutes after which I will stop for the introduction. Eight minutes and several paragraphs later, Brad Gioia, a friend and headmaster of Montgomery Bell Academy, introduced me, and although stitched together haphazardly, the talk ran smoothly, finishing so that the next presentation, a speech by William Frist, Republican senator from Tennessee, began on schedule. Many people saw me on television. Because the day was rainy, I borrowed an umbrella from the Marriott. Before speaking, I laid the umbrella on a dais behind me. At the end of the talk, I forgot to remove the umbrella. An hour later as Senator Frist finished talking, I returned to the chamber for the umbrella. "I didn't hear your speech," my cousin Ann recounted, "but I watched you get a white umbrella. You did it with style, creeping behind the senator, in your blue blazer looking like a big, friendly cat."

That night at the Country Music Hall of Fame, the Tennessee Humanities Council sponsored a party for festival participants. Worried about Eliza, I didn't stay at the party long. I inhaled a plate of barbecue, a dish Vicki never serves. The visit to the Hall lasted long enough for me to covet, however. The first thing I wanted was a green suit worn by Jimmy C. Newman and decorated with sequins, white flowers that seemed crosses between magnolias and snowdrops, and alligators, these last red with yellow backs, bellies, and jowls. The second item I coveted was Webb Pierce's 1962 white Pontiac Bonneville convertible, cow horns on the front bumper, a leather saddle riding the axle and dividing the front seat into halves, piggy banks of silver dollars glittering from doors, and an arsenal of guns, a rifle atop the trunk, and racked here and there at least seven pistols. "If I wore that alligator suit and drove this car around Connecticut," I said to a man, "the ladies would go wild." "And so would the gentlemen," he said. "Hell, yes," I said, "especially the men."

My flight left Nashville at one, Sunday afternoon. In Pittsburgh I changed planes. In the seats next to the one I'd been assigned sat a young married couple holding a baby girl. "If I see an empty seat," I said after I sat down, "I'll move." "I understand," the man said. "Children can be nuisances." "No," I said, "it's not that, not that at all. Your little girl is lovely. Hug her. These years are wonderful." Then I stopped talking, fear turning words to tears. I reached Storrs at 8:15. "Good news," Vicki said. "Eliza's kidneys are fine. She has thyroid trouble, and Ken wants her to see an endocrinologist. You make the appointment." Eliza saw the doctor at two the next afternoon. "The best way to understand the problem," he explained, "is to think about it as mumps of the thyroid. A virus made her lose weight. The virus is gone now, and she should start regaining flesh."

In the lives of the middle-aged, nine days are nothing. Most members of the English Department didn't notice my absence. Don noted it, however. On Tuesday in my mailbox appeared a review of my travels, entitled "An Innocent and Broads." "Sam Pickering," Don wrote,

> takes us to the musty back rooms of country book-
> stores to discover what really causes that musty
> smell. In his wake he leaves reviews of his readings
> in newspapers with circulations of 2,000. Pickering
> is known and loved as a Southern Raconteur, and
> his narrative pauses often to remind readers that
> shaggy dog stories have always swapped fleas
> among themselves, and that many of his anecdotes

resulted from his having hunkered down on the
front porches of country stores with a bottle of
Dr. Pepper and a few oldtimers. "Why," he drawls,
"if'n all this was true I couldn't hardly drag myself
home and my wife wouldn't let me in anyways."
In fact Pickering is now in the fourth month of an
extended tour to promote sales of *An Innocent and
Broads*. But he says he calls home at least once a
week, just to see which way the wind blows.

"Lordy," I thought, holding the review. "My little fling is over. How good it is to be home." ❖

News

I teach at eight every morning. I always get to class at seven-thirty. A handful of students also arrive early. I stroll the room and chum the air with remarks, hoping to hook paragraphs and topic sentences. Rarely does a student rise to a noun. Students haven't learned to mold thought into word. In hopes that someone has read the *Hartford Courant,* I eventually ask, "What's new in the world today?" Only once during the semester did a student surface to a by-line. "This morning my younger brother entered pre-school," a boy said. Because the class looked puzzled and eight o'clock snapped across the digital clock on the wall, the boy's news did not expand beyond sentence into story.

Although uncomfortable reporters, students papered the lecture hall with announcements. Pasted to the walls of the room one morning were twenty-two, eight-and-half-by-eleven-inch sheets of green paper. Stamped across the sheets in black type was the question, "Still looking for the love of your life?" Not Miss Lonelyhearts, but the InterVarsity Christian Fellowship posed the question. "Come meet Jesus," the Fellowship urged, implying that He attended gatherings in room 382 in the Student Union "Every Thursday @ 7:30." "Holy Cow," I said to the class. "Do you realize the implications of His appearance?" Alas, only two students had heard of the Second Coming.

"What did you expect?" Josh said later. "Money-changers and Pharisees have transformed American Universities into Temples to Athletics. In the *Sports Bible,* the good Samaritan is a booster, and Michael Jordan, the only deity capable of walking on water. Even if Jesus were to appear on campus, He wouldn't draw a crowd, and the student newspaper wouldn't cover the event, especially if the Huskies were playing basketball." "Not even if He performed miracles," I said, "healing the sick or feeding a multitude." "Fish and bread," Josh scoffed. "Students belong to the nacho and Big Mac generation. Even if He raised the grades of a couple of hopeless academic cases, He'd seem just another motivational speaker, no different from the hordes of flim-flam artists who tongue paths across campuses to riches."

In Carthage, the *Courier* covers religious news. In October a Presbyterian evangelist set up a cross and baptismal tub outside the Smith County courthouse, advertising himself as Ambassador of the King. "Brother," the Ambassador said, addressing Wiley Trefry who had just purchased a bucket of suppositories at Read's Drugstore, "To what denomination do you belong, and are you sanctified?" A goose that had hung too long having made him bilious, Wiley didn't have patience for indigestible words. "Denomination?" Wiley said, "I don't know nothing about no denomination. I attend First and Only Baptist on Main Street. That's where I was raised." "And," Wiley continued, "I'm not sanctified. I'm consti-pated and have bought these suppositories to soften my stool."

Talking to Josh makes me splenetic, and as I strolled back to my office, I longed for a cure-all, not the low sort Wiley purchased, but one high in spirits. Occasionally hankerings are rewarded. Under my door was a page torn from a spiral notebook, a newspa-per clipping stapled to it. "Professor," wrote Michael, a student in my class, "here is some real news." A couple in New Hampshire, the clipping reported, refused to pay the mortgage on their house, saying God had forgiven their debts. "It was our desire to be free from this mortgage," the husband explained to a judge. "Therefore we asked our Heavenly Father in the name of Jesus Christ to release us from the burden. He harkened to our prayer and broke the chains of bondage."

Francis has attended college for three months. Every fortnight he sends the family an email. The notes are short, and Francis doesn't mention class. Last week Francis went to New York and attended a concert by the Pet Shop Boys. "I had fun," Francis wrote; "Elton John danced in the crowd. I got within twenty feet of him." "Do you think Francis's newsletters worth the thirty-five-thousand-dollar subscription fee?" Vicki asked. "Yes," I said. For me, regimented stumbling kicks up more paragraphs than regimens of study. I spent much of October in the basement of the university library thumbing forgotten books. "Not when vicious inclinations are opposed to holy, but when virtue conflicts with virtue, is the real rending of the soul in twain," Rev. F. W. Robertson declared in the nineteenth century. "It is when fidelity to duty can be kept only by infidelity to some entangling engagement or the straight path must be taken over the misery of others."

Robertson's two sentences seemed true. In contrast, distortion often disfigures long articles. One evening, according to Palestinian story, Truth bathed in the Jordan River. Busy scrubbing off the tarnish of the world, Truth did not see Falsehood creeping through willows above the riverbank. Falsehood filched Truth's clothes. After slipping them on and tossing his rags into reeds, Falsehood vanished, taking the road to Nablus. When Truth discovered his clothes were missing, he pursued Falsehood. Unlike Truth, Falsehood was well turned-out, wearing stylish bespoke words, looking to the truth born. On meeting Falsehood, people embraced him and welcomed him into homes and lives. Because he was naked, villagers shunned Truth, and throwing kitchen slops and camel dung at him, chased him from town to town.

Instead of feature stories, I scan news for squibs and fillers. Form determines content. Consisting of one or two lines, squibs are naked and don't lend themselves to elaboration or falsehood. Many squibs are maxims, statements such as "violets don't grow as tall as nettles" and "the gnat is small, but she is not the servant of the cow." Taking up few column inches, fillers are immune to interpretation, the failing described by the old rhyme, "Commentators sometimes view / In Homer, more than Homer knew."

At breakfast I roam margins of the *Courant*. Like pedestals fillers swell at the bottoms of columns. Unlike headlines, fillers are often down-to-earth and jut out like plinths. Dress, I recently learned, determines whether or not an apparition is a ghost. Invariably, real ghosts appear nude. Cotton and wool, not to mention ersatz fabrics such as rayon, polyester, and GoreTex, lack soul and as a result decay. Although clothes can be in frightful, indeed shockingly, poor taste, they cannot be haunted.

Unlike features, fillers don't cause heartache. They are too short for accounts of man's inhumanity. Instead of tears, squibs sink to punch lines. In October a reporter for the *New York Times* overheard remarks made by a trustee of the Metropolitan Museum of Art. "I can't get a-holt of this Millennium business," the trustee said. "How can New Year's be the first day of 2000 if the world is four or five billion years old? It's no wonder American students stack up poorly against students from other countries in mathematics. Professors hereabouts in charge of adding and subtracting would be well-advised to return to the basics and see how folks in England figure the calendar."

Of course, reasonable people shouldn't pay attention to dates. Unfortunately social life presses thought into convention. Consequently people keep track of dates and chart change. Rather than celebrating continuation, people insist upon discovering change, convinced that the quiet and motionless are stagnant, even corrupt. I have taught for thirty years. Often, after I give a talk, people inquire about educational change. Treating questions seriously creates good will, and I manufacture one or two changes. In October I spoke at the university bookstore. Afterward a woman asked me to describe differences between the teaching that I did decades ago and that I do now. The talk having gone well, I told the truth. My teaching, I said, had not changed. It had remained static, "thorough and good," I explained. What had changed were relationships with students and colleagues. When I first taught, I was comfortable with students and knew many well. With colleagues I was often ill at ease. I disliked several teachers at Dartmouth. "For good reason," I added; "many were spoiled, petulant, insignificant turds." "Nowadays," I continued, "I like students. I help them learn. I want them to enjoy life, and I hope they will be lucky. But I do not befriend them." "For twenty years at

Connecticut I have taught with the same men and women," I said. "I am comfortable with them, and they are more than friends. They bring joy to my days. In fact I love them." Some mornings when I roam the English Department, I want to hug them and say, "you really are swell." The next day I received an email sent by a student in the audience. "Oh, Professor Pickering," she wrote, "so many students would like to be your friend. They could learn so much from you." "Maybe," Josh said after I showed him the email. "But would the knowledge living has brought you be good for them now? Students are young. Better to interest them in books, trees, furniture, anything but you. And warn them, as you do each semester, 'if someone my age wants to be your friend, watch out.'"

Later that week I received a letter from Kentucky. My correspondent had read *A Little Fling,* my latest collection of essays. "I admire your taste in poetry," the man wrote. "I'm town librarian. In evenings after I chase children from the building and bolt the door against the little Goths, I poke about. Enclosed are two stanzas I unearthed in September. "The Lord He made the ocean," the first selection began, "And then He made the Whale. / And then He made a raccoon / With a ring around his tail." Despite climbing from animal to human, the second excerpt lost none of the first selection's high seriousness.

> I know a nose no other knows.
> 'Neath starry eyes, o'er ruby lips it grows.
> Beauty in its form,
> And music in its blows.

The English poet Lord Byron got matters wrong in *Childe Harold* when he wrote, "life's enchanted cup but sparkles near the brim." The swigs my correspondent sent were dregs, heel taps bringing guffaws to the gullet.

Laughter is therapeutic, insulating mind from bile. That night I spoke to a poetry club at RHAM High School in Hebron. Afterward twenty students read their verse. "Count references to Columbine," Edward said before I left home. Never are poems by adolescents humorous. Although no one mentioned Columbine,

150 News

students' poems were doleful. I jotted down a haunting brew of lines and phrases: "brown worm thrashing in decay," "fetal mind bathed in blood," "floods of black teardrops," "withered nails seeping pus," and "my insides tumbled out sparkling like the sun." The next morning I sent a sampler of student verse to Kentucky. My correspondent replied by return mail, enclosing a stanza from a song.

> Some folks say preachers won't steal.
> But I found two in my cornfield.
> One with a shovel and t'other with a hoe,
> A diggin' up my taters row by row.

My days are back pages. This fall at the university I attended three football games, three volleyball matches, and three soccer games, two of these last being girls' games and one boys'. At the open house sponsored by the Natural History Museum, I noticed that the egg of an emu had been mislabeled and attributed to a herring gull. One Thursday early in November, I flew to Pittsburgh. That night I spoke at a college. A student borrowed a car from a friend and fetched me at the airport. As soon as she entered the interstate, she sped, reaching 87 miles an hour. I threatened to kick her foot off the accelerator, and she decelerated. The girl dropped me at Ramada Suites on Chatham, saying she'd return at five to take me to dinner. That afternoon I wandered Pittsburgh in search of lunch. At the bakery at Kaufman's Department Store on Fifth Avenue, I bought a sweet roll and a chocolate doughnut. At twenty after five, the girl appeared at the Ramada. Piled in the back seat like a cord of wood, one thigh atop another, were six freshmen, one girl and five boys. My escorts took me to a restaurant in a mall. The specialty of the house was blackened Cajun catfish. "Fresh from the Monongahela?" I asked. "I think so," the waiter said, "but I'm not sure. I'll have to ask the kitchen." One minute before my talk was scheduled to start, the girl delivered me to the building in which I spoke. No one planned to introduce me, so I introduced myself. After the talk, the girl returned me to the Ramada. "I'm supposed to take you to the airport tomorrow morning," she said. "No, no," I said solicitously, "you have done too much already. Stay in bed and get some beauty sleep. I'll take the airport limousine."

Automotive matters cluttered November. Edward took a driver's test. He passed, but on the report sheet, the examiner wrote, "Bad language while parking." That night Edward drove the Toyota to Chris Geary's house on Spring Hill. At twelve-thirty, Vicki shook me. "Edward's not home," she said. "What are you going to do?" I threw off the blanket, dressed, and at 12:42 backed the Mazda out of the garage. The night was cloudy and dark. Although I spotted lumps in the Gearys' driveway, I could not distinguish the Toyota, so I parked on Spring Hill. I slid out of the car and crept along the edge of the drive to the house. The Toyota was parked beside the kitchen. Just as I recognized the car, Edward walked into the kitchen and put on his jacket. I turned, ran down the driveway, and jumping into my car, hurried off, not switching on lights until I reached Maple Road. I beat Edward home by four minutes, time enough to slip the Mazda in the garage and myself into pajamas and bed. "Edward," I said the next morning, "I was asleep, but Mommy tells me you came home late last night. In future if you are going to be out late, call home and let us know. Otherwise I might come looking for you." "No," Edward said, "you wouldn't do that. Nobody's father would do that."

Thanksgiving weekend I telephoned my cousin Kathryn in Nashville. Kathryn is eighty-six years old and until four days before the holiday had driven a white Camaro. That morning she bought a hamburger at The Krystal. Half a mile down the road, a woman from Florida lost her way. Studying a map and not the road, the woman ran a stop sign and bashed into the side of Kathryn's car, destroying the Camaro and knocking Kathryn's seat loose from its moorings, pushing it across the transmission and against the door on the passenger side of the front seat. Kathryn wasn't hurt. Still, wreckers could not remove her from the car for an hour. A boy stopped and comforted her. The boy reached through a broken window, and rubbing Kathryn's back, said, "Don't worry ma'am. You are going to be all right." Then after a pause, he added, "You remind me a lot of my grandmother. She just passed."

During November fillers dominated news from Carthage. Loppie Groat found a hollow turnip stuffed with peas, the work,

Loppie judged, "of a garden mouse." From a peddler Loppie purchased a gold ring, supposedly forged from a hinge stolen from the coffin of Pontius Pilate. The ring, the peddler told Loppie, cured rheumatism better than "magnetic garters." Much news described folks who "passed" or were exiting rapidly. A colt kicked Grandy Vanlo in the stomach, rupturing his bowel, buying him a ticket, as Proverbs Goforth put it, "to that world where horses don't buck and sorrow and weeping don't snort and roll their eyes." Grandy's friends tried to visit him on his deathbed. But the disconsolate victim of bereavement to be, his wife Ruelle, refused them admittance. Sitting at the kitchen table eating steak and potatoes in order, she said, to fortify her spirits for the funeral and the will, she explained that Grandy was too busy dying to be disturbed. "He can't stop to chat," Ruelle told Turlow Gutheridge, adding, "besides tomorrow is market day, and I can't waste any more time in this house. I've got chores to do."

A week after Grandy cantered across the finish line, Prudie Schwitters turned in her feed bucket. Prudie was ninety-four when she died. "Two days before Mama took to bed with the staggers," Prudie's daughter Lana recounted, "she mended her stockings. Mama always had gentlemanly ways, and I reckon she heard the neighing of the mules pulling the hearse." "I certainly miss Mama," Lana told Turlow. "Every time I sits down to dinner, I see her across the table, reaching out her fork for the biggest potato."

Death rose yeasty in Carthage. Lonnie Donahoo, the baker, "borrowed" a tombstone from the cemetery below the Methodist church on Third Avenue. He used the stone as hearth in a new oven. Carved into the stone but weathered almost out of sight were a death's head and the word RESURGAM. Lonnie's eyesight was poor, and he didn't notice when the head and word appeared on the bottoms of loaves baked in the new oven. What Lonnie missed, others saw. Roscoe Toone discovered the death's head when he sliced a loaf for Sunday lunch. Thinking the end of the world was at hand, Roscoe fell to the dining room floor and confessed his sins, among which were indiscretions with Ione Mulkey, committed frequently and with enthusiasm over the past eighteen years, the knowledge of which irked Roscoe's wife Mildred considerably. "I've buried Mother and Father, a young husband, a baby, and any quantity of other connections," Mildred told Turlow, "but never have I felt so deprived."

Cold slows the percolation of yeast, and as fall kneaded leaves from trees, days in Storrs did not rise like Lonnie's bread. Still, if hours did not provide dough for trays of springy Wonder Bread, they furnished gluten for filler. On October 1, I wandered Mansfield. Above the Fenton River, fall trod summer grapes alcoholic. Atop pin oaks, leaves dried into orange twists. When I closed my hand around the inflorescences of green foxtail, they shimmered through my fingers like caterpillars. Woolly aphids wrapped alders in white gauze, and yellow berries bent horse nettle to the ground. Bluebirds bustled about a dead white oak. I sat on the ground and watched them. Suddenly I noticed two fledglings, late summer hatchlings, one sunning, pasting wings against the tree, the other hovering in a crook between trunk and limb, its breast mottled and hard to distinguish from shags of bark.

Not until the Sunday before Thanksgiving did I roam town again. As usual I saw the plumage of season, not the bird itself— gizzard, craw, and Pope's Nose. Below the sheep barn canes of multiflora rose switched the path under the power line. At the bottom of the hill, I removed twenty-eight deer ticks from my trousers. Near the pumping station, crab apples had turned soggy and begun to melt into small red sacks. A chipmunk squeaked and scurried between rocks. Overhead a goose honked. In the Ogushwitz meadow, winter crest shredded into ice. Near the beaver pond, buttons of mountain mint poked through tussock sedge. Students had picnicked near the landfill, and husks of the evening lay scattered about—cans that once contained beer, Budweiser, Busch Lite, and Red Dog—brown bottles once full of Hard Core, an apple cranberry cider, 6 percent alcohol; Negra Modelo, a dark beer imported from Mexico, and Harpoon IPA, India Pale Ale, on the corners of the label of which appeared, not winds fermenting and blowing, but orange lilies. While St. Pauli Girl and Molsen Ice came in green bottles, Mike's Hard Lemonade was in a clear bottle. On the neck of a Spanish Peaks bottle was a paper medallion. The phrase "NO WHINERS" curved around the top of the medallion. In the center of the medallion appeared the profile of a black retriever, around the dog's neck a collar with "CHUG" stamped on it.

On Thanksgiving, Vicki, the children, and I drove to Princeton and spent four days with Vicki's mother. Along Nassau Street leaves on sawtooth oaks turned bronze and metallic, crosscutting breezes. Days were warm, and cherries bloomed at the Seminary. Despite the sunshine, I spent most of the time inside, flipping through rooms, searching for fillers. The small and the out-of-the-way provide me endless pleasure. When the insignificant seems to outlast the important, as it so often does, my spirits hop a two-step. "Artifice appeals to you," Vicki said last week, "because you are addicted to saucing and rouging." "Maybe," I said, "but do you know what creatures thrived during the Flood?" "No," Vicki answered. "Fish," I said. "If you had spent hours rising to the hooks of back pages, you would have known."

Lining a trunk in the attic in Princeton was a newspaper, the *Morning World Herald,* published in Omaha, Nebraska on December 8, 1941. Sixteen pages long, the paper sold for three cents in Omaha and Council Bluffs and five cents "Elsewhere." The circulation was large. In November, the paper sold 189,492 copies daily, 84,709 of these in the city; 29,281 in the suburbs, and 75,502 in the country. On Sunday circulation increased to 190,891, subscribers in the country now outnumbering those in the city, 81,498 to 78,276, with people in the suburbs buying 31,117 copies. The number of subscribers was not so important as the news, at least to people sixty years ago. Across the top of the paper, WAR appeared in black type, the letters two-and-thirteen-sixteenths inches tall, the thick portions of each letter seven-eighths of an inch wide. Beneath the date and name of the paper, a black band stretched across the page. Stamped out of the band and proclaiming EXTRA! were white letters one-and-a-half inches tall. Below the band was a two-line headline, "Japs Bomb U. S. Bases in Far East; Report Heavy Loss of Life, Damage." "Japan today choose [*sic*] war with the United States," an article reported, black type streaming across a double column on the right side of the front page. "Like a thunderbolt in the midst of diplomatic shilly-shallying, she sent her bombers against the United States' great Pearl Harbor naval base in Hawaii." In the middle of the page was a picture of Pearl Harbor on a sunny, peaceful day. Below appeared a picture of a "twin-engined Japanese warplane." "The Attackers Fly Planes Like This," black type explained.

I turned pages slowly, my eyes caught by Tubruk and Rommel, Tula, the Rostov Front, and the Donets River Basin. Twenty-five years ago I spent three months in Leningrad, and when I saw the name of the city, I paused. "Russian smashes against entrenched Leningrad besiegers," the article recounted, "had been thrown back, while German siege guns rained shells on the city, particularly the north docks and machine tool factories." "We poured paint into water, boiled it, and drank it like soup," a friend who survived the siege once told me.

An article on the fourth page described the evolution of Japanese-American relations. The piece had been written in anticipation of war and withheld from publication until the bombing. "The Japanese belief that their national prestige and pride of race has received affronts from America is indisputably a factor in this crisis," a paragraph stated. "They resent bitterly our exclusion laws, which they say class them with other races they consider inferior. Many Japanese contend that the whole course of history since the world war might have been different had the white nations admitted them as full equals."

Instead of mulling war news, I searched the paper for knick-knacks, saucing, hiding the red wave behind decoration. At its core civilization may only be decoration and artifice, ornaments that keep human nature lisping. Household Finance offered twenty-five dollar loans "with no endorsees." Borrowers repaid loans in monthly installments, choosing six, nine, or twelve payments. If one chose to close his twenty-five dollar debt in six months, each payment was $4.49, the total paid amounting to $26.94. The payment for each of nine installments was $3.09, the total adding up to $27.81. For the twelve-month plan, each payment was $2.40 or $28.80 for the year.

The motto of Fitch, McEacheron, and Cole Mortuary was "An Institution Built Upon Reputation." "Ask Those Whom We Have Served," the advertisement urged, the grammar correct but the instruction difficult to follow. People napping in dirt are notoriously reticent. A five-car Lionel train cost $25.25, a fine Christmas present for a child, but probably not one appealing to those served by Messrs. Fitch, McEacheron, and Cole, "silent passengers riding rails in wooden kimonos," as Turlow Gutheridge put it. Weight wasn't about to force Mrs. C. D. Wells of Fort Worth to circle the drain, but the Ayds Candy Plan enabled her, an advertisement stated, to peg off fifty-two pounds, dropping from 170 to 118. The candy cost $2.25 a box, a quarter less than a Hickok Belt Set. Sold at Brandeis Department Store, the set contained a belt and a buckle, this last with "Kristol initials," both items set in a "clear glass ashtray."

For forty cents one could see Gary Cooper starring in *Sergeant York* at the Paramount. At the Arbor, Errol Flynn starred in *Dive Bomber,* and Eleanor Powell and Ann Sothern appeared in *Lady Be Good* at the Dundee. Admission to *You'll Never Get Rich* with Fred Astaire and Rita Hayworth cost thirty cents at the Beacon while at the State a seat for Johnny Mack Brown in *The Masked Rider* was twenty cents. Characters in comic strips were familiar: Blondie, Joe Palooka, Little Orphan Annie, Dick Tracy, Mary Worth, Moon Mullins, Li'l Abner, and Terry and the Pirates. In Moon Mullins, Lord Plushbottom assured Emma he would apologize to Mr. Peevy. Lord Plushbottom knew Emma would listen behind the door, and as soon as he entered the room with Peevy, Plushbottom shouted, "I want to apologize to you." Once he was out of Emma's hearing, however, Plushbottom snapped his fingers in Peevy's face and blew a raspberry. In Thimble Theatre, Admiral Popeye's ship was loaded and ready to sail for Spinachova. Ground collapsed beneath Dick Tracy, and falling into a drainage tunnel, he faced "Mole."

Amid the classifieds were advertisements for coal. Names of the coals sounded poetic: Tiger Lump, Broken Aro, Marvel Nut,

Star Semmut Run, Stoker, Dallas Nut Coke, and Sunnyglow Large Lump. "Cracks Nuts, Not Safes" stated the caption above a filler from St. Louis. "Isadore Edelstein, paroled life termer, when arrested here for possessing burglar tools had 30 pounds of walnuts in his room. A five-pound sledge hammer lay near the nuts. He told police the sledge hammer was his nut cracker." Atop the sports section appeared a picture six-and-a-half by eight inches. Standing side by side were the "Master Minds of Oregon State's Rose Bowl Outfit": Head Coach Lon Stiner, "the former Nebraskan"; Line Coach Jim Dixon; Backfield Coach Hall Moe; and End Coach Bill McKalip. The masterminds wore long-sleeved sweat shirts, football pants resembling striped knickers, high-toped cleats, and white socks so short that the men flashed broad hunks of calf.

Despite the photograph, the feature story discussed football at the University of Texas. "The greatest team in Southwest conference history," the Longhorns had once been ranked first in the nation. On successive weekends, however, Baylor tied and Texas Christian branded the Longhorns, momentarily polling them and turning them into steers. Some "youngsters," the account stated, "spent too much time reading about their greatness." On sports pages articles are upbeat, and the horns were "reborn," goring Texas A&M, knocking them from "unbeaten ranks" 23-0 then trampling Oregon, 71-7, a team that lost to Rose Bowl–bound Oregon State by only five points. Texas was the team, the article concluded, "that couldn't afford to lose its self-respect." A small dose of athletic respect cloys, and after the tale of the Longhorns' journey "down the hazardous gridiron trail," I read squibs. "Joe Hubka, the Dodge, Neb. Adonis," a paragraph stated, "will get back into an Omaha ring Monday night when he meets Pete Sherman in the opening match on the Auditorium rassle card. Jumping Joe Savoldi will meet Lou Thesz, former champion, in the main event. Orville Brown will tackle the giant, Bob Stewart, and Lord Alfred Mills will meet Alf Johnson in other matches. Joe Zikmund will be the referee."

"Read this," Edward said, handing me a scrap of paper. Edward had spent the morning rummaging through old books. Ink on the paper had faded and spread like mold. Nevertheless, a stanza of verse was visible.

> Tho we allow that milk is good,
> And say the same of grass,
> The one to babes is food,
> The other for an ass.

Edward discovered the paper in the first volume of *The History of the Bucaniers of America*, the fourth edition published in London in 1741. I looked at the book. Written inside the front cover was "Bought in Panama in 1850 by C. F. W. McClure on his way home from California." Before McClure purchased the book, it belonged to Joseph Rumrill, a child living in Boston. On margins throughout the book, Rumrill practiced writing his name. Sometimes he wrote in ink, other times, in pencil. Often he wrote *Boston*. On several pages he wrote dates, 1822 and 1827 each once, then 1830 three times. On the back of woodcuts in the book he drew pictures. Behind Henry Morgan he drew a man shaped like a peanut and wearing a top hat. Shorn of headgear, the same man or his cousin strolled a thin street, unaware that "Puerto del Principe Taken & Sackt" was occurring in back of him.

"Daddy," Edward said after looking at *The Bucaniers,* "rooting is great fun." "Yes," I agreed. An hour later, Edward brought me a scrapbook he found in the basement. Measuring eight by ten inches and bound in green cloth, the book contained forty-eight pages, a sheaf of pages near the middle of the book having been sliced out with a razor. On the first page was the inscription "To My Dear Wife, Omaha Feb'y 9th 1869," the letters square and leaning backwards. The scrapbook book resembled one of my notebooks, its contents miscellaneous items of the sort I paste into essays. Glued neatly to pages of the scrapbook were fillers gleaned from newspapers and magazines. People collect then arrange clutter in order to define and create. By clipping and pasting, one masters chaos and fosters the illusion of control. Ultimately, of course, time transforms everything into filler. Glue decays, and history slips from memory, leaving pages wrinkled but empty. Event loses significance, and readers pause longer over the names of coal than over the names of emperors and presidents.

After being shuffled, contents of the scrapbook slipped into suits: science, anecdote, morality, and people. Sketches of the plague and consumption fell under science, the latter disease responsible for slightly less than one-fifth the deaths in Boston and New York and one-sixth in Baltimore and Washington. According to a note, Maine contained 1,568 lakes. "It is claimed that no other area of equal extent in the world possesses so much water power." Some scientific clippings were sensational. From West Prussia came an account of "a blooming young woman" who gave "birth to a female child." The baby was "perfectly healthy" except for a tumor as large as "two fists" on her back. "In the tumor," the article related, "there moves very plainly an unborn babe, whose well-formed limbs can be felt through the skin of the tumor. Its size corresponds with that of a foetus five or six months old." The girl's father asked a doctor to remove the tumor. After an examination, however, the doctor "declared that there was a possibility of the foetus arriving at maturity" "No physician," the doctor concluded, "would be justified in destroying this wonderful life," observing "the new born girl is very beautiful and strong and imbibed her mother's milk with rare appetite."

For the parent burdened with a child who wept more than she lapped, the *Rock Island Union* offered a remedy. "To quiet a crying baby it is only necessary to prop it up with pillows, if it cannot sit alone, and smear its fingers with thick molasses, then put half a dozen feathers into its hands. It will sit and pick off the feathers from one hand to the other until it falls asleep. When it wakes up, more molasses and more feathers." "This recipe," the *Union* concluded, "is worth thousands of dollars. If we get five hundred for it we shall be content."

The scrapbook was thick with anecdotes. From England a correspondent reported that a blind boy could "repeat not only the whole one hundred and fifty Prayer Book Psalms, and a large number of metrical psalms and hymns, as well as a considerable amount of modern poetry, including Goldsmith's 'Deserted Village,' but the whole of Milton's 'Paradise Lost,' with marginal notes and a biography." Several stories were humorous as well as apocryphal. When a veteran of the Revolution ran for Congress against a youngster "who had never been to the wars," the old campaigner described hardships he endured. After noting he'd bled for his country, fighting both the British and Indians, the man scaled poetic heights, declaring, "I have slept on the field of battle with no other covering than the canopy of Heaven. I have walked over the frozen ground till every footstep was marked with blood." The speech greatly affected a countryman in the audience. Wiping "tears from his eyes with the extremity of his coattail," he interrupted the speaker, asking if he had really fought the British and Indians, slept on the dirt "without any kiver," and walked until his feet ran blood. On the speaker's saying *yes,* the rustic sighed and said, "I'll guess I'll vote for t'other fellow, for I'll be blamed if you ain't done enough for your country."

While ambling a country lane, a preacher came upon a member of his congregation breaking rocks with a pickaxe. The man knelt "to get at his work better," a squib explained. "Ah, John," the preacher mused, "I wish I could break the stony hearts of my hearers as you are breaking those stones." "Perhaps, master," the man replied, "you do not work on your knees." Another clipping described initiation into the Masons. After presenting himself at Lodge Room "No. 36,666," the initiate entered a foyer. "Five or six melancholy chaps, in sashes and embroidered napkins" received the man, after which they turned "back somersaults." "A big fat fellow" commanded, "Sinner from the other world advance." After a display of nonsensical verbal acrobatics, the initiate was blind-folded and "pitched" on to a goat's back. Eventually the handkerchief slipped from the narrator's eyes, and he discovered the goat was imaginary, the "squalls" he experienced being part of the initiation rite. At the conclusion of the ceremony, the man reported, his brothers "were dancing a war-dance around a big skull, turning hand springs, and the big fat fellow was standing on his head in a corner."

Descriptions of actual people constituted some clippings, for example, Strauss "the Second Orpheus" and John B. Gough, a temperance lecturer who earned twelve hundred dollars for a speech. "This beats," the article stated, "the earnings of the leaders of the bar, popular preachers, and stars of the stage, and eclipses all Greek and Roman fame." According to Captain C. W. Lawton of the Fourth Michigan Calvary, the "arch-traitor" Jefferson Davis was captured while wearing "woman's attire." Over a suit of Confederate gray, he wore "a lady's waterproof cloak, gathered at the waist, with the shawl drawn over the head, and carrying a tin pail." A reporter for *The Times* described a reading Charles Dickens gave in Washington. "In a century or two from now," the man concluded, "when your Rothchilds, your Astors, and your T. A. Stewarts will be altogether forgotten, the fame of this man will scarcely have begun to expand into a glorious fullness of refulgence which will shine with its most genial warmth into every household, Christian or Pagan, on the habitable globe." Unlike his glowing performance, Dickens's dress had "a flash appearance." "Gold chain-cables" swung from each pocket. Attached to the cables were large charms, resembling "ancient chain armor," smacking of "Jew peddlers, or gentlemen in the circus or negro-minstrel line of business."

Accompanying a sketch of the humorist Petroleum V. Nasby was Nasby's account of "His Little Hatchet." "I commenced being good at a very early age and built myself up on the best models," Nasby recollected. "I was yet an infant when I read the affecting story of the hacking down of the cherry tree by George Washington, and his manly statement to his father than he could not tell a lie. I read the story and it filled me with a desire to surpass him. I was not going to let any such a boy as George Washington, if he did afterwards get to be President, excel me in the moralities." Nasby proceeded to chop down his father's most valuable cherry. After felling the tree, he went Washington one better and dug the roots, "so that by no means could the variety be preserved." Nasby eagerly anticipated confessing and being "wept over and forgiven"

162 News

because of his "extreme truthfulness." The plan failed. "I was very much like George Washington, but the trouble was that my father didn't resemble George Washington's father." On being asked, "did you chop down the cherry tree?" Nasby responded, "Father, I cannot tell a lie. I did it with my little hatchet." Nasby then struck "the proper attitude for the old gentleman to shed tears on me." Alas, his father said that "he had rather I had told a thousand lies than to have cut down that particular tree, and he whipped me until I was in an exasperated rawness."

The book contained signatures of moral verse, poems entitled "Deeds, Not Words," "The Other Side," "To Stella in Heaven," "The Master's Touch," "The Voyage of Life," "The Little People," and "Cometh A Blessing Down."

> My bosom has Aeolian chords
> That warble wildly to the soul
> And oft the strain takes form in words
> That echo like a death-bell's toll,

began "An Aeolian Melody." "How the Night Comes Down" also contained memorable stanzas.

> Just over the hilltops, in the valleys doth roll
> A ruby-red river of girasole;
> It sinketh, it swelleth in golden motion,
> Like a river of gold to a golden ocean.

"What sound so sweet," began "Summer Rain," "After a day of fiery heat, / And sun-strokes in the dusty street." Occasionally I feel bound to a wheel of nouns and verbs, and the first lines of "Let Me Rest" smacked of sometime feelings.

> I am weary; let me rest
> Underneath the nodding clover,
> With the grass upon my breast,
> And the daisies bending over.

Devotees of fillers prefer low to high culture, and I enjoyed the poetry. At dinner I read a description of childhood.

When sticks of peppermint possessed
A sceptre's power to sway the breast,
And heaven was 'round us, while we fed
On rich ambrosial gingerbread.

"Is that good poetry?" Edward asked. "No," I said, "but I like it."

Many stories in the scrapbook were also inspirational or instructive. Christ, a column explained, was "the door," the mediator between God and man. Other doors existed, but they all "failed." The door of Self-Righteousness was cheap, "full of knots and holes, thinly veneered over and varnished, so as to imitate the genuine wood." The door of Self-Torture or Penance was painful and bloody and led to doubt and despair. The door of Universal Salvation opened away from punishment but not sin. This last was "in fact no door, but the breaking down of all doors or boundaries between sin and holiness, right and wrong," transforming "heaven from a walled city into an enclosed common." The Sectarian door assumed sundry forms. Sometimes it was "rounded into a Roman arch, and carefully guarded by a man wearing a triple crown, calling himself successor of St. Peter." Other times the door rose to a "Gothic point" as "in the English or Episcopal manner." In contrast the Presbyterian or Puritan door was "a severely square form, disdaining ornament and emblazoned with elaborate confessions of faith." No door other than Christ, the piece concluded, provided "exclusive access to God, to holiness, to heaven." "Hear and remember the words of Christ," the last sentence urged, "I am the door. By me, if any man enter in, he shall be saved." "Eternity has no gray hairs," a squib began. "The flowers fade, the heart withers, man grows old and dies; the world lies down in the sepulchre of ages, but time writes no wrinkles on the brow of eternity."

Several clippings consisted of conventional advice. "The proverb tells us," began a paragraph entitled "Idleness," "that idle persons can never find time for any thing; and the reason is that they have always a bundle of arrears to engross their attention. They can do little or nothing because they are always intending to do a vast deal." Domesticity was the subject of much concern.

Women would enjoy more success keeping "Men At Home" if they "were taught to feel the angel duty that devolves on them, to keep the wandering steps of those who are tempted so much more than they, in the paths of virtue and peace—to make them feel that in the busy world is noise and confusion—that at home there is order and repose." "Let a wife," an article advised, "in her whole intercourse with her husband, try the efficacy of gentleness, purity, sincerity, scrupulous truth, meek and patient forbearance, an invariable tone and manner of deference, and if he is not a brute he cannot help respecting her and treating her kindly; and in nearly all instances, he will end by loving her and living happily with her."

Glued into the book as illustrations were prints, most moral or precious. In the middle of "It Was Not Me," a mother opened a door into a room. Scattered across the floor in front of her were shards of a porcelain statue. To the mother's right and in her vision stood a small girl holding a whiskbroom in her left hand. In her right hand the girl clutched a doll. The doll's feet brushed the floor limply, and her head was buried in the child's midriff, as if she were weeping, asking forgiveness for a misstep. Hidden from the mother's view behind the door stood two other children, a little boy and a little girl. Attached to the wall above them was the pedestal on which the statue had stood. While the girl pressed her hands against the sides of her head in fright, the boy held a string in his left hand. Attached to the end of the string was the foot of the statue.

More playful was "The Mustache." While a young music teacher dozed in a chair, a violin and the sheets of "Home Sweet Home" in his lap, his student, a budding girl, drew a black mustache on his upper lip. The girl's younger sister sat a table behind the teacher giggling, behind her George Washington framed on the wall, in front of her a book resting on a sheet of paper, across the top of which was written "Sunday School." In the left front of the print, a spaniel perched on a pillow and gazed at the teacher. Behind the dog, coals blazed in a fireplace. On the mantle stood an ornamented flagon and a vase overflowing with flowers. Hanging on the wall behind the mantle was the portrait of a woman, hands pressed together in prayer. The Holy Bible stood on a bookshelf. Next to the shelf a window opened onto a village green. Across the green stood a church.

"I prefer Nasby and the cherry tree," Edward said looking at the print. "I like them both," I said. Scrapbooks don't lend themselves to judgment. Their contents are trinkets. Ironically, however, lives are fabrics of scraps. On returning to Storrs, I found a letter from Kentucky. "Think you will like the enclosed," the librarian wrote. "I discovered the lines in an old farce. I've now decided to call myself a poetic resurrectionist or quatrain snatcher."

> And thus began their cooing,
> And now they would be wooing,
> And then they would be doing,
> And then commences rueing,
> And then the boo-hoo hooing.

The next morning I roamed the broken land near the sewage treatment plant. A pair of red-tailed hawks floated over the old landfill. Doves rang into flight, and juniper gleamed green and silver. Four crows harassed a sharp-shined hawk perched in a bigtooth aspen. The day was hot, and the fragrance of manure rose baked from a field. A mockingbird sat atop wild rose and scissored its tail. Near a stonewall lay remnants of a gray squirrel. A blue jay flew racketing through a white oak. I stood quietly for a moment then said aloud, "this is enough for a day—enough for a life." ❖

Shadow

Winter is shadowy. Clouds overlay the land; the florid colors of other seasons pool into gray, and bark blooms unobtrusively. In December, I roamed field and wood. White oaks shingled a ridge, and green slipped from hemlocks along the Fenton River, at dusk yellowing the air. At the bottom of Ski-Tow Hill, buds bunked along willow twigs, scales pinched about them. At the edge of the Ogushwitz meadow, plates peeled from the trunks of red maples. Nearby, laurels twisted, limbs contorting, almost dancing, bark clinging to them like tights. From an ash a broken limb jutted into a faucet. Scattered around the lip were shards of acorns. Beside a fence stood a lone sugar maple. While lower branches sagged like old boots, upper branches splintered, stenciling the sky.

Winter appeals to the middle-aged. As clarity vanishes, life becomes harmonious, and truth appears more arbitrary than during other seasons. In contrast spring imposes fluorescent certainty upon days, attracting youth, people who haven't lived long enough to understand that decency and compassion grow best in shadows. Inexperience is the consort of vigor and dogmatism. As a result societies that celebrate youth are narrow and heartless. "Only the young or people whose development has been arrested by ambition," Josh said recently, "could be prosecutors."

During winter, people mull idea into fiction. As winds curl around houses like scarves, people sink into rooms. Stories that wilted under the glare of summery analysis flourish during winter. Last Friday in Ankerrow's Café, Turlow Gutheridge told the lunchtime crowd an instructive tale. "Many years ago," Turlow recounted, "when Europeans could sling blue tails over limbs," a mastiff chased a little dog through a forest. Just as the mastiff raised his right paw to swat the dog into Alpo, a magician saw the animals. Taking pity upon the small dog, the magician transformed him into a lion. Immediately the lion killed the mastiff. While the lion gnawed the mastiff's entrails, the magician fled to the coast, hired a boat, and vanished into a distant land, explaining, "I'm the only living person who knew that lion when he was a puppy."

Like all lessons, those of story are fleeting. For its part, however, fiction endures longer than abstract truth, often so long that fictions themselves evolve into truth, in the process starting their declines. Fictional landscapes flower in winter. For eleven years, a friend in Iowa has mailed me reports, describing doings of characters that come out of hibernation during winter. In December I received a box from Ames. The box contained a white sack. Stamped in red on the sack were a mortar and pestle and the words "D and H Drug Store." The store had two branches, both in Columbia, Missouri, the first located at 1001 West Broadway, the second, at 1812 Paris Road, both "Open every day to serve you."

The sack contained signatures of cure-alls, each page lifting spirits. The first letter I ever received from Ames was written by Mrs. Neoscaleeta Pemberton, founder of The Carts for Wienie Dogs Foundation, "TCFWDF," a charity established to aid crippled dachshunds. Four years ago Mrs. Pemberton and the Rev. Rusty Zwanger attended a conference in Kansas City. Zwanger himself had founded RIO, the Remain Intact ORGANization, a group dedicated to preventing male circumcision, "the unkindest cut of all." At the Raphael Hotel in Kansas City, Mrs. Pemberton and the reverend fell from grace and tumbling into fleshy embraces, behaved in such an athletic and untoward manner that they wrecked Zwanger's suite. "Destroying," the hotel manager wrote me, "a new Hoover vacuum cleaner." After receiving awards for their efforts on behalf of dogs and small boys, Zwanger and Mrs.

168   Shadow

Pemberton vanished. Two years ago Zwanger surfaced in Ames. Reborn as the Rev. Zevs Galaxy, he founded the Nudist Christian Church. His stay in Ames was short, long enough, however, to rekindle the passion of Starlene Zwanger, his abandoned wife. Consequently when Rusty disappeared for the second time, Starlene hired a private detective to run him to ground, Merle T. Oderman, whose agency was located at "$9\frac{1}{2}$ East St. NW (Behind the Laundrymat)" in Sibley, Iowa, "Peace Bond Swearing Out and Custom Stump Grinding Our Specialties."

When the package arrived, I was reading *Wild Fruits,* Henry David Thoreau's "Rediscovered Last Manuscript." Zwanger's doings proved so enticing that I haven't nibbled *Fruits* for five weeks. "Nor," Vicki said, "the Koran or *The Brothers Karamazov,* both of which have collected dust under the bed for a dozen years." Mrs. Ivadell Teeverbaugh Naslund, "Fund Raising Chair Pro Temp" for TCFWDF mailed the package. "Professor Pickelring," she wrote, "Am only doing as was asked in forwarding the enclosed. These things now in your hands and the Lord bless you in your stewardship of them." "P.S.," she concluded, "you are invited to join us at the open house at Morton Norton and Tinsie Stanky's in honor of their newborn triplets—Unique, Boutique, and Clinique."

Under Mrs. Naslund's letter lay a memo written by Detective Oderman and dated December 4, 1999. The memo described the apprehension of the Rev. Zevs Galaxy. "OPERATION BARE NUDITIES," Oderman recounted, "proceeded as per our arrangement and plan. After we learned that Arizona and Utah law was after Zwanger/Galaxy, my operatives Deedub Wall and Ataturk Spivey put together a retrieval posse. This posseafication led to subject being returned to Ames jail where he was booked into custody by Chief Noville Fenton. Subject now in Story County jail awaiting trial. There is talk about work release to preach at his church near campus as there is agitation to resume services among students. Ames Nudist Christian T-shirts being brought to jail daily for conversion of other inmates."

At the end of the memo, Oderman observed that the Carts For Wienie Dogs Foundation needed to thank "these OPERATION BARE NUDITIES posse members for their assistance even if they did not retrieve Mrs. Pemberton." Forty-eight men belonged to the posse, including Rooney Booheister, Terald Hargis, Rardell Clemens, Lamar Sump, Elam Sheldahl, Marcus Pido Yamshido, Etheredge Feaker, Lonnie Lee Gaumer, Nort Fiscus, Buseter Gene Handlos, and Colothoian Devonde Tate. Thirty members of the "posse Ladies Auxiliary" also assisted in Galaxy's capture, among others, Verena Skalicky, Genevieve Lodene Flaspohler, Tonya Tarbell-Nolting, Wanda Pringnitz, Neoma Coonradt, Valicicty Rayhons, Clarice Farquart, Mrs. Pamline Pertile, Gretta Semelinski, Tranquilla McCaw, and Arlene Charlene Stanky.

Oderman noted that Galaxy instructed that property "confiscated by Chief Fenton" be sent to "Prof. Sam Pickelring," adding "he would know what to do." I received four items: the business card of Marcus J. Anderson, "Special Agent" assigned to the "Omaha Field Office" of the "Defense Security Service"; a membership card to the J.C. Penney Bra and Panty Club, no panties but four bra's stamped as purchased—two more and Zevs or Mrs. Pemberton would have received a free bra; a deck of playing cards, the backs yellow, printed on them in black, the Statue of Liberty then the words "Lederman Bail Bonds," "Oskaloosa 673-6670," and "Toll Free 1-800-564-8898"; and lastly *The Book of Zevs*, "subject's divinely-inspired words," Oderman explained, "that come to him in the Zion Wilderness National Park to be placed in Pickelrings bible after Revelations or Nahum if of the Jewish persuasion."

The Book of Zevs consisted of a cover, an introductory epistle, and five chapters, the whole being six pages long, each page four and a half inches wide and seven and a quarter inches tall. Three columns appeared on each page of text. The book was printed by hand, and the script was small, the third column of the fourth page, for example, consisting of sixty-three lines. To read the *Book,* I magnified and reproduced the pages. On the cover the Reverend stood "Clothed with the Sun," his posture straight and his endowment, his Methuselah, as Baptist brethren label such things, Masonic, identifying him as one of the "giants in the earth." In the Epistle Zevs described God's visiting him in the Nudist National Wilderness, located on the border of Utah and Colorado. God directed Zevs to "the Blessed Cave" where He instructed Zevs to fast. Eventually God called Zevs from the cave. Once outside, Zevs saw three luminous figures hovering in the air. "They looked like," Zevs wrote, "3 Long Texas Bull Horns and they were lit up at the top like torches because the Hot Fervent Flame was coming from each one of them. Their light enabled me to see that there were writings on each one of them. There were three vertical columns on every one of the Three Long Horns. The writings on the 3 Long Horns were written in the awesome Greek Language."

The Lord instructed Zevs to translate the Greek and afterward convey the message to "people in the State of Iowa and the Midwest" on three "priceless papyrous plates." Beside the *Book of Zevs,* three P's appeared on the plates, signifying, "Peace, Production, Prosperity or Triple Peace." To help Zevs, God sent the Angel Ephygenia, "wild rose scented, beautiful, and sharp-eyed." In the *Book* Zevs railed against polygamy and the Mormon Church, calling Joseph Smith, "a fortune teller, witchcraft believer, and psychic treasure hunter." In justifying his mission to Utah, Zevs wrote, "it was more important for God's Holy Plan to send me there than to go out in the Swamp States," this last phrase referring to moldy portions of the southern United States.

In the second chapter God transported Zevs to the "Galaxian Heavens." God spent three days, three hours and three minutes with Zevs. Afterward Zevs wandered the Heavens for five hours. "The Holy Naked Father" then became The Great Schoolmaster. After urging Zevs to deliver "the people from cults and paganism," He preached tolerance. "You must always remember my son not to force our Christian beliefs on the Muslim people for they are humble people and they are the flock of Mohamed. And do not force our Christian beliefs on the Buddhist people for they are humble people and they are the flock of Buddha. And do not force our Christian beliefs on the Hindu people for they are very humble people and they are the flock of Yogi. And do not force our Christian beliefs on the Evolutionist people for they are people of great learning and they are the flock of Science."

At the conclusion of the Sermon in the Heavens, Ephygenia returned Zevs to earth, asking, "in what way would I like to descend on the planet Earth; on a Flying Horse, on a Space Craft, on a Waterbed, on a Hot Air Balloon, or on a Andean Condor." After choosing the spacecraft, Zevs landed in Arizona, northwest of the Grand Canyon. Here, God informed him, was "the Holy Land of the Nudist Christian People." Here the City of Galaxy was to be built "with primitive look alike houses and ancient look alike settlements and ancient temples." "Your people," God assured Zevs, "will have the necessary Sciences. Your people will have resourceful gardens and orchards, plenty of milk and cheese of the Blessed Goat. In this Blessed Arizona Strip cherries and watermelons and other juicy fruits will refresh your mouths in the summer days, where man and woman, male and female will have Godly respect and admiration for one another, and for each other's nakedness and wholesome natural body."

"Daddy," Edward said, after glancing at the enlargement, "the person who wrote this is nuts." "No," I answered; "she's my age, and she is absolutely sane." Edward looked puzzled, so I continued, asking, "did you hear about the garrulous man who went deaf for want of practicing his hearing?" "No," Edward said, walking away and leaving me alone to peruse the rest of the package. At sixteen Edward appreciates explanations clear as tile. Only years bring the capacity to enjoy the lacquered dark.

Records of the Ames police accompanied the items. Five and a half by seven and a half inches, three sheets composed the first record, the top sheet being white, underneath, two copies, one pink, the other yellow. Reverend Galaxy was Case Number 99-15072314. Fenton, the record showed, arrested Galaxy and brought him to the Ames jail where Harvey Dingler searched him, removing Zevs's possessions, including, as Fenton wrote, "Bible?" The second record was the Inmate Intake Screening Form. The Arrestee's Name appeared on one side, followed by Nearest

172   Shadow

Relative, in this case, two relatives, Starlene, Zevs's wife, and Darrell, his dog. Under current medical problems, Dingler wrote, "says feelings are hurt." Zevs's only medication was "Gookin Headache Powder," and he was allergic to "Marigolds and Claustrophobia." The names of sixteen ailments appeared on the sheet, Zevs having been treated for only one, Sexually-Transmitted Diseases. Stamped in black under the ailments was the instruction, "If YES to any of the above questions, obtain the most recent date and description of their treatment." When queried about the disease, Zevs responded, "see Mrs. Pemberton and ask her." While in jail, Zevs, the record showed, only made one telephone call, this being to Darrell the dog.

On the lower half of the sheet appeared twenty lines, providing space for cell checks. Five jailers observed Zevs during his stay in Ames. One wrote with a pencil, letters in longhand and drifting over lines like a steeplechaser falling sideways over rail fences. Another used a pen containing black ink; this man's writing was controlled, his letters packed together like books on a shelf. A third jailer wrote with a red pencil. The fourth appeared left-handed, printing letters that tilted backward, slipping off foundations. The fifth jailer used a ballpoint pen filled with blue ink, his handwriting a sprawl of print and script. Zevs's incarceration was uneventful. At 2:40 in the morning, he removed his clothes and spent the next hour "preaching and exhorting." At 7:15 he banged his head against a wall and chewed his mattress, cutting his forehead and chipping a tooth. Five minutes later Dingler doused him with Gookin Headache Powder. At nine o'clock he ate a McDonald's Happy Meal for breakfast. On the back of the sheet appeared Release Information, Jail Checklist, and Screening Questionnaire, this last consisting of seven questions, asking, for example, if the inmate showed "signs of depression" or was under the influence of drugs or alcohol. The only question that received *yes* for an answer was, "Is the inmate acting or talking in a strange manner?" At the bottom of the page under Release Information appeared the print from Zevs's "Right

Index" finger, Zevs having been freed at ten o'clock, November 11, a bond of thirty thousand dollars having been posted, a court appearance scheduled for December 5.

Zevs himself filled out the Personal Information Sheet, listing his address as "Zion Nat. Wilderness" in the state of "Disrobed." For his telephone number, he wrote 1-800-BEE-NUDE; for his Social Security Number, NO-DEVIL-THING. Russell Zwanger was his Maiden Name, and his address in Ames was "#15 Ballerina, Swan Lake Country Club Mobile Home Park." As children he listed "Darrell (Dog)" and "Booger (Dog)," noting that this last was "Deceased." On the line following "In Emergency Notify," he wrote, "Prof. Sam Pickelring" whose "Phone" was "At Connecticut." Beside Occupation, he wrote "Preacher-Prophet." In past years, he noted he worked as "Wienie Dog Cart Installer," having finished the "Wienie Dog Cart Installation Short Course" at Iowa State University, the "Extension." He also attended Sibley High School and "Uncircumcision U." His height was "tall." His weight was "medium." His eyes were "deep," and "his nationality was "Nudist." "Daddy," Edward said, holding the sheet, "the answers are made up, but this paper is the Personal Information Sheet of the Ames Police." "You bet," I said, puzzling Edward again by adding, "the answers may be wintry, but they are real."

Sometime every winter I explore the attic and rummage through scrapbooks of old photographs. Time has crazed many pictures. Edges flake, and shadows spread across houses and faces. Often people in the pictures are strangers. Still, as I study photographs, imagination lures me to recognition. Amid the browns and yellows appear hints of the familiar, the tilt of a chin, a brambly brow, an eye, its focus wavering. In December I also mail Christmas cards to people who hover dim in memory, their presence not strapped to particulars but forming the texture of the shaping past. A snapshot of Vicki, the children, and me appeared on this year's card. I sat on the floor, and Vicki and the children, on a blue sofa behind me. Despite my position in front, I seemed background. While Vicki's and the children's faces glowed, my skin was thin and

174 Shadow

pale, creating a cloudy translucence. The lid of my right eye drooped like a slat that had slipped two rungs down the ladder tape of a blind.

Although I enjoy meandering the half-light of winter, the season makes others uncomfortable. Such people prefer hours black and white and cards crisp with tree and snow. The last day of class someone slipped two tracts under the door of my office in the English Department: "The Governing Principle of the Body of Christ" and "A God Who Hides Himself," the second tract written by Witness Lee and published by Living Stream Ministry in Anaheim, California. Three years ago Uncle Coleman died in Houston, Texas. Every week I receive mail addressed to him. On the day I found the tracts, I received a packet from Howard Phillips, soliciting money from Uncle Coleman. Phillips was the presidential candidate of the Constitutional Party, a man whose certainty turned dark into light and banished doubt from mind. Running for president, he declared, was "not a game." "This is a campaign to rescue America from its downward slide." "The Bible and the Constitution," he emphasized, "are our Foundation." Phillips promised to reject "One World Imperialism" and close down the Establishment's "Ministries of Truth." "The propitious smiles of heaven," he wrote, "can never be expected on a nation that disregards the eternal rules of order and right, which heaven itself has ordained." "My fellow Americans," he said, "our country has walked far from those eternal rules of order and right ordained by God." Phillips opposed funding the National Endowment for the Arts and "Executive Branch Employment of Practicing Homosexuals." "Only in the executive branch?" Edward asked, adding, "do you think Galaxy will run for office? After all how many people has the Holy Naked Father praised as 'copper-bearded, curly-haired, goat-nourished, and sure-footed'?"

This past fall semester I taught a course in children's books. For extra credit students wrote fairy tales. A third of the class wrote tales, twenty-one students handing in tales before December and thirty-two, the last day of class. Early in the term I read quickly. In December, despite the greater number of tales, I meandered paragraphs, enjoying the smoky patina of fiction. Magical willow trees grew in groves, the only magic tree that rooted. Six heroines were named Rose. While one Rose haunted a forest and had "hair like a honeycomb," another lived in a rundown castle and had "skin white as snow and long, flowing golden hair." A third Rose "saw nothing but the great willow tree, the green grass, and yellow dandelions bobbing in the wind." A witch changed people into wind chimes. For her orchestra the witch sought different types of people. "Some were dancers, painters, and inventors; others were explorers or poets." Needing "a virtuous princess" for the orchestra, the witch enchanted a Rose who had a heart of gold.

A menagerie of animal helpers frolicked through stories: a raccoon, two gray squirrels, three foxes, a pink caterpillar, an owl, and a timid green dragon named Gargle. A kindly "Ogra," one presumably with Egyptian ancestors, rescued a baby from a basket floating down a river. Students' spelling was poor. On a winter night, though, correct spelling doesn't matter. Eight rain deer pulled a slay. Despite misspellings, the deer did not lose their way amid dark clouds on Christmas Eve, and Santa succeeded in delivering presents "to all the good boys and girls, and most of the naughty ones, too."

Although Richie Wealthenbrat was "a snotty, pretty boy with rippling muscles, a dazzling smile, golden skin, and a firm jaw," characters were generally selfless. Every day Zeema collected snails in order to save them from becoming escargot. Students at the McQuaid School of Conformity ridiculed George the Gigantor. In truth, George was "downright ugly, with a head big as a basketball, beady eyes hidden under wrinkles of skin, and a mound of shaggy hair thick as steel wool. Outdoors his ghostly skin reflected light, giving him an ogreish appearance. His legs were round as tree stumps, and his fingers large as carrots." Teasing didn't bother George. He tried out for crew, and when a storm threatened to sweep an eight over a dam, George grabbed a tree limb and single-handedly hauled the boat ashore. Stories ended optimistically. "She had what she wanted, and as the story goes, they lived happily." "The princess was happy because she found a husband with a kind heart." "The two rode off together along the banks of river, beneath the starry sky, and silvery moon in the faraway land of Jagarwood Forest."

Even sorcerers were kindly, causing mishaps through inadvertence, one imprisoning the sun in a marble because he thought stars lovely. Another brewed a spell to make himself immortal. Unfortunately, he miscalculated, and the elixir caused him to inhabit inanimate objects. When an object broke into pieces, the wizard's soul entered something else. The wizard fended off melancholy by doing good deeds. Confined to a baseball, he met Amaya when he smacked her in the forehead. Instead of pain, main characters endured laughter. Because he wouldn't come downstairs to dinner and stayed in his bubble bath too long, Harry Bixler was imprisoned in a huge bubble. The bubble blew out the bathroom window and floated over a baseball field on which Harry's friends were playing, exposing all of Harry to ridicule.

Occasionally modernity touched tales. A queen searched for the "ideal partner." Prince Bobby suffered from birth defects. Doctors predicted he would die before he was three, but he lived to be thirteen. For years, he communicated "by hand gestures, facial expressions, and moans." Eventually Jack, a retired scientist, invented a talking machine for him. Immediately thereafter Bobby took command of the army and saved his kingdom from "barbarians." After the great victory, Bobby died, "mourned by everyone." "For years," the author of the story told me, "I took care of a handicapped boy. At his birth a doctor said he wouldn't live more than three years. In October he died. He was thirteen." The imaginary appointments of winter days were brighter than reality. "I can't talk long about my tale," said a boy, who described three enchanted oranges, the first containing a brooch shaped like an Iris and sparkling with rubies bright as dew; the second, a handkerchief stitched with gold thread and adorned with black pearls; and the third, a silver palace complete with alabaster furnishings and a king's daughter "more beautiful than a blue river." The boy lived in New London. He drove to Storrs on Tuesdays and Thursdays and took five classes, one after the other, each class eighty minutes long. On Mondays, Wednesdays, and Fridays, he worked in a high school, caring for a retarded student. On Saturdays he managed a juice store in a mall.

Winter is the season of habit, not experiment. For fifteen years Vicki and I have bought Christmas trees at Hye Acres Farm on Route 44, spending an afternoon roaming the hillside behind the house, debating merits of sundry trees. For several years Mr. Talmadge, the owner of Hye Acres, has not planted new trees, and trees that escaped cutting Christmas after Christmas have grown long in the trunk. On the Saturday before Christmas, I decided to vary routine, and Vicki, Eliza, and I drove to a tree farm off Route 32. Like biscuits in trays, cars jammed a lot near the farm. Ribbons hung from trees, blue ribbons, for example, on trees six feet tall, yellow, on seven-footers, prices mounting foot by foot. A man driving a forklift brought trees down from a field above the house. He dumped the trees on the ground where a machine spun twine around branches, making carting them home easy. "This farm is nice," Eliza began then stopped. At Christmas efficiency seems unseasonable. Half an hour later, we were trudging Hye Acres. Mr. Talmadge gave us chocolate chip cookies. As usual I tossed my cookie into privet when Mr. Talmadge looked away. From a pile of limbs, Vicki extracted boughs of white pine for the mantle. "See you next year," Eliza said to Mr. Talmadge, as Vicki and I struggled to tie the tree on the roof of the car. On the way home Vicki and Eliza discussed pinks shuttering through the sunset. Colorblind, I saw only brown. At home I clipped the top of the tree to prevent it from scraping the ceiling. Two of the four screws on the stand twisted across the trunk of the tree instead of boring into it. Consequently, Vicki lashed the trunk to the fireplace insert and set thirty pounds of barbells on one leg of the stand. "Christmas as usual," she said, "too big a tree from Mr. Talmadge and this terrible stand. Next year I am going to buy a new stand." "No, you won't, Mommy," Eliza said. "You said the same thing last year. The stand is a Christmas tradition."

As soon as the tree was stable, I rushed to the university. The registrar scheduled the examination for Children's Literature for

December 22. Because many students work during holidays, I set an earlier, alternative examination on Saturday at six in the evening. Fifty-four students took the early examination, forty-four girls and ten boys. Five students were left-handed, all girls. During the examination, I started coughing, so I bought a Coca Cola for seventy-five cents. In winter I roam shadows and discover parts for sentences. As I dropped my empty soft drink bottle into the waste can, I wondered what the can contained. Contents were various, among victuals, a banana peel; an apple core, brown and the remnant of a red delicious; and a pack which once held four Fig Newton cookies. While two of the cookies had been eaten, two others had been nibbled. Instead chewing them singly, the purchaser of the pack had treated these last two as a layer cake and had bitten into them at the same time. The purchaser had a pronounced overbite as his upper teeth sliced into the top cookie at a wide angle.

Lurking in the can were a dozen cups, all of which once contained coffee, nine of the cups from Café Origins and three from Dunkin' Donuts. Crushed against the side of the can was a box that had held five "Toscano Style" cigars. The box was two and a half inches wide, three and a half tall, and half an inch deep. Manufactured by Parodi Cigars in Scranton, Pennsylvania, the cigars cost $2.25 at CVS Drugstore. Printed on the front of the box was a seal within a seal. In the middle of an ornamental seal, a mammalian seal reared upward, the better to stare into the distance. A green band circled the animal. Printed in white along the band were two stars, the name *Parodi,* then the slogan "Seal of Perfection." Also crammed into the can was a bale of examinations, most from Political Science 121, Communication Sciences 102, and Sociology 102 and 269. Near the bottom of the can lay a blue book soaked with coffee. James Potter began an essay for English 127, but after writing one sentence, threw the book away, choosing to write about another topic. In my class Potter's single sentence would have received at least a *B,* and during winter, probably an *A.* "After reading both *Daisy Miller* and *The Female Quixote,*" Potter wrote, "I am most certain that I will never understand a woman."

Imagination thrives in shadow. Not only does imagination clothe the indistinct, but in winter it also blows life into nothing. I soon lost interest in the contents of the can. Before I reached bare metal, fancy molded objects out of inclination. Printed on a scrap of paper was the beginning of a speech made to the university's board of trustees. "Lentlemen, gadies, students and other honorable members of the proletariat, hermaphrodites in tights, hardened speculators, blatant adventurers, Methodists, and anti-ballistic shields." Beneath a mouse stuffed with capers and hearts of pimento lay the famous Russian novel, *The Great Gatsby* written by F. Myron Goldberg. Sticking out of the book was the calling card of Tychic Laboe Stonehocker, vice-president in charge of domestic accounts at Fleet Bank. Printed on the bottom of the card was "Our Night Suppository is Always Open, particularly to Catholics." Hunkered next to a lilac bagpipe was a Jehovah's Witness with a red mustache and wearing a bowler hat covered with blue and yellow sprinkles.

Because I write, I peel my eyes for words, especially when I dig through nothing. Scribbled on brown paper was a stanza composed by Conklyn Terrell on the occasion of his visiting the grave of his wife Luella in Carthage, two months after she died in childbirth.

> Be not upset, my dearest Life.
> Sleep on. I've got another wife,
> And cannot waste my time with thee,
> For I must go to bed with she.

On another sheet of paper appeared Gizzard Markley's last, inspirational words. "When this mortal coil loosens and the pearls of my being roll away like silk," Gizzard said to his son Udell, "when the final flickers of life's golden lamp quiver like the toes of premature babies, when prayers ascending to the ivory Throne of Grace waft my soul to the green Garden beyond the evening star, when I give the last sonofabitching kick, grab the money box under the bed or your damn sister Peggy will steal it."

Once a person grows accustomed to shadow, life becomes a garden. On walks I noticed more than bark: sparrows hanging like bulbs from brambles; leaves of mugwort, dried and corkscrewing through black and white; across a shady hillside, princess pine, staghorn clubmoss, and lattices of running cedar. In the Ogushwitz meadow, a pigmy shrew nested under a board. Behind the beaver pond liverwort covered humps of moss. Beside a cornfield seeds tumbled from Jimson weed, pattering across leaves like hard rain. Ice wrapped a stream, water thumping beneath like a xylophone. Atop a log lay the fresh scat of an ermine, a small black pile, ends tapering into hooked filaments. One afternoon the sunset turned clouds rising from the university steam plant golden, the swirls dropping and sweeping, fit domicile, I thought, for a god.

After students finished the examination, I drove to Hartford and picked Francis up at the railway station. On the way home I stopped at Wing Express and bought takeout for the family: vegetable biryani, chicken mughlai, dal makhani, lamb saag, four samosas, and an extra order of rice. Sunday afternoon I drove Eliza to East Hartford for volleyball practice. As I drove through Coventry, a red pickup truck approached. Sitting in the passenger's seat of the truck was Santa Claus, a big Santa with a full beard and a face as round as a pumpkin. "Look, Daddy," Eliza said and pointed at the truck. "Wow," I said. "That's wonderful, Eliza, just wonderful." ❖

The Last Book

"Daddy," Eliza said walking into the study, "what are you going to call the collection of essays?" "*The Last Book,*" I said. "But," Eliza said, pausing for a moment, "suppose you write another book. What will its title be?" "*The Next to Last Book,*" I said. I'm sixty years old and have written fifteen books, twelve of them collections of autobiographical essays. Like society my essays are custom-made. Although I shake different seasonings over them, the thoughts that sift through paragraphs have long remained the same. Moreover as I age, instead of rising in sweet confections, days often remain flat, heartache overheating the mind. On Christmas Eve I received a letter from a former teacher. My correspondent was old, and the letter was incoherent. The next morning I telephoned a cousin. She'd been ill for two years, and over the last months her speech had deteriorated. On Christmas I did not understand anything she said. That afternoon I called my godfather and asked about his family. He had forgotten the names of his children. "Begin an essay," Vicki said, after I described the last conversation. "Paragraphs are mazes. Clambering over adjectives and under adverbs is work, and before you reach the bottom of a page, you'll have jettisoned worry."

People eventually become their habits, and I suspect I won't stop writing. For Christmas Vicki gave me a "Lap Counter and Timer." Worn on the index finger, the counter records swimming distance. "During swim you will be able to think about things

182 The Last Book

other than numbers," Vicki said. Freed from counting laps, I now toy with numbers, swimming, for example, two hundred yards of crawl, followed by a series of seventy-five-yard swims consisting of fifty yards of breaststroke followed by twenty-five yards of crawl. Once the number of yards of breaststroke equals that of crawl (eight groups of seventy-five yards does the trick), I begin a different mix of strokes.

In implying that writing is therapeutic, Vicki was partly right. By observing closely, the essayist frees himself from quotidian reality, and often from worry. To study gable and bargeboard, I so narrow vision that roof itself blurs. The first two weeks of January were a swirl of bits, not wholes—quoins, corbels, and soffits. Thursday after New Year's, Eliza, Edward, Vicki, and I drove to the Museum of Fine Arts in Boston to see "Pharaohs of the Sun," an exhibit of Egyptian art. We didn't realize the exhibition had been sold out for weeks. My Storrs is far from Boston, and I did not think to purchase tickets in advance. Writing creates contentment, however. Instead of bemoaning the what-could-have-been, I enjoy what-is. "I'm such a blunderer," I said as I parked the car, "that I can't pull a boot on without putting my foot in it."

At the Museum was a display of the paintings of Martin Johnson Heade. I have long admired Heade's salt marshes, hay humped on straddles above the tide; the grass chartreuse, yellow in sunlight and dark green in shadows; salt creeks curving in question marks, mallards dozing and men poling gundalows. For twenty minutes, I studied "April Showers." On the right side of the painting, clouds slipped over hills like a nightshirt. On the left, pencils of yellow and silver streaked the sky. Across the right foreground, a creek bent into an elbow, willows sweeping banks, behind them, green fields still as ponds. Across the left foreground, a stonewall dragged like a long line of poetry. A wooden gate slumped, its meter broken, and rocks sank low and inaudible into the ground. At corners of fields, apple trees blossomed in pink puffs. The roof of a farmhouse tilted orange behind a tree, smoke trickling from a chimney. "A farm far from cholera, hookworm, and tuberculosis," Vicki said. "Apple trees clean as wallpaper, the cider fresh as spring, not wintry and bitter with incest and suicide." "The landscape of my essays," I said. "The bruises of The Fall make me melancholy. That's why I may stop writing."

In salt marshes July is haying season. For me January is viral, and I tend to ailments. Last April my feet began going numb, and after Christmas I endured a series of tests. Doctors jabbed needles into muscles and jump-started reactions, running electricity through nerves. One test made my right arm spring up from the elbow. To administer the test a technician leaned over my right side and applied a shock to a nerve high in my arm. Each time she shocked the nerve, my hand rose in a cup and lifted her right breast. "How many times did the woman shock your arm?" my friend Josh asked after I described the test. "Many times," I said, adding that I could not control my hand. "I assume the technician became red in the face and in a frenzy increased the tempo of the shocks," Josh said. "No," I said. "Suppose," Vicki opined that night, "she had shocked your spine and something else rose from the grave. That would have been embarrassing." No matter the season, Vicki ploughs fertilizer into medical furrows. The morning after returning from Boston my right ear was plugged. Vicki searched the medicine cabinet for eardrops. "Why don't I pour a bucket of stool softener into your ear," she said as I lay in bed. "That always loosens the impacted."

My inner ear was infected, and nothing Vicki squirted brought relief. The infection made me wobbly, and I spent the next day reading Gore Vidal's memoir *Palimpsest*. In the book Vidal described broad literary doings. That night after dinner Edward discovered the book on my bedside table. Edward read for an hour than came downstairs to the study. "Daddy," he said, "take that book back to the library. Reading it isn't good for you." Edward's concern invigorated me. The next morning I sent a fax to a company in White Plains, New York. In November, I spoke at Duquesne University. The company booked the speech, arranged flights, and handled payment. Speech and flight went smoothly, but payment hit turbulence. When I telephoned to ask about my money, I was shunted to the dead end of voice mail. Lively letters

184   The Last Book

became moribund, and email refused to spark. "You've been stiffed," Vicki said. "We'll see," I said, after returning *Palimpsest* to the library. In the fax, I said that delays caused by illness or financial problems were understandable. Losing the fee did not bother me. But not responding to inquiries was reprehensible. On weekdays I have coffee at the Cup of Sun, a café in Storrs. Three friends join me: Ellen Zahl, Lee Terry, and Roger Crossgrove. In the message, I stated that if the company did not respond by week's end, I would consult a friend, "a partner in the firm of Zahl, Terry, and Crossgrove." On Friday I received payment. Going to the imaginary law works as well as talking to a real lawyer and is less expensive, an hour of a fictional lawyer's time costing relatively little.

Once I would have telephoned the Museum of Fine Arts and inquired about tickets. Years in Storrs have worn grooves in my behavior, however. Instead of thinking about doings in Boston or New York, I wander field and hill, the land a magical canopic jar, gold and vital, circling the bowl, a cartouche carved by seasons. On New Year's, a male marsh hawk glided engraved over a cornfield, underwings white, the tips of its primaries black. A white-throated sparrow perched in sumac, and from a wood rolled the drumming of a pileated woodpecker. Foxtails swam a breeze. At the edge of a furrow stood a shaft of mullein, flowers dried to beaks. On multiflora rose, thorns swept upward from gray divots. Cherries shrunk into tart sweetness, and crab apples folded into sugary seams. While buds on bigtooth aspen clung waxed to twigs, field birch exploded into wiry red branches. Unnamed Pond was a tired mirror, frosted and crazed. At sunset green spread mossy and low under clouds; above, gray melted into pink then slowly hardened into purple. I walked home in the dark. On my desk Eliza had put a knot of pods from honey locust. The pods were dry and black and between nine and fifteen inches long. They coiled across the desk, and when I picked them up, seeds rattled.

Carnivals pitch paragraphs, and parades trip through my essays. In January I always spend time in the house, becoming susceptible not only to earaches but also to the blare of trumpets and barkers. Imagination expands beyond door and sill and transforms days into circuses. Words tumble clownishly in sawdust then hopping into rings prance through tricks. The acts are familiar. The femme fatale on the trapeze is pudgy. The Mongolian warhorse is swaybacked. Big cats look like mothy sofas. Lines don't crackle, and paragraphs stick to the gullet like cotton candy. Since none of my shows will ever travel the interstate to Bestseller, I can be willful. When the son of the femme fatale grows four inches in sixth grade, he can become "The World's Tallest Midget."

Despite the cold, the pods pulled along the desktop, sidewinding into idea. Four days later, in July, the Carthage Chamber of Commerce sponsored the "Cruel, Cruel Sarpent Festival," the title of the festival lifted from Orson Nady's eighteenth-century epic describing the fall of man. An Englishman and physician, Nady lived in Somerset, in Combe Florey, a house later occupied by the divine and wit Sydney Smith, and still later by the novelist Evelyn Waugh. In 1787, at his own expense, Nady published "Golden Lamps of Heaven, Farewell." The American Revolution influenced the epic, Nady explained, saying he intended to democratize poetry. "By using the language really spoken by men, I hope to interest common people in the story of Adam and Eve. I utterly reject mechanical devices of style, such as those employed in the last century by the Puritanical and Regicidal John Milton in *Paradise Lost*." In Nady's epic, Adam succumbed to the temptations of Eve and the apple on Karn Hattin, later the mountain on which Christ preached "The Sermon on the Mount." The verse that provided the festival's title occurred in Book IX of the epic. Having eaten the apple, Adam became engorged with pride and climbed to the top of the mountain so he could address God as an equal. "As he went on to the mountain high," Nady wrote, "A rattlesnake did Adam espy. / And all at once he then did feel / That p'ison critter bite his heel." Immediately thereafter Adam began to descend, sliding more than walking, "crying aloud, as down he went, / 'Oh, cruel, cruel, sa-ar-pent.'"

For the festivities the Eastern Star sponsored a flower show. Participants fashioned arrangements out of coat hangers and flowers, first bending the hangers in the shape of snakes then binding flowers to the wires. Carmella Waddle exhibited two arrangements, "Serpens Caput" and "Serpens Cauda," weaving asters thick through the hangers. Junie Millsap entitled her exhibit "Creation," first twisting coat hangers into a circle eighteen inches in diameter, then tying orchids and orchid buds to the wire. Alice Twombey's arrangement "Mousing" differed slightly from other exhibits. Alice bent three wires into arches. To the front of each arch, she attached an anthurium, the spadix dangling like the tail of a snake investigating a mouse hole.

Few members of the Eastern Star gave arrangements titles. While one snake struck, its upper body supported by struts made from balsa wood and its mouth a day lily gaping in bloom, another stretched out breast-feeding a litter of eight: the mother's body poppies; its teats butterfly peas; the young, lizard's tails; their eyes buttercups and violets. Another mother wrapped herself around eggs, a batch of closed gentians. In a serving dish a snake woven from hydrangea coiled in thin pool of gold water. Patterns bloomed eclectically across the skins of many snakes, milkweed, yellow bedstraw, pansies, zinnias, and devil's paintbrush, blossom by blossom. Instead of the melony aroma of blacksnake, the exhibition was fragrant with home—narcissus and deep blue Iris.

The exhibit was popular, "a great triumph," said Sister Leonora Tomiyama, Grand Secretary of the Star. Despite this success, however, I changed the festival into a patent medicine jamboree, influenced in part by HMO fairs blossoming across Connecticut. More importantly, however, I like snakes. For the festival to have been successful, Carthaginians would have been forced to catch tubs of serpents, bringing to mind rattlesnake roundups sponsored by venomous imbeciles in the southwest and attended by prehensile morons, low dolts not at all like the good folk of Carthage. Only one of the acts planned for the festival remained in the jamboree. Crying "snake-bit," six men carried a coffin along Main Street. Orin Grookin lay in the coffin, his one-legged hen Baha nesting on his forehead. When the pallbearers reached Read's Drug Store, Kenrick Confer burst out the door, a bottle of Warner's Tippacanoe Tonic in his left hand. Shouting "Tippacanoe and Grookin, too," Kenrick dumped the tonic down Orin's throat. Immediately Orin sat upright, grabbed Baha, and said, "where's the frying pan? That snake's done give me a prodigious appetite. I'm ready for fried chicken."

Drummers set up booths around the courthouse, hawking, among other things, Murray's Charcoal Tablets, Gatta's Acid Phosphate, Ditman's Trusses, Jambeck's Gastricine, Cuticura Resolvent, and Mother Morton's Cherry Pectoral. Friedrichshall Natural Bitter Water cured, a drummer claimed, "constipation, head and heart ache, hemorrhoids, indigestion, gravel, gout, catarrh both the yellow and the high green, impurities of the blood, and all diseases peculiar to females." Imperial Hair Rejuvenator turned gray hair every shade "from light ash to deep gold, blonde, chestnut and auburn, red sunset, and brown and black." "Not only that, but Turkish and Russian baths don't hurt the colors, and just a taste kills nits and pinworms." Prices were low. "Birds in the bush sell for a song," Turlow Gutheridge said.

After listening to a drummer, Hink Ruunt bought an Electro-Voltaic Belt for Buster, his Jersey bull, Buster having recently gone off feed and cows. "For all men, animal, vegetable, and mineral, who are suffering from nervous disability, lost vitality, wasting weakness, and all diseases of a personal nature, resulting from abuses, accidents, and other causes," the drummer declared. "Speedy relief and complete restoration to health, vigor, and manhood guaranteed." "Buckle the belt around the stump in your front yard, plug it in, and leave it overnight. The next morning that stump will be a tree, not no quaking aspen or weeping willow neither, but a butternut, sixty feet tall and vigorous and straight." "If George Washington had owned a belt, his little hatchet wouldn't be rusting in the Potomac now. He'd have strapped the belt around that cherry, and the next morning, his pappy would have found a full-grown apple tree in the yard, heavy with summer fruit, Sops of Wine, Early Joe, and Red Astracan."

The jamboree lured crowds to Carthage. A truck came all the way from Chattanooga to deliver Double Cola to Woody Ankerrow's Café. Barrow's Grocery did holiday business as Woody ordered crates of deviled ham, potted meat, and Vienna sausage. For lunch-time customers, Clevanna Farquarhson baked sixty sweet potato pies. Four bowls of pickled eggs sat atop Woody's counter, all the eggs pink because Clevanna added beet juice to the marinade. "Boarders" at the School for the Afflicted in Buffalo Valley attended the jamboree. Most had never seen pink eggs. "That's nothing," one of the more sophisticated boarders said after scrutinizing the bowls. "I once saw an egg so big that it took seven hens to lay it." Despite my intention of purging serpents from the mind, snake talk lingered about town like castoff skins. "I read," Loppie Groat said, "that Hindus are reasonable people, but I wonder. Every year snakes kill fifty thousand people in India. Instead of reasonable, that seems out of hand. Why, despite all the preachers in East Tennessee dumping strychnine in Holy Water and congregations playing catch with copperheads and rattlers, not more than two or three true believers die from snakebite a year."

To elevate the cultural tone of the festivities, the *Courier* scheduled its annual poetry contest during the jamboree. Buster inspired Hink. Unfortunately like Buster himself, Hink broke down and couldn't finish what he started, in this case a bovine version of Tennyson's "Charge of the Light Brigade." "Heifer leg, heifer leg, heifer leg onward," Hink wrote before foundering. Proverbs Goforth's "I Sting Therefore I Be" took second prize. "O frolicsome insect, though far you may roam, / Bee it ever so bumble, there's no place like comb." Rumor buzzed that Proverbs spent two days hovering about the library before the contest. "If Proverbs' honey isn't adulterated," Hoben Donkin said, "then he robbed a hive." Gossip aside, Vester McBee's "My Mother" took laurels.

> Tell me, mother, tell your daughter.
> Tell me truly, do not scoff.
> Tell me if you think I oughter
> Take these derned old flannels off.

Life is not an unbroken festival. Mortality gatecrashes, in the case of the jamboree, however, unobtrusively and not disrupting the party. On Friday night, Lester Cone died suddenly. Twenty-eight years old, Lester had been married for five months, leaving behind

Eva a widow, aged twenty-four. Saturday morning Eva braved downtown and sent a telegram to her father in Pass Christian, Mississippi. "Lester died last night at ten o'clock. Loss fully covered by insurance." Also on Saturday Loppie Groat met Junior Peavy in Ankerrow's Café. Five weeks earlier Junior's twin brother Senior had been injured when a still detonated. "Junior," Loppie said, "how's Senior coming along. I haven't heard about him recently." "Part of him is still on this earth," Junior said. "It don't talk much and flops around on its belly. But with the Lord's help, I'm hoping to get it up to a knee before putting in the corn next spring."

In Tennessee crowds attract holy as well as secular pitchmen. Reverend Devil preached on the dangers of drink at The Church of the Chastening Rod. The reverend got his name because he'd once been a demon for alcohol. "Like a tomcat pouncing on a saucer of buttermilk, I lapped up whiskey. Before the Lord plucked me red-faced from the jug, I used to cry, 'Barkis is willin', but the flesh is weak.' After I quit drinking, the King baptized my belly, christening it Hades, the place of departed spirits." "I can't answer all your questions," the Reverend told the congregation. "I don't know why angels climbed up and down Jacob's Ladder when they had wings. But this much I know is true: more people drown in wine than water, and the whis-key unlocks the door to damnation."

Reverend Devil bellowed like ten bulls and waved his arms in a thunderstorm. Blue veins ran down his tongue. When the Spirit moved him, the veins swelled, making him hiss, astonishing congregations and increasing the take considerably. "You might lose sight of Death by running around a bend in the long road," he warned, "but Death knows a short cut through the woods. Bankruptcy might wipe your slate clean in Tennessee, but St. Peter won't listen to pleas of spiritualruptcy. The wages of sin is death, and payday is bound to come, sooner or later. Trust the Lord, but don't fool around with Him." "Bolting the door with good resolutions doesn't keep Sin out of the house," the Reverend continued. "A man of words and not of deeds is a garden full of weeds." "When the Lord visits, don't serve the bald-headed rooster. Bring out grandma's corn cakes and egg bread, watermelon rind pickles, ham cured by charity, egg plant, fried okra, and tomatoes stewed in righteousness, ambrosia and plum pudding topped with sweet devotion."

Reverend Devil was large. In sermons he always mentioned food, and determined to keep slugs away from their vegetables, congregations fed him handsomely. "Daddy," Eliza asked after I read her parts of his sermon, "have you ever written about Reverend Devil before?" "No," I said. "Then you will have write more about him in *The Next to Last Book*." "I suppose," I said, adding that I should also write about his brother The Singing Undertaker. Two years ago he took third place in the poetry contest, singing,

> I know that I shall die.
> Love so my heart bewitches.
> It makes me hourly cry.
> Oh, how my elbow itches.

"Enough jamboree," I thought, and putting down the pen, left the house. Two days earlier snow fell. The afternoon was cold—seven degrees. After half an hour, I forgot the temperature. At dusk I stood in the Ogushwitz meadow. Stems of goldenrod and Joe-Pye weed stuck red through the snow, rough as calluses. Along the edge of the field, alders clumped gray and purple. Above the Fenton River, hemlocks cast brown shadows. Branches of red maples looked like fans sketched on screens. The moon rose. In the west, clouds smoldered into blackened orange and smoking blew gasping over the ridge. I stood beside the beaver dam. Snow glazed the ice, and willows shrank into switches. I walked into the woods, unconsciously following deer paths. Bony trees creaked, and wind throbbed, its pulse rapid with cold. Shadows smudged the snow, and I pondered something Josh said. As men grow old, friendships melt. In contrast as women age, the number of their friends increases. Over time a wife stops not only being her husband's companion but also his friend. "Men die from heart attacks," Josh said, "caused by plugged affections, not plugged arteries." "A matter to consider in another book," I mulled as I pushed through black locusts, thorns hooking my cap, the sky above, enameled, hard and blue. ❖